WORLD HISTORY Volume 2
FROM THE SEVENTEEN-SEVENTIES

Also by Robert Pascoe

World History, Vol. 1

Nat Bonacci: No Ordinary Australian

VOL 2 – HUMAN DESTINY IN HUMAN HANDS

WORLD HISTORY

FROM THE SEVENTEEN-SEVENTIES

ROBERT PASCOE

connorcourt
PUBLISHING

Published in 2013 by Connor Court Publishing Pty Ltd

Copyright © Robert Pascoe 2013

ALL RIGHTS RESERVED. This book contains material protected under International and Federal Copyright Laws and Treaties. Any unauthorised reprint or use of this material is prohibited. No part of this book may be reproduced or transmitted in any form or by any means, electronic or mechanical, including photocopying, recording, or by any information storage and retrieval system without express written permission from the publisher.

Connor Court Publishing Pty Ltd.
PO Box 224W
Ballarat VIC 3350
sales@connorcourt.com
www.connorcourt.com

ISBN: 978-1-922168-757 (pbk.)

Cover design: Ian James

The image on the cover is *Liberty Leading the People* by Eugène Delacroix. It is an 1830 reference back to the French Revolution. This painting inspired New York's Statue of Liberty.

Printed in Australia

World History is both the story of humankind and an introduction to the discipline of History. This book (in two volumes) will give you greater confidence in understanding, organising and revising your content knowledge of World History, but will also introduce you to the techniques used by historians to analyse and explain the past. History demands a specific set of techniques and a mode of thinking. Any history book or article that you read began life as the application of these techniques to a body of evidence, known as 'primary sources'. Each unit here is accompanied by one or more relevant primary sources, as well as suggestions of books, articles and websites for further reading.

Vol. 1 World History to the 1770s:
People and Their Gods

Vol. 2 World History from the 1770s:
Human Destiny in Human Hands

Robert Pascoe is Dean Laureate and a Professor of History at Victoria University, Melbourne. This book covers his first-year subject over two semesters in World History.

CONTENTS (both volumes)

Introduction: How to use this book (both volumes)
Volume 1: People and Their Gods: The deo-centric world

Units 1-4: The ancient Middle East

Unit 1 Before patriarchy
The death of Derbforgaill
Unit 2 The river valley cultures
The story of The Flood
Unit 3 Monotheism and the Axial Age
The Jewish calendar
Unit 4 The Greeks and the idea of the West
Sophocles, Oedipus Rex

Units 5-8: Classical and medieval Europe

Unit 5 Rome
Tacitus, Germania
Unit 6 Byzantium and the Muslims
Narratives of the First Crusade
Unit 7 Feudalism
Quantification in History
Unit 8 The City in History
Maps of town and country

Units 9-12: Europe and the known world

Unit 9 Peasants and revolts
Tudor rebellions
Unit 10 Catholic Renaissance and Protestant Reformation
The nine stories in Renaissance and Reformation art
Unit 11 Maritime imperialisms
World population by century and region
Unit 12 The Columbian Exchange
Montezuma and Cortés

Volume 2: World History from the 1770s

Human Destiny in Human Hands: Anthro-centric alternatives

Units 13-16: The Revolution in France

Unit 13 Absolutism   3
Thomas Hobbes, Leviathan

Unit 14 Removing the King: The English, American and French Revolutions   39
The American Declaration of Independence *and the French* Declaration of the Rights of Man and Citizen

Unit 15 Enlightened Despotism: Catherine and Friedrich   71
Jonathan Swift, A Modest Proposal

Unit 16 Mandarins and Mughals   95
The Memoirs of Jahāngīr *and Kangxi's* Sacred Edict

Units 17-20: The British revolution

Unit 17 The Industrial Revolution   123
Thomas Spence, The Real Rights of Man, *and Thomas Paine*, Agrarian Justice

Unit 18 1848, Nationalism and the Commune   153
Adam Smith, The Wealth of Nations, *David Ricardo*, On the Principles of Political Economy and Taxation, *and John Stuart Mill*, Principles of Political Economy

Unit 19 Colonialism and the Scramble for Africa   189
Karl Marx and Friedrich Engels, The Communist Manifesto, *and Emile Zola*, Germinal

Unit 20 The Great War and Bolshevism   **225**
Narratives of the Great War

Units 21-24: The Rise of the United States

Unit 21 Fascism, World War 2, Postcolonialism   **259**
Anne Frank, The Diary of a Young Girl, *and Charlotte Delbo,* Auschwitz and After

Unit 22 The Long Boom   **297**
The nine stories, as retold by Hollywood, 1945-1962

Unit 23 The Sixties and the undermining of Western hegemony   **323**
Students for a Democratic Society, The Port Huron Statement

Unit 24 Neo-liberalism and the New World Order   **363**
Barack Obama, A New Beginning, *Cairo, 4 June 2009*

Acknowledgements   **396**

Index   **397**

Introduction:
How to use this book (both volumes)

World History is both the story of humankind and an introduction to the discipline of History. This book (in two volumes) will give you greater confidence in understanding, organising and revising your content knowledge of World History, but will also introduce you to the techniques used by historians to analyse and explain the past. History demands a specific set of techniques and a mode of thinking. Any history book or article that you read began life as the application of these techniques to a body of evidence.

In Volume 1 we mostly focus on distinguishing primary sources from secondary sources.

What is a primary source? How do we recognise a true eyewitness account?

Decoding primary sources: How do historians deconstruct one or more accounts of an event or a period?

Measurement in History: What are some of the basic ways historians analyse spatial, demographic and other quantifiable data?

In Volume 2 we begin to practise using these techniques to develop more extended arguments of the kind found in history essays.

Texts as social products: how do we recognise the clues inside the document that tell us what social forces led to its creation?

Texts as analysis: how do we compare and analyse documents that purport to give an account of historical developments?

Texts as cultural documents: How can we apply literary techniques to the interpretation of primary source documents?

Volume 2:

Human Destiny in Human Hands: Anthro-centric alternatives

From the 1770s more and more people began to think that human history was not entirely directed by divine forces, but instead was amenable to human endeavours. Two revolutions were essential to this end. The French Revolution showed the power of the urban masses -- the collective action of citizens joined together in common purpose could unseat even monarchs whose rule seemed God-given.

The Industrial Revolution in Britain had economic consequences as profound as these political changes. Feudalism finally capitulated to this new mode of production, capitalism.

These political and economic developments began in Europe, but in the twentieth century a new power arose, that of the United States. With the defeat of the Soviet Union in 1989, America emerged triumphant as the greatest empire the world had known.

Units 13-16: The Revolution in France

The French Revolution should be understood as the hinge on which the anthro-centric change turned. The tumultuous events in 1789 Paris were a popular response to the concentration of governmental power known as Absolutism. Absolutism can be conveniently divided into Western and Eastern halves. Eastern Absolutism shared the same institutional framework as that of the West, but differed in its detail. This model of Eastern Absolutism can be deployed beyond Eastern Europe and the Ottoman Empire to deepen our appreciation of the great empires of India and China.

Unit 13

Absolutism

Shakespeare recognised Absolutism for what it was and was critical of it. His so-called History plays – *Richard II*, *Henry IV, Part I*, *Henry IV, Part II*, and *Henry V* – are concerned with how to balance the official 'divine right of kings' with more subtle Machiavellian ideas of political rule. Consider the famous speech by John of Gaunt, loyal to Richard II:

> This royal throne of kings, this scepter'd isle,
> This earth of Majesty, this seat of Mars,
> This other Eden, demi-paradise;
> This fortress built by Nature for herself,
> Against infection and the hand of war,
> This happy breed of men, this little world,
> This precious stone set in the silver sea,
> Which serves it in the office of a wall,
> Or as a moat defensive to a house,
> Against the envy of less happier lands;
> This blessed plot, this earth, this realm, this England,
> This nurse, this teeming womb of royal kings,
> Fear'd by their breed, and famous by their birth.

This is a man who has grasped the essence of Absolutism, and has given himself to it. In this speech are references to some of the key institutions of the Absolutist State, such as its military reach, and the continuity of its royal dynasties.

Defining Absolutism

Absolutism is a deceptively simple idea.[1] During the 1500s, 1600s and 1700s individual governments (States) across Europe and the Middle East were able to accumulate greater power. This so-called Absolutism saw the end of the 'parcellised sovereignty' that we associated with feudalism. The aristocrats had enjoyed considerable independence in the classic feudal period: now, right across Europe, in the late mediaeval era, they increasingly found themselves marshalled and disciplined by the monarchies.

Where did this new power come from? How was this power used? What were the new institutions created by the Absolutist State to further its ends? In what parts of Europe and the Middle East were these Absolutist States most powerful? Is there a pattern to this? And, finally, what forces developed to challenge this new Absolutist State?

Absolutism meant economic consolidation: although the aristocrats lost certain political rights they had enjoyed in the feudal period, at the same time they made significant economic gains. Late feudalism finally broke free of the continent: the economic advances were now truly international, in distant places like Louisiana, Hudson Bay, even the Antilles. This meant an entirely new extension of European power. The mercantile bourgeoisie developed in size and strength during this era because the older principle of 'parcellised sovereignty' had meant that generally towns could develop independently of what was going on in the rural world dominated by the aristocracy (although this process was by no means even).

Late medieval governments faced two threats, one from this rising bourgeoisie, the other from the old peasantry. Absolutism can therefore be seen as the monarchies' response to two quite different but equally important challenges to their position: the threat posed by peasant

---

[1] This discussion owes a great deal to the work of Perry Anderson, *Lineages of the Absolutist State*, Verso, London, 1979 [1974].

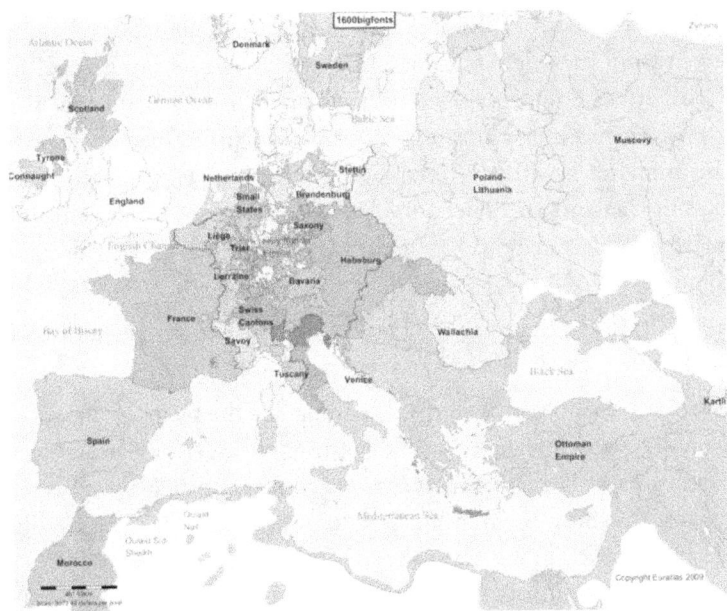

The map of Europe in 1600 is clearly divided between those Absolutist States with large unified territories and the smaller realms

unrest; and the ascent of the urban bourgeoisie. Absolutism relied on a combination of old law and new institutions.

The old law was Roman. Roman Law was important to this accumulation of State power, because it dealt with both 'jus' (economic relations between people) and 'lex' (relations between the State and its subjects). Roman Law provided a more secure basis for the re-conceptualisation of European society than had been provided by the localised understandings of the feudal period. In England, however, Roman Law was not required by the English Absolutist State because it was already a unitary State on account of the Norman Conquest of 1066; here common law developed instead of Roman Law. Elsewhere across Europe Roman Law was deployed by the monarchies with the assistance of the university graduates from places like Bologna where it was re-introduced into the curriculum.

This newer form of Roman Law began to be understood as being different from the original Roman Law, which had set out general social rules and precepts (as developed by Justinian in his *Institutes*). Now Roman Law evolved more as a means of compelling the subjects to conform to the monarch's wishes. (Even here there were limits, however: the Tudors in England introduced the Star Chamber and other instruments of increased central power, but these were destroyed by the English Revolution of 1640.)

The Absolutist State relied for its power on five key institutions: the army, its bureaucracy; taxation; trade; and diplomacy.

The early modern army looked nothing like the professional modern army. With their reluctance to arm their own peasants, the Absolutist State placed a great reliance on mercenaries. Famous among these were the Croatians, to whom the humble bowtie owes its origins. The Croatians, serving the French in the Thirty Years' War, wore a cravat as a good-luck charm around their neck. War was important to the development of the Absolutist State. As the Italian political theorist Niccolò Machiavelli put it, quite simply: 'War is the only art expected of a ruler'.

A period actor in the bowtie made famous by the Croatian mercenaries of the early modern period

Territorial accumulation was at the heart of the Absolutist exercise. So the sixteenth and seventeenth centuries were, above all else, centuries of international war. War was expensive and two-thirds or more of State revenues were consumed by it, with armies usually paid by plunder.

Important new military technologies appeared in the period from the late 1500s to the Battle of Waterloo in 1815. The infantry line and drill was introduced by Maurice of Orange in the struggle for Dutch independence against the Spanish in the late 1500s. The charismatic Swedish king Gustavus Adolphus added the cavalry salvo to his army's repertoire in the Thirty Years' War, during the early 1600s. He also developed a more integrated deployment of the artillery, cavalry, and infantry. The concept of a unitary vertical command was associated in the same Thirty Years' War with the cold-blooded Czech general, Albrecht von Wallenstein.[2]

These growing armies meant that each State faced an internal political problem. The increasing militarisation of the Absolutist period led to a drain on royal income and an increased need to tax the Estates. The 1600s was a century of rebellion against the excessive spending on the military, but only in England did this rebellion succeed, with the English Civil War.

It was such a violent period of European history that writers like the Englishman Thomas Hobbes assumed that this was a normal situation. In *Leviathan* Hobbes replaced the 'contract' of vassalage to a particular lord with a 'social contract'. His opening assumption, to see a brutal life as one where the State does not exist, reflects the bellicose times in which he lived, a condition produced by the Absolutist State itself! Nonetheless this text is regarded as the quintessential primary text for modern political theory.

After the tumult of the 1600s, the eighteenth century was one of

---

2 The Thirty Years' War (1618-1648) began as a religious war stemming from the option given to each of the 225 local German leaders as to whether their realm was to convert from Catholicism to Protestantism; it soon escalated into a full-blown war.

Diplomacy was a critical institution in the construction of the Absolutist State: Hans Holbein the Younger, *The Ambassadors*, 1533 [National Gallery, London]

relative peace between the monarchy and the nobility. Military conflict now followed the pattern of trade in shifting outside Europe. The first of these major conflicts was Seven Years' War, 1756-63, a war essentially between England and France, but conducted in distant North America – this was the first major inter-continental war in modern times, and so has been nicknamed 'the first world war'. This war would have significant implications, well beyond the 1760s.

The second major institution to grow in the Absolutist period was that of the bureaucracy. The early-modern bureaucracy comprised 'offices' that could be bought and sold, a natural progression from feudalism: an office gave one the power to make money by selling licences of various kinds. Samuel Pepys (1633-1703) was a London bureaucrat, famous as a diarist who gives us insights into the public and private life of these early bureaucrats. Pepys developed a detailed knowledge of naval materiel that would prove invaluable in the formative years of the Royal Navy. Typically these bureaucrats possessed specialised knowledge that helped the Absolutist State exercise control over key aspects of government.

A third institution was the taxing power. We have seen how taxation has been linked to elite control of society since river valley times, but now it was increasingly sophisticated – and unfair. The burden of taxation fell unevenly on the poor, one of the causes of peasant revolts. Feudalism did not have universal taxation. The Estates-General had to be called together by the monarch to raise taxation, and this was a point of vulnerability for the Absolutist State.

The Great Chain of Being was an early-modern invention to explain how human social structures were part of the natural order

The fourth key institution in the rise of the Absolutist State was that of trade. Mercantilism was the logical economic system of this period, with each State jealously guarding its own trade, prohibiting the export of its bullion and encouraging the export of its own goods, the very opposite of the laissez-faire economy that Adam Smith would recommend in 1775. Its zero-sum logic was to support the development of a war economy. Nonetheless, the period of maritime imperialism produced wealth on a scale that neither the Europeans nor the Ottomans could have imagined. The advent of the American trade led to a guaranteed income stream for the European nobility.

Finally, there was modern diplomacy, re-invented by the Absolutist State (it was originally a Byzantine creation). Diplomacy aimed to probe the weaknesses in other jurisdictions, made possible by the newly centralised monarchies that were replacing the older pyramidal social structures.

The ideology of Absolutism

So the Absolutist State was inherently unstable, full of contradictions and conflicts, with local variations. What Absolutism was not: it was in no sense nationalistic, for the early-modern State had no interest in mobilising the patriotic sentiments of its would-be citizens. Absolutism was working toward uniformity across its jurisdiction, such in the construction of legal codes, and this made a path for the rise of the bourgeoisie. Absolutist power grew not because the European dynasties expected to create nation-states, but because of its internal logic of territorial accumulation, and it did so within the existing linguistic-ethnic mosaic of Europeans.[3]

---

3 The work in this area of the Norwegian political scientist Stein Rokkan (1921-1979) deserves to be better known. See Charles Tilly, 'Stein Rokkan's conceptual map of Europe', CSRO Working Paper No 229, Center for Research on Social Organisation, University of Michigan, February 1981, mimeo, 21 pp. [available at http://deepblue.lib.umich.edu/bitstream/handle/2027.42/51003/229.pdf, accessed 9 July 2013].

A crucial element in the ideology of Absolutism was the 'divine right of kings'. This was a device intended to elevate the monarchy well above their vassals by proposing a ladder of intermediary entities (the divine, angels, monarchs, aristocrats, and all the rest down to sticks and stones) that put everyone firmly on their rungs. The Great Chain of Being placed the Absolutist ruler close to the apex in a deo-centric worldview, but had the less fortunate effect of coupling the deo-centric world with the anthro-centric alternative, as it invited a consideration of the events occurring well below the purview of the gods.

To understand how this idea of Absolutism played out, we will consider a number of major European dynasties.

Spain

Table 13.1: Notable Kings and Queens of early-modern Spain, 1474-1714

Isabella I of Castile	1474-1504
Ferdinand of Aragon	1479-1516
Joanna the Mad	1516-1555
Charles I and V	1516-1556
Philip I	1556-1598
Philip II	1598-1621
Philip III	1621-1665
Charles II	1665-1700
Philip IV	1700-1705
Charles III	1705-1714

There were two key factors in the early success of Absolutist Spain: the plunder of the Americas, and the success of the Hapsburgs in creating a family dynasty. Ferdinand of Aragon (Barcelona) and Isabella of Castile (Madrid) brought together the two realms and asserted their power as aristocrats over the urban bourgeoisie. Absolutist Spain, from the time of Ferdinand and Isabella, proved to be very successful. This

Ferdinand of Aragon (Barcelona)

aristocracy was able to resist the rise of a local bourgeoisie of the kind observed elsewhere in Europe. Its wool industry made it the 'Australia of the Middle Ages'. By 1492 the Reconquista had driven the Moors from Granada. In Castile the persecution of the 'conversos' (supposed Christians concealing their true beliefs) led to the flight of Jewish capital. The Spanish Absolutist government moved to create a local Catholic church that would be independent of the Papacy.

However, the monarchs Ferdinand and Isabella were unable to integrate their two realms – in the end there was no common currency, tax system, or legal code. Indeed, their only unifying institution was the Spanish Inquisition! Charles V (originally known as Charles I of Spain) expanded the Hapsburg Empire into Europe. He was able to prove divine support for his reign through the successes of Hernán Cortés in Mexico and Francisco Pizarro in Peru. The continuing flow of wealth from Mexico and Latin America meant that a centralised Iberian State

There was so much gold in New Spain that pieces like this, now at the Bogota Gold Museum, were not needed in Spain

was not an economic necessity. The size of the Spanish plunder from the New World was staggering. Even today, the Bogota Gold Museum still holds 60,000 pre-Hispanic pieces. This colonial bullion, however, made up only 20-25 per cent of the total income coming into Spanish coffers during the Absolutist period.

Spanish success continued into the sixteenth century. 1571 saw the naval defeat of the Ottoman fleet at the battle of Lepanto, in the Gulf of Corinth, ending Ottoman ambitions in the Mediterranean. From 1580 to 1640 the Spanish absorbed Portugal (an episode that strengthened the sense of Portuguese nationality). In the decades leading up to its formal control in 1599, the Spanish undertook the settlement of the Philippines, the most daring European conquest of this period, leading to the imposition of European feudal laws in the archipelago and a dominion that would survive until 1898. The Spanish also maintained a large standing Hapsburg army, especially in the Low Countries of Europe. But the defeat of the Spanish Armada by the English in 1588, and the Spanish defeat in the Thirty Years' War, were signs of the limits to Spanish power. The 1640s saw Spain's borders contracted, mostly thanks to French expansion.

France

Table 13.2: Some rulers of France, 987-1804

Capetian dynasty	
987-996	Hugh Capet
Valois dynasty	
1328-1350	Philip VI
Bourbon dynasty	
1589-1610	Henry IV
1643-1715	Louis XIV (the Sun King)
1715-1774	Louis XV
1774-1792	Louis XVI
First Republic	
1799-1804	First Consul: Napoleon Bonaparte

Unlike Spain, France did not have the economic benefit of an empire (until much later, under Napoleon). However, the Capetians did not have the challenge of competing against rival realms of equivalent size and power. Their success meant that France was a unified kingdom with a population of 20 million people, double the size of Spain. The sheer size of France made it difficult to rule. When the Hundred Years' War with England (1337-1453) was finally concluded, France was left with a large standing army and an Estates-General with enhanced power.

The population continued to grow, rising from 18 million to 26 million between 1700 and 1789. The Government employed only 1000 bureaucrats, but could rely upon a total troop strength of 300 000, as well as a permanent police force, created in Paris in 1667, and then expanded to patrol all of France by 1699.

However, there was an underlying crisis. The wars of the 1700s cost the French State dearly, and led directly to damaging conflicts between the monarchy and the nobility. Merchants (and then the Enlightenment intellectuals) increasingly began to prosper outside of the orbit of this State. The American War of Independence (beginning in 1776) deepened this fiscal crisis without bringing the French State any obvious benefits from its support for the rebels.

England

Table 13.3: Some rulers of England, 1066-1685

1066-1087	William I (The Conqueror)
1189-1199	Richard I (The Lionheart)
1377-1399	Richard II
1399-1413	Henry IV (House of Lancaster)
1413-1422	Henry V
The Tudors	
1485-1509	Henry VII
1509-1547	Henry VIII
1547-1553	Edward VI
1558-1603	Elizabeth I (The Virgin Queen)
The House of Stuart	
1603-1625	James I
1625-1649	Charles I
Commonwealth	
1653-1658	Oliver Cromwell (Old Ironsides)
1658-1659	Richard Cromwell
House of Stuart (restored)	
1660-1685	Charles II

A potent symbol of English Absolutism: Henry VIII and his wives

Certain factors explain the particular qualities of English Absolutism. England's feudal monarchy was more powerful than that of France, but its Absolutism was short-lived, thanks to the English Civil War. English towns had not enjoyed the same independence as their continental counterparts, with power here securely based in the royal capital of London. The Estates system of France had no equivalent in the unitary government of England. The conquest of 1066 had created quite different conditions. There was also a more devolved sense of local power, with the Sheriffs in England drawn from the local gentry; indeed, the Justices of the Peace constituted a uniquely English institution, with no equivalents on the Continent.

The ongoing conflict with the French helps explain the particularity of English Absolutism. For much of this period, the English were able to control parts of France across the barrier of the English Channel. These attacks on France were part of the same pattern that saw English military incursions on Scotland, Portugal, Castile, and elsewhere. The English did not maintain a professional army, but retained private plunderers for the lords who engaged them. This was the same model that underpinned English piracy. England's growing capacity in naval combat was not questioned, as maritime battles were not relevant to the Hundred Years' War. In 1386 the French did contemplate a sea-borne invasion of England, but thought better of the project. (This idea then lay dormant until Napoleon in 1805.)

The Absolutist period saw a change in the balance of power between England and France. The English had the upper hand at first because of their unified aristocracy and, when finally evicted by the French from the Continent, descended into the internecine War of the Roses and the rise of the Tudors. After Henry VIII's marriage crisis of 1527-28, the Reformation gave the Tudor State access to all the properties and power previously held by the Catholics. But Henry VIII's reckless military campaigning in Europe meant that much of his new wealth was dissipated. With their conquests in America, France and Spain were suddenly more powerful in relative terms.

The English victories at Crécy and Agincourt have usually been portrayed as significant. The traditional view is that Agincourt proved that humble archers could defeat patrician French knights. But the English nobility from now on gained very little military experience – they turned instead to commercial agriculture. Their only genuine military success was Ireland, colonised in 1604.

English Absolutism is materially represented in several ways by the Tower of London, its Crown Jewels and assemblage of towers making it a popular destination for toursts to England.[4] Although the site, on the northern bank of the Thames, dates back to Roman and Anglo-Saxon

---

[4] Visitors find it unrelentingly grim: 'Cold and dark. Fake jewels', wrote one young modern visitor from Australia. (Rosemary Clerehan, pers. corr., 16 June 2013).

times, only in medieval times did it attain a central role in the government of England. It was restored by the Normans in 1086, two decades after their successful invasion. Kings like Edward I and Edward III developed its fortification further and used it as a temporary refuge during times of political strife, such as during the big Peasant Revolt of 1381. Royals slept there intermittently, but only when they needed protection from enemies – but they were more likely to use it as a place of incarcerating their opponents.

However, the Tower's more germane significance lies in the particular institutions associated with the Absolutist State that became located there. One by one, agencies that would prove critical to the success of Absolutism were bundled into the physical boundaries of the Tower of London. One was obviously the military, with the Tower performing the vital role of serving as an armoury for the weapons that shaped the course of early modern battles on land and sea. Another was the economic role played by coinage, since the Mint was moved to the Tower and remained there until modern times. England's trading prowess was represented by the bestiary within the Tower, a kind of medieval zoo that contained specimens from the world over. Shuttered up within the Tower of London are clues aplenty as to how English Absolutism was actually experienced, by rulers and ruled alike.

Over time English Absolutism changed to fit the conditions of a changing world. Under the Tudors England gradually became a naval power, with piracy as a training ground. The defeat of the Spanish Armada in 1588 was a critical moment. The Royal Navy would prove more useful for trade than an English army. When the Scottish Stuarts took the English throne after 1603, their attempt to impose a new form of Absolutism failed – they prorogued Parliament, but then had to recall it with the invasion of the Scots in 1640 and the Irish rebellion of 1641. The English Civil War of the 1640s was driven by London's gentry. English Absolutism had reached a dead end.

Italy

Curiously, Absolutism drew from Italy many of its instruments of power, but in Italy itself there was no Absolutism, no unified national government, owing to the precocity of urban mercantile elites in north Italian cities such as Florence and Venice. These cities were of course the cradle of the Renaissance. Even the artists of the Renaissance belonged to urban guilds. These Italian city republics gradually became local tyrannies, such as the Medici rule in Florence, except where they had maritime empires. Machiavelli's advice to 'The Prince' was not particularly relevant to Absolutist monarchies, as he was writing for a prince ruling one city rather than an entire kingdom. One of the ways of thinking about the development of the Italian peninsula, and Sicily, is to see these regional governments as highly creative in developing the key institutions of Absolutist rule (diplomacy in Venice, trade in Genoa, taxation in Florence, etc), but not in bringing then into a coherent pattern. Italy remained a constellation of principalities until modern times, perhaps (some would say) until 1943.

Sweden

Table 13.4: Some rulers of Sweden, 1389-1654

1389-1412	Margaret
House of Vasa	
1523-1560	Gustav I
1560-1568	Eric XIV
1568-1592	John III
1592-1599	Sigmund
1604-1611	Charles IX
1611-1632	Gustav II Adolph ('the Great')
1632-1654	Christina (played by Greta Garbo in a 1933 film)

Sweden was a curious mix of Western and Eastern Europe. It comprised a free peasantry, which lent it a Western flavour, but the absence of large cities and towns (and hence an insignificant urban bourgeoisie) was more Eastern, as was the small size of its aristocracy. Together, these factors meant that Sweden saw a limited development of feudalism. Sweden was also unusual in that a fourth Estate was created for its peasantry.

Swedish Absolutism survived for several reasons. One was the wealth produced in Sweden's iron and copper mines. These resources were also used in building a local armaments industry. In 1527 the monarchy usurped all the church properties in the Reformation. Gustavus Adolphus led a successful military intervention in the Thirty Years' War, as a result of which Sweden controlled much of northern Europe. Sweden was unusual in having a standing conscripted army, formed in 1544. In 1680 Charles XI was declared to be of divine right, a fiction endorsed by the Swedish parliament.

Challenges to Absolutism

Across Western Europe Absolutism was reasonably consistent, with certain features in common. These included: the accumulation of State power through the use of Roman Law and the five key institutions – the army, taxes, diplomacy, trade, and the bureaucracy. Missing from this quintet of Absolutist institutions was the Church: the Church was no longer as important politically as it had been. Each of these five institutions of Absolutist power had a logical connection, but together they contained some contradictions; these contradictions opened up combined and uneven developments. For one thing, the deo-centric worldview would soon come under serious attack.

Primary source: Thomas Hobbes, *Leviathan*

The Second Part: Of Commonwealth

Chapter XVII

Of the Causes, Generation, and Definition of a Commonwealth

THE final cause, end, or design of men (who naturally love liberty, and dominion over others) in the introduction of that restraint upon themselves, in which we see them live in Commonwealths, is the foresight of their own preservation, and of a more contented life thereby; that is to say, of getting themselves out from that miserable condition of war which is necessarily consequent, as hath been shown, to the natural passions of men when there is no visible power to keep them in awe, and tie them by fear of punishment to the performance of their covenants,

The frontispiece to *Leviathan* depicted the State as a large man

and observation of those laws of nature set down in the fourteenth and fifteenth chapters.

For the laws of nature, as justice, equity, modesty, mercy, and, in sum, doing to others as we would be done to, of themselves, without the terror of some power to cause them to be observed, are contrary to our natural passions, that carry us to partiality, pride, revenge, and the like. And covenants, without the sword, are but words and of no strength to secure a man at all. Therefore, notwithstanding the laws of nature (which every one hath then kept, when he has the will to keep them, when he can do it safely), if there be no power erected, or not great enough for our security, every man will and may lawfully rely on his own strength and art for caution against all other men. And in all places, where men have lived by small families, to rob and spoil one another has been a trade, and so far from being reputed against the law of nature that the greater spoils they gained, the greater was their honour; and men observed no other laws therein but the laws of honour; that is, to abstain from cruelty, leaving to men their lives and instruments of husbandry. And as small families did then; so now do cities and kingdoms, which are but greater families (for their own security), enlarge their dominions upon all pretences of danger, and fear of invasion, or assistance that may be given to invaders; endeavour as much as they can to subdue or weaken their neighbours by open force, and secret arts, for want of other caution, justly; and are remembered for it in after ages with honour.

Nor is it the joining together of a small number of men that gives them this security; because in small numbers, small additions on the one side or the other make the advantage of strength so great as is sufficient to carry the victory, and therefore gives encouragement to an invasion. The multitude sufficient to confide in for our security is not determined by any certain number, but by comparison with the enemy we fear; and is then sufficient when the odds of the enemy is not of so visible and conspicuous moment to determine the event of war, as to move him to attempt.

And be there never so great a multitude; yet if their actions be directed according to their particular judgements, and particular appetites, they can expect thereby no defence, nor protection, neither against a common enemy, nor against the injuries of one another. For being distracted in opinions concerning the best use and application of their strength, they do not help, but hinder one another, and reduce their strength by mutual opposition to nothing: whereby they are easily, not only subdued by a very few that agree together, but also, when there is no common enemy, they make war upon each other for their particular interests. For if we could suppose a great multitude of men to consent in the observation of justice, and other laws of nature, without a common power to keep them all in awe, we might as well suppose all mankind to do the same; and then there neither would be, nor need to be, any civil government or Commonwealth at all, because there would be peace without subjection.

Nor is it enough for the security, which men desire should last all the time of their life, that they be governed and directed by one judgement for a limited time; as in one battle, or one war. For though they obtain a victory by their unanimous endeavour against a foreign enemy, yet afterwards, when either they have no common enemy, or he that by one part is held for an enemy is by another part held for a friend, they must needs by the difference of their interests dissolve, and fall again into a war amongst themselves.

It is true that certain living creatures, as bees and ants, live sociably one with another (which are therefore by Aristotle numbered amongst political creatures), and yet have no other direction than their particular judgements and appetites; nor speech, whereby one of them can signify to another what he thinks expedient for the common benefit: and therefore some man may perhaps desire to know why mankind cannot do the same. To which I answer,

First, that men are continually in competition for honour and dignity, which these creatures are not; and consequently amongst men there ariseth on that ground, envy, and hatred, and finally war; but amongst these not so.

Secondly, that amongst these creatures the common good differeth not from the private; and being by nature inclined to their private, they procure thereby the common benefit. But man, whose joy consisteth in comparing himself with other men, can relish nothing but what is eminent.

Thirdly, that these creatures, having not, as man, the use of reason, do not see, nor think they see, any fault in the administration of their common business: whereas amongst men there are very many that think themselves wiser and abler to govern the public better than the rest, and these strive to reform and innovate, one this way, another that way; and thereby bring it into distraction and civil war.

Fourthly, that these creatures, though they have some use of voice in making known to one another their desires and other affections, yet they want that art of words by which some men can represent to others that which is good in the likeness of evil; and evil, in the likeness of good; and augment or diminish the apparent greatness of good and evil, discontenting men and troubling their peace at their pleasure.

Fifthly, irrational creatures cannot distinguish between injury and damage; and therefore as long as they be at ease, they are not offended with their fellows: whereas man is then most troublesome when he is most at ease; for then it is that he loves to show his wisdom, and control the actions of them that govern the Commonwealth.

Lastly, the agreement of these creatures is natural; that of men is by covenant only, which is artificial: and therefore it is no wonder if there be somewhat else required, besides covenant, to make their agreement constant and lasting; which is a common power to keep them in awe and to direct their actions to the common benefit.

The only way to erect such a common power, as may be able to defend them from the invasion of foreigners, and the injuries of one another, and thereby to secure them in such sort as that by their own industry and by the fruits of the earth they may nourish themselves and live contentedly, is to confer all their power and strength upon one man, or upon one assembly of men, that may reduce all their wills, by plurality of voices, unto one will: which is as much as to say, to appoint one man, or assembly of men, to bear their person; and every one to own and acknowledge himself to be author of whatsoever he that so beareth their person shall act, or cause to be acted, in those things which concern the common peace and safety; and therein to submit their wills, every one to his will, and their judgements to his judgement. This is more than consent, or concord; it is a real unity of them all in one and the same person, made by covenant of every man with every man, in such manner as if every man should say to every man: I authorise and give up my right of governing myself to this man, or to this assembly of men, on this condition; that thou give up, thy right to him, and authorise all his actions in like manner. This done, the multitude so united in one person is called a COMMONWEALTH; in Latin, CIVITAS. This is the generation of that great LEVIATHAN, or rather, to speak more reverently, of that mortal god to which we owe, under the immortal God, our peace and defence. For by this authority, given him by every particular man in the Commonwealth, he hath the use of so much power and strength conferred on him that, by terror thereof, he is enabled to form the wills of them all, to peace at home, and mutual aid against their enemies abroad. And in him consisteth the essence of the Commonwealth; which, to define it, is: one person, of whose acts a great multitude, by mutual covenants one with another, have made themselves every one the author, to the end he may use the strength and means of them all as he shall think expedient for their peace and common defence.

And he that carryeth this person is called sovereign, and said to have sovereign power; and every one besides, his subject.

The attaining to this sovereign power is by two ways. One, by natural force: as when a man maketh his children to submit themselves, and their children, to his government, as being able to destroy them if they refuse; or by war subdueth his enemies to his will, giving them their lives on that condition. The other, is when men agree amongst themselves to submit to some man, or assembly of men, voluntarily, on confidence to be protected by him against all others. This latter may be called a political Commonwealth, or Commonwealth by Institution; and the former, a Commonwealth by acquisition. And first, I shall speak of a Commonwealth by institution.

CHAPTER XVIII:

OF THE RIGHTS OF SOVEREIGNS BY INSTITUTION

A COMMONWEALTH is said to be instituted when a multitude of men do agree, and covenant, every one with every one, that to whatsoever man, or assembly of men, shall be given by the major part the right to present the person of them all, that is to say, to be their representative; every one, as well he that voted for it as he that voted against it, shall authorize all the actions and judgements of that man, or assembly of men, in the same manner as if they were his own, to the end to live peaceably amongst themselves, and be protected against other men.

From this institution of a Commonwealth are derived all the rights and faculties of him, or them, on whom the sovereign power is conferred by the consent of the people assembled.

First, because they covenant, it is to be understood they are not obliged by former covenant to anything repugnant hereunto. And consequently they that have already instituted a Commonwealth, being thereby bound by covenant to own the actions and judgements of one, cannot lawfully make a new covenant amongst themselves to be obedient to any other, in anything whatsoever, without his permission. And therefore, they that are subjects to a monarch cannot without his leave cast off monarchy and return to the confusion of a disunited multitude; nor transfer their person from him that beareth it to another man, other assembly of men: for they are bound, every man to every man, to own and be reputed author of all that already is their sovereign shall do and judge fit to be done; so that any one man dissenting, all the rest should break their covenant made to that man, which is injustice: and they have also every man given the sovereignty to him that beareth their person; and therefore if they depose him, they take from him that which is his own, and so again it is injustice. Besides, if he that attempteth to depose his sovereign be killed or punished by him for such attempt, he is author of his own punishment, as being, by the institution, author of all his sovereign shall do; and because it is injustice for a man to do anything for which he may be punished by his own authority, he is also upon that title unjust. And whereas some men have pretended for their disobedience to their sovereign a new covenant, made, not with men but with God, this also is unjust: for there is no covenant with God but by mediation of somebody that representeth God's person, which none doth but God's lieutenant who hath the sovereignty under God. But this pretence of covenant with God is so evident a lie, even in the pretenders' own consciences, that it is not only an act of an unjust, but also of a vile and unmanly disposition.

Secondly, because the right of bearing the person of them all is given to him they make sovereign, by covenant only of one to another, and not of him to any of them, there can happen no breach of covenant on the part of the sovereign; and consequently none of his subjects, by any pretence of forfeiture, can be freed from his subjection. That he which is made sovereign maketh no covenant with his subjects before hand is manifest; because either he must make it with the whole multitude, as one party to the covenant, or he must make a several covenant with every man. With the whole, as one party, it is impossible, because as they are not one person: and if he make so many several covenants as there be men, those covenants after he hath the sovereignty are void; because what act soever can be pretended by any one of them for breach thereof is the act both of himself, and of all the rest, because done in the person, and by the right of every one of them in particular. Besides, if any one or more of them pretend a breach of the covenant made by the sovereign at his institution, and others or one other of his subjects, or himself alone, pretend there was no such breach, there is in this case no judge to decide the controversy: it returns therefore to the sword again; and every man recovereth the right of protecting himself by his own strength, contrary to the design they had in the institution. It is therefore in vain to grant sovereignty by way of precedent covenant. The opinion that any monarch receiveth his power by covenant, that is to say, on condition, proceedeth from want of understanding this easy truth: that covenants being but words, and breath, have no force to oblige, contain, constrain, or protect any man, but what it has from the public sword; that is, from the untied hands of that man, or assembly of men, that hath the sovereignty, and whose actions are avouched by them all, and performed by the strength of them all, in him united. But when an assembly of men is made sovereign, then no man imagineth any such covenant to have passed in the institution: for no man is so dull as to say, for example, the people of Rome made a covenant with the Romans to hold the sovereignty on such or such conditions; which not performed, the Romans might lawfully depose the Roman people. That men see not the reason to be alike in a monarchy and in a popular government proceedeth from the ambition of some that are kinder to the government of an assembly, whereof they may hope to participate, than of monarchy, which they despair to enjoy.

Thirdly, because the major part hath by consenting voices declared a sovereign, he that dissented must now consent with the rest; that is, be contented to avow all the actions he shall do, or else justly be destroyed by the rest. For if he voluntarily entered into the congregation of them that were assembled, he sufficiently declared thereby his will, and therefore tacitly covenanted, to stand to what the major part should ordain: and therefore if he refuse to stand thereto, or make protestation against any of their decrees, he does contrary to his covenant, and therefore unjustly. And whether he be of the congregation or not, and whether his consent be asked or not, he must either submit to their decrees or be left in the condition of war he was in before; wherein he might without injustice be destroyed by any man whatsoever.

Fourthly, because every subject is by this institution author of all the actions and judgements of the sovereign instituted, it follows that whatsoever he doth, can be no injury to any of his subjects; nor ought he to be by any of them accused of injustice. For he that doth anything by authority from another doth therein no injury to him by whose authority he acteth: but by this institution of a Commonwealth every particular man is author of all the sovereign doth; and consequently he that complaineth of injury from his sovereign complaineth of that whereof he himself is author, and therefore ought not to accuse any man but himself; no, nor himself of injury, because to do injury to oneself is impossible. It is true that they that have sovereign power may commit iniquity, but not injustice or injury in the proper signification.

Fifthly, and consequently to that which was said last, no man that hath sovereign power can justly be put to death, or otherwise in any manner by his subjects punished. For seeing every subject is author of the actions of his sovereign, he punisheth another for the actions committed by himself.

And because the end of this institution is the peace and defence of them all, and whosoever has right to the end has right to the means, it belonged of right to whatsoever man or assembly that hath the sovereignty to be judge both of the means of peace and defence, and also of the hindrances and disturbances of the same; and to do whatsoever he shall think necessary to be done, both beforehand, for the preserving of peace and security, by prevention of discord at home, and hostility from abroad; and when peace and security are lost, for the recovery of the same. And therefore,

Sixthly, it is annexed to the sovereignty to be judge of what opinions and doctrines are averse, and what conducing to peace; and consequently, on what occasions, how far, and what men are to be trusted withal in speaking to multitudes of people; and who shall examine the doctrines of all books before they be published. For the actions of men proceed from their opinions, and in the well governing of opinions consisteth the well governing of men's actions in order to their peace and concord. And though in matter of doctrine nothing to be regarded but the truth, yet this is not repugnant to regulating of the same by peace. For doctrine repugnant to peace can no more be true, than peace and concord can be against the law of nature. It is true that in a Commonwealth, where by the negligence or unskillfulness of governors and teachers false doctrines are by time generally received, the contrary truths may be generally offensive: yet the most sudden and rough bustling in of a new truth that can be does never break the peace, but only sometimes awake the war. For those men that are so remissly governed that they dare take up arms to defend or introduce an opinion are still in war; and their condition, not peace, but only a cessation of arms for fear of one another; and they live, as it were, in the procincts of battle continually. It belonged therefore to him that hath the sovereign power to be judge, or constitute all judges of opinions and doctrines, as a thing necessary to peace; thereby to prevent discord and civil war.

Seventhly, is annexed to the sovereignty the whole power of prescribing the rules whereby every man may know what goods he may enjoy, and what actions he may do, without being molested by any of his fellow subjects: and this is it men call propriety. For before constitution of sovereign power, as hath already been shown, all men had right to all things, which necessarily causeth war: and therefore this propriety, being necessary to peace, and depending on sovereign power, is the act of that power, in order to the public peace. These rules of propriety (or meum and tuum) and of good, evil, lawful, and unlawful in the actions of subjects are the civil laws; that is to say, the laws of each Commonwealth in particular; though the name of civil law be now restrained to the ancient civil laws of the city of Rome; which being the head of a great part of the world, her laws at that time were in these parts the civil law.

Eighthly, is annexed to the sovereignty the right of judicature; that is to say, of hearing and deciding all controversies which may arise concerning law, either civil or natural, or concerning fact. For without the decision of controversies, there is no protection of one subject against the injuries of another; the laws concerning meum and tuum are in vain, and to every man remaineth, from the natural and necessary appetite of his own conservation, the right of protecting himself by his private strength, which is the condition of war, and contrary to the end for which every Commonwealth is instituted.

Ninthly, is annexed to the sovereignty the right of making war and peace with other nations and Commonwealths; that is to say, of judging when it is for the public good, and how great forces are to be assembled, armed, and paid for that end, and to levy money upon the subjects to defray the expenses thereof. For the power by which the people are to be defended consisteth in their armies, and the strength of an army in the union of their strength under one command; which command the sovereign instituted, therefore hath, because the command of the militia, without other institution, maketh him that hath it sovereign. And therefore, whosoever is made general of an army, he that hath the sovereign power is always generalissimo.

Tenthly, is annexed to the sovereignty the choosing of all counsellors, ministers, magistrates, and officers, both in peace and war. For seeing the sovereign is charged with the end, which is the common peace and defence, he is understood to have power to use such means as he shall think most fit for his discharge.

Eleventhly, to the sovereign is committed the power of rewarding with riches or honour; and of punishing with corporal or pecuniary punishment, or with ignominy, every subject according to the law he hath formerly made; or if there be no law made, according as he shall judge most to conduce to the encouraging of men to serve the Commonwealth, or deterring of them from doing disservice to the same.

Lastly, considering what values men are naturally apt to set upon themselves, what respect they look for from others, and how little they value other men; from whence continually arise amongst them, emulation, quarrels, factions, and at last war, to the destroying of one another, and diminution of their strength against a common enemy; it is necessary that there be laws of honour, and a public rate of the worth of such men as have deserved or are able to deserve well of the Commonwealth, and that there be force in the hands of some or other to put those laws in execution. But it hath already been shown that not only the whole militia, or forces of the Commonwealth, but also the judicature of all controversies, is annexed to the sovereignty. To the sovereign therefore it belonged also to give titles of honour, and to appoint what order of place and dignity each man shall hold, and what signs of respect in public or private meetings they shall give to one another.

These are the rights which make the essence of sovereignty, and which are the marks whereby a man may discern in what man, or assembly of men, the sovereign power is placed and resideth. For these are incommunicable and inseparable. The power to coin money, to dispose of the estate and persons of infant heirs, to have pre-emption in markets, and all other statute prerogatives may be transferred by the sovereign, and yet the power to protect his subjects be retained. But if he transfer the militia, he retains the judicature in vain, for want of execution of the laws; or if he grant away the power of raising money, the militia is in vain; or if he give away the government of doctrines, men will be frighted into rebellion with the fear of spirits. And so if we consider any one of the said rights, we shall presently see that the holding of all the rest will produce no effect in the conservation of peace and justice, the end for which all Commonwealths are instituted. And this division is it whereof it is said, a kingdom divided in itself cannot stand: for unless this division precede, division into opposite armies can never happen. If there had not first been an opinion received of the greatest part of England that these powers were divided between the King and the Lords and the House of Commons, the people had never been divided and fallen into this Civil War; first between those that disagreed in politics, and after between the dissenters about the liberty of religion, which have so instructed men in this point of sovereign right that there be few now in England that do not see that these rights are inseparable, and will be so generally acknowledged at the next return of peace; and so continue, till their miseries are forgotten, and no longer, except the vulgar be better taught than they have hitherto been.

And because they are essential and inseparable rights, it follows necessarily that in whatsoever words any of them seem to be granted away, yet if the sovereign power itself be not in direct terms renounced and the name of sovereign no more given by the grantees to him that grants them, the grant is void: for when he has granted all he can, if we grant back the sovereignty, all is restored, as inseparably annexed thereunto.

This great authority being indivisible, and inseparably annexed to the sovereignty, there is little ground for the opinion of them that say of sovereign kings, though they be singulis majores, of greater power than every one of their subjects, yet they be universis minores, of less power than them all together. For if by all together, they mean not the collective body as one person, then all together and every one signify the same; and the speech is absurd. But if by all together, they understand them as one person (which person the sovereign bears), then the power of all together is the same with the sovereign's power; and so again the speech is absurd: which absurdity they see well enough when the sovereignty is in an assembly of the people; but in a monarch they see it not; and yet the power of sovereignty is the same in whomsoever it be placed.

And as the power, so also the honour of the sovereign, ought to be greater than that of any or all the subjects. For in the sovereignty is the fountain of honour. The dignities of lord, earl, duke, and prince are his creatures. As in the presence of the master, the servants are equal, and without any honour at all; so are the subjects, in the presence of the sovereign. And though they shine some more, some less, when they are out of his sight; yet in his presence, they shine no more than the stars in presence of the sun.

But a man may here object that the condition of subjects is very miserable, as being obnoxious to the lusts and other irregular passions of him or them that have so unlimited a power in their hands. And commonly they that live under a monarch think it the fault of monarchy; and they that live under the government of democracy, or other sovereign assembly, attribute all the inconvenience to that form of Commonwealth; whereas the power in all forms, if they be perfect enough to protect them, is the same: not considering that the estate of man can never be without some incommodity or other; and that the greatest that in any form of government can possibly happen to the people in general is scarce sensible, in respect of the miseries and horrible calamities that accompany a civil war, or that dissolute condition of masterless men without subjection to laws and a coercive power to tie their hands from rapine and revenge: nor considering that the greatest pressure of sovereign governors proceedeth, not from any delight or profit they can expect in the damage weakening of their subjects, in whose vigour consisteth their own strength and glory, but in the restiveness of themselves that,

Thomas Hobbes, the first modern political scientist
[John Michael Wright, *Thomas Hobbes*, National Portrait Gallery, London]

unwillingly contributing to their own defence, make it necessary for their governors to draw from them what they can in time of peace that they may have means on any emergent occasion, or sudden need, to resist or take advantage on their enemies. For all men are by nature provided of notable multiplying glasses (that is their passions and self-love) through which every little payment appeareth a great grievance, but are destitute of those prospective glasses (namely moral and civil science) to see afar off the miseries that hang over them and cannot without such payments be avoided.

Questions for discussion:

During Units 13-16 we examine texts as social products, looking inside them for clues to the social forces that were contingent on their creation. We begin with *Leviathan*, written by a seventeenth-century Englishman, Thomas Hobbes.

Thomas Hobbes (1588-1679) is famous for his assertion that life is 'nasty, brutal and short', but in this regard he is usually misquoted. What he said was that in the state of raw nature people's lives are miserable. In societies that are more developed, he argued, people's living conditions improve dramatically. But there is a price to pay for this new-found prosperity and happiness: namely, acceptance of a ruler who directs our lives. This ruler he calls Leviathan. *Leviathan* (1651) is regarded as the first modern treatise in political science. Much of what has followed has accepted some of the critical assumptions and arguments made by Hobbes.

What is happening in England in the time Hobbes is writing? Why does Hobbes accept Absolutism as a preferable way of organising human societies?

What is missing from his account is this justification – would the Absolutist monarch necessarily accept the Hobbesian justification for his power? (Slavery still existed at this time, but most monarchs in the Absolutist period did not see it quite as Hobbes did – they preferred a different justification for their rule.)

What is the difference between a Judaic Covenant and a Hobbesian contract?

Fear is a recurring theme in the life of Hobbes. He was born prematurely during the coming of the Spanish Armada in 1588, because his mother (like many English people) was afraid of this invasion. How does Hobbes use fear as an explanatory tool?

There are several jurisdictions today which use the term

'Commonwealth'. One is the American state of Massachusetts; what is another?

What powers does Hobbes say are the exclusive right of the monarch? In contemporary America, who has these rights?

Why does Hobbes ignore the feudal period in his historical references and go back to the Romans? What were the contracts used in feudalism?

Going further:

Perry Anderson, *Lineages of the Absolutist State*, Verso, London, 1979 [1974]

Jeremy Black, *Tools of War: The Weapons that Changed the World*, Quercus, London, 2007

Charles Tilly, 'Stein Rokkan's conceptual map of Europe', CSRO Working Paper No 229, Center for Research on Social Organisation, University of Michigan, February 1981, mimeo, 21 pp. [available at http://deepblue.lib.umich.edu/bitstream/handle/2027.42/51003/229.pdf, accessed 9 July 2013]

E.M.W. Tillyard, *The Elizabethan World Picture*, Vintage Books, New York, 1953

Unit 14:

Removing the King: The English, American and French Revolutions

One of the plays that has most confused, angered and scandalised generations of theatre-goers and critics is John Ford's *'Tis Pity She's a Whore*, with its central tale of the incestuous siblings, Giovanni and Annabella, and its lurid violence.[5] In the final scene the brother appears before the Cardinal and members of the Parma nobility with his sister's heart skewered on a sword. He explains to the astonished assembly:

> For nine months space, in secret, I enjoy'd
> Sweet Annabella's sheets; nine months I lived
> A happy monarch of her heart and her;
> Soranzo, thou know'st this; thy paler cheek
> Bears the confounding print of thy disgrace;
> For her too fruitful womb too soon bewray'd
> The happy passage of our stolen delights,
> And made her mother to a child unborn.

One nobleman dies in shock. Murder and mayhem ensue before the Cardinal brings the drama to an end with these lines:

> CARDINAL. We shall have time
> To talk at large of all; but never yet
> Incest and murder have so strangely met.
> Of one so young, so rich in nature's store,
> Who could not say, 'Tis Pity She's A Whore?

---

5 This edition is © University of Adelaide Library. Retrieved from http://ebooks.adelaide.edu.au/f/ford/john/pity/ 9 July 2013.

One reading of this play is that it is prescient of the era of murder and mayhem into which the dramatist's society was about to plunge – the English Civil War. This war was part of a broader problem besetting early-modern Europe and America.

As they entered the modern period, England, America and France were becoming increasingly different societies, and their experience of Absolutism differed widely. Of the three revolutions, the French Revolution (and the Napoleonic period that followed) opened up the political story of the modern era in World History. Many historians would argue that the French Revolution was the single most important event in human history. Now, after 1789, 'anthro-centric' alternatives to the 'deo-centric' worldview begin to emerge. Feudalism and the *ancien régime* came to an end. The changes were political, economic, cultural and social – we need to understand how these were related and at the same time distinct, and how they played out differently in different countries, especially England, America and France. The American and the French Revolutions shared in common one important background factor: the Enlightenment.

The English Civil War, 1640s-1650s

The rise of the Absolutist state was connected with the era of Spanish hegemony (the 1500s) and the parallel rise of the Ottoman Empire centred on Constantinople. The following century, the 17th Century, was a period of conflict between the monarch and the people, especially in Spain, France, and England. Only in England did it reach civil war. James I and Charles I, the Stuarts, tried to raise money without the consent of Parliament. Civil war broke out between armies of the Parliament and of the King, leading to the establishment of the republican Protectorate under Oliver Cromwell.

The Protectorate moved further Left and lost majority public support. Eventually this led to the Restoration of the Stuarts under Charles II, but James II was replaced in the Glorious Revolution by William and Mary.

Sovereign power was limited and defined by the Bill of Rights, 1689, with agreement in the formula of King-in-parliament. This showed the English genius for compromise, and meant that England would be unique in undergoing its political and economic revolutions separately. The political revolution of the 1680s was a century before the Industrial Revolution began in the 1780s. Most societies do not have this luxury of dealing with their political and economic revolutions as separate events, and their modernisation is more painful as a consequence.

The Scientific Revolution: Copernicus, Galileo, Newton, 1680s

Three key scientists subverted the dominant paradigm of Western science at the end of the deo-centric period. One was the devout Catholic Copernicus, whose *On the Revolution of the Heavenly Spheres* (1543) proposed an abstract solution that would resolve the anomalies that had crept into the Ptolemaic system and thus restore God's role. The second was Galileo, author of *The Starry Messenger* (1610). He was a lecturer at the University of Padua who used telescopes to confirm the Copernican theory but was banned from saying so. Finally Isaac Newton, in *Principia* (1687), established that constant laws of motion operated throughout the universe.

Despite these quite significant breakthroughs, educated people continued to hold on to superstitions of various kinds – even Newton was also an alchemist. As late as the nineteenth century the Victorian English were obsessed with communicating with the other side, and wanted to believe in the power of the 'séance'. Of course, among the peasantry, pagan ideas continued in the Christian West. The Spanish Inquisition, 1478, began as a means of patrolling the nation for Jews and Muslims and then was turned on women and peasants. Japan and China had the abacus already, but the slide rule was not invented until 1633 (in the West). This so-called 'Scientific Revolution' was in some ways a technical revolution.

In the New World the Europeans made surprising finds. There were animals that seemed to fit none of the recognised categories, such as the llama, the beaver, and (later) the platypus. The discoveries of the New World questioned the authority of the ancients – even though the various Old World powers approached its exploitation differently, its remarkable floral and faunal curiosities controverted acceptable knowledge in the West, including the story of Noah's Ark.

The Enlightenment was fostered by the European exploration of the Pacific Ocean – it was more scientific than the Atlantic explorations had been – opening up another new world that pushed the boundaries of European thinking even further. New questions emerged: for instance, was there one God who created the world, or two?

Enlightened individuals

The scientific breakthroughs of the Age of Enlightenment began to disturb the medieval worldview. Some Absolutist monarchs were enlightened, famously Frederick the Great (Prussia), Joseph of Austria, and Catherine the Great (Russia). During the 1700s intellectuals across Europe began to advocate the application of science, reason and rationality to the solution of human and social problems, listed in what follows by date of birth.

John Locke (1632-1704) attacked the Absolutism of the period in his 'contract' theory of government (*Two Treatises of Government*, 1660-62, published 1689). Not surprisingly, he was in exile in The Netherlands from 1683 to the Glorious Revolution of 1688.

Voltaire (François-Marie Arouet, 1694-1778) was not particularly original, but helped popularise the Enlightenment and became an important adviser to the Enlightened despots. He was affronted by the ignorance of Absolutist power, such as the wrongful execution of Jean Calas in Toulouse in 1762 or the conflict with a nobleman that led him to flee to London. Voltaire used his three years in England to draw unflattering comparisons with France, such as pointing out the beneficial role of the English Parliament in that society's governance.

Jean-Jacques Rousseau

In the American colonies, Benjamin Franklin (1706–1790) was born to Puritan parents in Boston who taught thrift and equality; he grew up in Milk Street opposite the Old South Church. Franklin believed in the practical Yankee ethos – he was an inventor, printer, propagandist for the Revolution, and a diplomat representing the revolutionaries in Paris. He led an Enlightened life. He wrote a famous autobiography addressed to his son William, but this son was born to another (unknown) woman a year before Benjamin married Deborah Read. In this autobiography he set out his worldview, advocating modesty in all things, keeping one's own counsel, and valuing others. In his lifetime he crossed the Atlantic seven times, and remained insatiably curious throughout. He sought to serve God through helping others, beginning with the newspaper he founded, the *Pennsylvania Gazette*, and his participation in the Philadelphia militia; this was followed by his involvement in the 1754 Albany Congress and later the 1775 Second Continental Congress.[6]

Jean-Jacques Rousseau (1712-1778) was the author of the famous line: 'Man was born free but is everywhere in chains'. Civilisation and

---

6 Edmund S. Morgan, *Benjamin Franklin*, Yale University Press, New Haven CT, 2002.

society corrupt the human, he argued – if freedom is only understood as actualising our capacities and pursuing our ambition, we lose time for our inner life, reverie – the freedom not to be forced to interact with society is just as important. In *Confessions* Rousseau wrote the first modern autobiography – favouring slowness, idleness and contemplation, a non-vocational life over what most people considered to be freedom, such as enterprise for its own sake. Rousseau was a populariser, using his *Confessions* and his novels to circulate Enlightenment ideas in an era which saw the rise of the urban middle-class reader. (A modern equivalent would be the mass television audiences for Oprah.) Rousseau's appeal to natural law made him more radical than the other Enlightenment figures – he was interested in knowing the origins of people's present condition, not merely extending it. He argued that sovereignty was not merely to be based on popular will but that when citizens came together the body politic was stronger than the sum of the parts – this he called 'general will'. The sum was greater than the parts. Rousseau favoured equality over balancing public and private interests. Rousseau wanted women to be educated, but to serve men nonetheless. Passion for him was as important as reason – this is why he differed from some other Enlightenment intellectuals.

Denis Diderot (1713–1784) was the founder of the *Encyclopédie*, subtitled the *Reasoned Dictionary of the Sciences, Arts and Trades*. This work comprised 17 volumes of text and 11 volumes of illustrations, published between 1751 and 1772. It apparently sold 25,000 sets by 1779, with articles by leading Enlightenment intellectuals. The *Encyclopédie* was very anti-religious, seeing religion as merely a category of philosophy.[7]

Immanuel Kant (1724–1804) wrote a famous essay 'What is Enlightenment?' (1784) for a newspaper. The newspaper itself was an important invention of this period. Kant was writing exactly mid-way between the American and the French Revolutions, both of which were consequential upon the Enlightenment.

---

7 Modern scholars are presently translating it into English. See http://quod.lib.umich.edu/d/did/

Thomas ('Tom') Paine (1737-1809) was an Englishman who moved to the American colonies in 1774 and wrote *Common Sense*, one of the major pamphlets of the American Revolution. He later moved to Paris and supported the French Revolution. His *Agrarian Justice* (1797) also links him to the English Radicals.

Thomas Jefferson (1743-1826) was a farmer in Virginia, living at Monticello. The *Encyclopédie* opposed slavery – though of course some Enlightenment leaders, including Jefferson, had their own. The alleged descendants of Jefferson and his Black partner were denied a role in the Monticello story until quite recently. Jefferson's finest moment came with the writing of the American Declaration of Independence, a document that powerfully connects the Enlightenment ideals and the political needs of an embryonic republic.

Mary Wollstonecraft (1759-1797) was a British writer, author of *A Vindication of the Rights of Women* (1792). In this she argued that women had the same capacity for reason as men. She took the Enlightenment critique of monarchy and applied it to the family. Wollstonecraft was not alone as a female voice in the Enlightenment. (Madame) Anne Louise Germaine De Staël (1766-1817) was a Parisian equivalent. There was also a decidedly feminist thrust in the novel *Dangerous Liaisons* (written by Pierre Chodelros de Laclos, 1741-1803). Wollstonecraft showed that women could construct complex philosophical arguments equal in intellectual measure of the men's, and that the Enlightenment ideals were consistent with feminist notions of the time. Her book was surprisingly modern in its conclusions, even if politically unattainable until the emergence of mass political parties and the suffragette movement of the late 19th Century, the first-wave feminists. The second-wave feminists of the late 20th Century rediscovered Wollstonecraft and some, like the Australian Germaine Greer, also subverted male philosophical arguments in a similar style. There were several talented Wollstonecrafts. Her nephew Edward Wollstonecraft (1783-1832) established the eponymous Sydney suburb in 1821. Her daughter Mary Wollstonecraft Shelley wrote the famous novel *Frankenstein*.

Friedrich Schiller (1759-1805). There were some, such as Schiller in Germany, who objected to the excessive emphasis on rationality against other domains, such as aesthetic judgment, so the Enlightenment was a contested project from the start. In judging works of art, said Schiller, we are elevated to a higher level – we can be inter-subjective together, to be playful and creative, not merely to harness nature. Politics should not be solely about the economy, but also about creating an aesthetic public sphere.

There was a musical corollary in the high baroque and the classical, and in the artistic world in the neo-classical – as always, intellectual ideas ran parallel with developments in the arts. Bach's *Mass in B Minor* was the masterwork of the baroque style (1730s).

The 'ancien régime' was seen in hindsight as tyrannical, superstitious and irrational. Notions of social improvement were based on the new understandings in science. The Enlightenment had immediate politically revolutionary consequences for America and France, while the Scottish Enlightenment was an important regional version of what was going on across Europe and North America.

This complete rejection of the ancien régime led to some interesting myths, such as the supposed right of the lord to a night with each new bride in his domain (repeated in films like *Braveheart*), for which there is no reliable evidence.

The Enlightenment thinkers across the eighteenth century were not uniform in their views and arguments. Rousseau, in particular, did not agree with everything said by his contemporaries – he was often the odd man out in his views. Recent scholarship suggests a fundamental dichotomy between one set of Enlightenment thinker who were less democratic than their contemporaries.[8] What they had in common was their confidence in applying scientific method to all branches of knowledge. As the Europeans encountered fresh issues in their

---

8 Jonathan I. Israel, *Enlightenment Contested: Philosophy, Modernity, and the Emancipation of Man 1670-1752*, Oxford University Press, Oxford, 2006.

exploration and conquest of the New World (such as the place of Indigenous people) and as they encountered a new interest in gender issues, the Enlightenment thinkers sought rational understandings of these new issues.

One of the most significant events in the Enlightenment was the trio of voyages led by Captain James Cook, from 1768 to 1779. Cook was a true creature of the Enlightenment, including his careful observations of the Pacific Ocean and its peoples. Not one of his sailors died from scurvy, thanks to his scientific interest in better nutrition for his seamen – so it was something of an irony that he himself was killed in his infamous encounter with the people of the Sandwich Islands (Hawaii).

The making of the Yankee

In the meantime the North American settlers were becoming different people from what they had been: they were becoming Yankees. There were three aspects in which the physical environment of North America differed from what the Europeans knew: it had plentiful wood, fast streams, and limitless land. It became the home for transplanted English institutions. One of the most important of these were the justices of the peace – they were local gentry invested with considerable power, despite an absence of formal legal training. JPs were supported by the petty constable and the churchwarden, again roles transplanted from England. The New England towns were settled by groups of between three and 40 families, usually known to each other from England, with dissidents 'hiving off' to create their own towns. Each town thus had a strong sense of collective identity.[9]

Further south, the Middle Colonies were different. The Chesapeake County differed from New England with fewer women and children. Its settlers were mostly 'adventurers' who cared little for community, and planted tobacco for profit. Here there was also greater ethnic diversity,

---

9 David Freeman Hawke, *Everyday Life in Early America*, Harper & Row, New York, 1988, pp. 9-17.

with Germans and Swedes in Pennsylvania, Dutch in the Hudson Valley, and English in Virginia. If New England's symbol was the individual clap-board house, here it was the log cabin and the collective barn-raising.[10] The colonial Americans adapted European technology for this new environment. Two examples will make this point. One was the Kentucky rifle, adapted in Pennsylvania from the German Jaeger. Another was the Conestoga wagon, capable of carrying four times the English load.[11]

The Protestant Yankee work ethic became evident early on in this settlement. Carving a farm from the wilderness required the colonial Americans to be more industrious than their English contemporaries. They were also adaptive. They learnt 'girdling' (ring-barking) from the Indians, they erected post-and-rail fences, they modified the axe into the lighter American version, and they adopted corn as their staple. The early Americans also learned to be frugal, adopting the credo, 'All the hog was used, except its squeal!' (The meat from just four hogs salted down in barrels could keep a family alive though winter.) The colonist, in short, became a 'jack-of-all-trades'.[12]

Home life in colonial America revolved around the hearth. The colonial hearth was large enough both to heat the house and cook the meals. The family ate at 'board', with only one chair (for the head of the house, known as the chairman), and the rest sitting on benches. People sat in pairs to spoon the food from a wooden trencher. Later, forks were introduced to spear the food. (This helps explain American eating customs.)

The rites and ceremonies of these colonists included the traditional European holidays, such as Lady's Day (25 March), Midsummer (24 June), Michaelmas (29 September), and Christmas (25 December). Sundays

---

10 Hawke, *Everyday Life in Early America*, pp. 20-30.
11 The Conestoga wagon has become a children's toy, now made, for example, by the Orvieto toymaker, Il Mago di Oz.
12 Hawke, *Everyday Life in Early America*, pp. 31-46.

were the weekly highlight. Funerals were more important than weddings as social occasions. Civic life centred on town meetings in the North, and court hearings in the South. Until the adoption of Thanksgiving in 1863, there was no recognised national holiday.[13] The first Halloween jack-o-lanterns appeared in 1837.

The Americans spoke a version of English that became increasingly their own. In their vocabulary were survivals of an older English, with words like 'deft', 'scant', and 'bub' (boy). In the new country they needed to name new plants and creatures: these words included 'popcorn', 'eggplant', 'bluebird', 'mockingbird', 'groundhog', 'bullfrogs', and 'rattlesnakes'. They named new types of watercourse ('branch', 'fork', 'run') and weather patterns ('cold snap', 'Indian summer'). They made use of certain borrowed words, including 'chowder' (from the French 'chaudière'), 'yacht', 'stoop', 'spook' (all Dutch), and 'squash', and 'canoe' (Indian).[14]

American men became used to service in the militia, following behind the fife and the drum as they beat their martial rhythm. Unlike the selective English militia, all male colonists were required to muster for training. They soon adapted to combat with the Indians, with moccasins replacing boots, lighter backpacks, buckskin uniforms, shorter brown-coated muskets, hatchets instead of swords, and formations of dispersed patrols guarded by scouts. The Indian uprisings of 1622, 1637, 1644 and 1675-76 were brutally put down.[15]

This was a pre-scientific society: most of these colonists believed in divine punishment, such as Indian uprisings. Most had superstitions, such as the need to jump backwards if one walked over a grave, for fear a kinsman would die. Almanacs informed farmers of the phases of the moon: crops should be sown during a new moon; cows will give better meat during a full moon. The Salem witch-trials saw 20 women

---

13 Hawke, *Everyday Life in Early America*, pp. 88-100.
14 Hawke, *Everyday Life in Early America*, pp. 101-04.
15 Hawke, *Everyday Life in Early America*, pp. 131-42.

executed (a small number given the half a million who perished in medieval Europe).[16]

There were some changes during the 1700s. Colonial life was still rough and ready around 1700, even though everyday life was safe, without the threat of any more Indian uprisings. Country life was friendly: goods could still be bartered in the old way. Northerners more commonly assumed an equality among men, but in the North there were far fewer Blacks and slaves. In the South as much as one-third of the first free settlers had lost their farms to the big plantations and life was not quite as equal.[17]

The American Revolution

The Enlightenment ideas had become 'self-evident truths' to these colonists. Colonial Americans resented the style of English rule. They drew particularly on the ideas of John Locke to write the American Declaration of Independence in 1776. France joined the Americans to defeat the English – they undertook a huge spending in undertaking this cause. An analysis of the signatories to the Declaration of Independence will show that the American Revolution was a rebellion of latecomers to a freshly growing set of British colonies.

It was also an argument about the control of the North Atlantic waters – New England was by now a maritime economy, and its prosperity was worth fighting over. The British war with the French (the so-called Seven Years War, 1756-1763) gained Canada for the British but also provided military training for the American colonists (which would prove useful for them) and led to increased taxation to pay for the war. The French and Spanish support for the revolutionaries was also crucial. (It is curious that no other New World rebellion succeeded until the 1820s, and that

---

16 Hawke, *Everyday Life in Early America*, pp. 157-67. The Salem witch trials won notoriety through Arthur Miller's play, *The Crucible* (1953), which used them as an allegory for the Communist witch hunts of 1950s America. The 2013 production of this play deploys the witch hunt in contemporary obsessions with identifying terrorists.
17 Hawke, *Everyday Life in Early America*, pp. 168-77.

these societies, typified by Bolivia and Peru, remained militarised to a greater extent than the young American republic.

Not all American colonists supported this revolution. Indeed, the thirteen rebellious American colonies were disloyal by comparison to the northern colonies (Canada) and the tropical (Caribbean), with some exceptions. One group of Loyalists included those Americans connected to the British Empire through occupation or industry (like New York traders, Massachusetts officials, and fewer people in Philadelphia). The planters in the South were fearful of a major slave insurrection inspired by a Revolution. Some colonists supported British authority on religious grounds, such as the Dutch and the Scottish Highlanders on the Hudson River, while, some, like the Quakers, remained neutral.[18]

The French Revolution

The French Revolution was arguably the single most important event in world history, for reasons that are worth exploring. In the 1950s, the first premier of the People's Republic of China, Zhou Enlai, is supposed to have replied, when asked about the impact of the French Revolution: 'It's too early to tell!' This was a compliment indeed.

The Revolution was centred on Paris. What was it like to be living in Paris at this time? Paris grew prodigiously from 180 000 people in 1600 to more than 500 000 in 1800. This helps explain the sense of urban ennui experienced by its inhabitants. The Swiss-born Jean-Jacques Rousseau said he was disappointed when he first saw Paris – all the mud and dirt made the city less glamorous than its reputation promised. Paris was by now sharply divided between rich and poor with the development of each 'faubourg' (suburb).

The events of 1789 indicated that this was a society profoundly in conflict with Louis XVI. The Revolution showed that even a monarchy as powerful as his could be overthrown. The French Revolution was

---

18 D. W. Meinig, *The Shaping of America*, vol. 1, *Atlantic America, 1492-1800*, Yale University Press, New Haven CT, 1986, pp. 307-22.

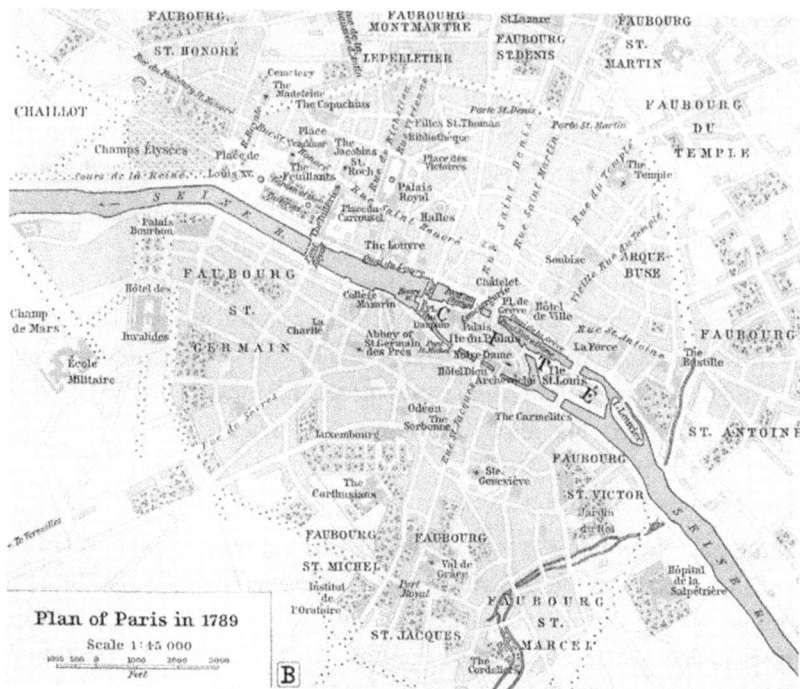

Plan of Paris in 1789, the epicentre of the world's most famous revolution
[www.lib.utexas.edu/maps]

not just a political event; it was also a social revolution. As it went on, increasingly the revolutionaries stressed equality, rather than mere liberty. This caused great alarm abroad. By 1793, at the height of the Reign of Terror, thousands were being packed off to the guillotine. This encouraged other countries to stamp out revolution at all costs.

Why was it France where this first modern revolution took place? Despite having the largest population in Western Europe, and arguably the most advanced economy, France was in many respects very old-fashioned. Its monarchy was Absolutist; it still contained pockets of classic feudalism; it had tolls; it had no systematic weights and measures. The bourgeoisie was taxed heavily; the nobility was not taxed, nor was the Church (and church leaders were often nobles in any event). The lesser townsfolk (the 'sans culottes') had problems in merely surviving: bread prices in 1789 went up 88 per cent. There was looting in Brittany, Flanders, and Provence.

The king sat at the very apex of government – he could choose or dismiss ministers at will. However, by the late 1780s he faced a deepening financial crisis (it was made worse by French aid to the colonists in the American War of Independence). Desperate, the king summoned the Estates-General to their first meeting since 1614. (The Estates-General was a meeting of the nobility, the clergy, and the Third Estate.) The deputies who came to Paris to this meeting of the Estates-General had been elected by local assemblies. They brought with them 'books of grievances' – lists of complaint compiled in each district of France. In June 1789 this meeting gave itself the title of a National Assembly. In August they enacted the Declaration of Rights of Man and Citizen (a document that in its assumptions was less deo-centric, and far more anthro-centric).

Killing the king: Louis XVI is beheaded, 21 January 1793, as illustrated by Charles Monnet (1732-1808) [Bibliothèque nationale de France]

The 'sans culottes' and the poorer women were now demanding weapons as civil disorder grew. On 14 July 1789, a date which became famous in world history, a Paris mob stormed the Bastille. There were outbreaks of violence throughout France. The monarchy could raise support from the rest of Europe (which was naturally enough quite alarmed), from aristocrat-led armies massing at the French frontiers; from the church; and even from some peasants (with the uprising in Vendée, 1793). Now the king was virtually under arrest; he made a foolish and unsuccessful attempt to escape. Now war broke out, and quickly became a total war. In response, the revolutionary French Government organised a conscription of its male citizens (a 'levee en masse'), an innovative step. Meanwhile the revolution continued to gather strength — all men were now to have the vote, to enjoy universal franchise.

Incredibly, this new revolutionary government not only managed to repel the invaders, but conquered additional territory, thereby exporting the Revolution. In this changing climate, the moderate Girondins were overtaken by the radical Jacobins. A Republic was proclaimed in 1792; the king was tried, and then guillotined in January 1793. The Terror of 1793-94 emerged out of a reaction to the invasion of France by Austria and Prussia, with the complicity of Louis XVI. The Terror was led by Robespierre and the Jacobins. Robespierre was an alluring figure: ladies found his austere habits to their liking.[19] The Revolution's violent turn can be deduced in the very last line of the Marseillaise, which calls for troughs of the 'impure' blood of aristocrats and traitors.

Symbols of the revolution were everywhere. The new anthem was written in 1792, and, although banned by Napoleon, re-emerged after 1879 as the official anthem in both Left and Right governments (albeit performed at different speeds, depending on who was in power). The Revolutionary Calendar was officially adopted in France on 24 October 1793 and abolished on 1 January 1806 by Napoleon. The 365 days were

---

19 John Carr, *Robespierre: The Force of Circumstance*, St Martin's Press, New York, 1972, p. 64.

divided into 10 months with names like Thermidor that reflected the changing seasons. The French also established a new clock, in which the day was divided into ten hours of a hundred minutes of a hundred seconds – producing exactly 100,000 seconds per day.

Napoleon

With Napoleon came a revolution with a lower-case 'r'. This was not a Revolution in the English, American or original French sense. Napoleon has to be understood as completing the French Revolution. Many of the English sources concerning Napoleon are quite hostile – we need to look beyond these views of Napoleon to grasp his significance in the history of France. He was born in Corsica, in 1769, into the minor nobility. He was trained as artillery officer, and was promoted on merit, an innovation of the Republic. He worked out strategies for handling the vast new armies of the Republic to best effect, using mobility and surprise. Napoleon was originally a supporter of Robespierre, but later supported the new government. He won military promotion through his spectacular victories in Italy. Egypt was not as successful a campaign.

Nonetheless, Napoleon was increasingly popular, and seized power. He promulgated a new constitution that made Bonaparte the First Consul, of three. The French people approved this change through a referendum. In 1804, in front of the Pope, he crowned himself the Emperor of the French. In 1810 he took a trophy wife, Marie Louise, from the Hapsburgs.

Napoleon reorganised France internally, with a new government based on the 'department', each headed by a prefect, a model that was exported with the growth of the Empire to other parts of the French-speaking world. In short, Napoleon sought to strike a balance between the old 'ancien régime' and the achievements of the Revolution. He created the Bank of France in 1800, providing a bank that was both national and central. The revolutionaries had issued promissory notes, pending the sale of confiscated property, and had thereby inadvertently caused inflation. Napoleon ended the old feudal dues and introduced centralised taxation. He codified the famous Code Napoleon in 1804.

Napoleon established the Concordat of 1801. His view was that the church was needed to provide social cement. In turn the Church recognised its loss of lands. Henceforth all clergy salaries were paid by the State. In the area of education, Napoleon set up high schools and the first Ministry of Education. Like the army, entry and promotion into civil service was now to be based on merit. Napoleon created a bureaucracy that was expected to be industrious and loyal. French people were now forbidden to hold meetings or demonstrations (Napoleon thought there had been plenty enough of them during the Revolution). He set up a network of secret police and informers, and people could be arrested without trial.

Napoleon enjoyed a special relationship with the French Jews. Napoleon removed the restrictions on Jews that required them to live in ghettoes, and gave them equality with Protestants and Catholics. He was motivated partly by the cynical need to attract wealthier Jews into France, and partly by the ideals of the Revolution. The German Prince von Metternich (1773-1859) warned that Napoleon might be the long-awaited Messiah. During his unsuccessful siege of Acre, in 1799, Napoleon allegedly proposed a Jewish homeland, a suggestion which inspired some Zionists in the 20th Century.

The English feared a French invasion across the Channel. Around 1805 Napoleon massed troops in preparation for moving across the Channel, considering the use of pontoons, balloons, even a tunnel. He had a creditable military record by this time. Italy had been conquered. In 1806 Napoleon abolished the Holy Roman Empire, and reorganised Germany. Napoleon's brothers were installed on the thrones of Spain and Naples.

Napoleon's military strategy was to deal with France's opponents one by one. He imposed a trade blockade against Britain, but Britain enjoyed greater naval strength. In 1812 he embarked on the disastrous Russian campaign – leaving 250,000 French soldiers dead. 1812 was his real defeat – Waterloo was but a coda. Not long afterwards, the allies reached Paris. Napoleon was exiled, but escaped and regrouped, leading to the battle of Waterloo in 1815. Napoleon was defeated by both Britain and Prussia. Napoleon was exiled to St Helena and died there in 1821.

The French Revolution was profoundly significant in world history. The ideal of 'the sovereignty of the people' entered general currency. The ideals of these Revolutions continued well past the material conditions that produced them – they were cited by revolutionary movements throughout the twentieth century, sometimes together with the American Revolution, as in the case of the Vietnamese, and sometimes singly. Bastille Day (14 July) was recognised internationally. The idea of 'the citizen' was now at the heart of political discourse, replacing 'the subject'. Napoleon proved to be one of a new kind of leader, the 'enlightened despot'.

Primary sources:

The American Declaration of Independence, and the French Declaration of the Rights of Man and Citizen

The American Declaration of Independence, 1776

IN CONGRESS, July 4, 1776.

The unanimous Declaration of the thirteen united States of America,

When in the Course of human events, it becomes necessary for one people to dissolve the political bands which have connected them with another, and to assume among the powers of the earth, the separate and equal station to which the Laws of Nature and of Nature's God entitle them, a decent respect to the opinions of mankind requires that they should declare the causes which impel them to the separation.

John Trumbull, *Declaration of Independence* [Capitol Building, Washington DC]

We hold these truths to be self-evident, that all men are created equal, that they are endowed by their Creator with certain unalienable Rights, that among these are Life, Liberty and the pursuit of Happiness.--That to secure these rights, Governments are instituted among Men, deriving their just powers from the consent of the governed, --That whenever any Form of Government becomes destructive of these ends, it is the Right of the People to alter or to abolish it, and to institute new Government, laying its foundation on such principles and organizing its powers in such form, as to them shall seem most likely to effect their Safety and Happiness. Prudence, indeed, will dictate that Governments long established should not be changed for light and transient causes; and accordingly all experience hath shewn, that mankind are more disposed to suffer, while evils are sufferable, than to right themselves by abolishing the forms to which they are accustomed. But when a long train of abuses and usurpations, pursuing invariably the same Object evinces a design to reduce them under absolute Despotism, it is their right, it is their duty, to throw off such Government, and to provide new Guards for their future security.--Such has been the patient sufferance of these Colonies; and such is now the necessity which constrains them to alter their former Systems of Government.

The history of the present King of Great Britain is a history of repeated injuries and usurpations, all having in direct object the establishment of an absolute Tyranny over these States. To prove this, let Facts be submitted to a candid world.

He has refused his Assent to Laws, the most wholesome and necessary for the public good.

He has forbidden his Governors to pass Laws of immediate and pressing importance, unless suspended in their operation till his Assent should be obtained; and when so suspended, he has utterly neglected to attend to them.

He has refused to pass other Laws for the accommodation of large districts of people, unless those people would relinquish the right of Representation in the Legislature, a right inestimable to them and formidable to tyrants only.

He has called together legislative bodies at places unusual, uncomfortable, and distant from the depository of their public Records, for the sole purpose of fatiguing them into compliance with his measures.

He has dissolved Representative Houses repeatedly, for opposing with manly firmness his invasions on the rights of the people.

He has refused for a long time, after such dissolutions, to cause others to be elected; whereby the Legislative powers, incapable of Annihilation, have returned to the People at large for their exercise; the State remaining in the mean time exposed to all the dangers of invasion from without, and convulsions within.

He has endeavoured to prevent the population of these States; for that purpose obstructing the Laws for Naturalization of Foreigners; refusing to pass others to encourage their migrations hither, and raising the conditions of new Appropriations of Lands.

He has obstructed the Administration of Justice, by refusing his Assent to Laws for establishing Judiciary powers.

He has made Judges dependent on his Will alone, for the tenure of their offices, and the amount and payment of their salaries.

He has erected a multitude of New Offices, and sent hither swarms of Officers to harrass our people, and eat out their substance.

He has kept among us, in times of peace, Standing Armies without the Consent of our legislatures.

He has affected to render the Military independent of and superior to the Civil power.

He has combined with others to subject us to a jurisdiction foreign to our constitution, and unacknowledged by our laws; giving his Assent to their Acts of pretended Legislation:

For Quartering large bodies of armed troops among us:

For protecting them, by a mock Trial, from punishment for any Murders which they should commit on the Inhabitants of these States:

For cutting off our Trade with all parts of the world:

For imposing Taxes on us without our Consent:

For depriving us in many cases, of the benefits of Trial by Jury:

For transporting us beyond Seas to be tried for pretended offences:

For abolishing the free System of English Laws in a neighbouring Province, establishing therein an Arbitrary government, and enlarging its Boundaries so as to render it at once an example and fit instrument for introducing the same absolute rule into these Colonies:

For taking away our Charters, abolishing our most valuable Laws, and altering fundamentally the Forms of our Governments:

For suspending our own Legislatures, and declaring themselves invested with power to legislate for us in all cases whatsoever.

He has abdicated Government here, by declaring us out of his Protection and waging War against us.

He has plundered our seas, ravaged our Coasts, burnt our towns, and destroyed the lives of our people.

He is at this time transporting large Armies of foreign Mercenaries to compleat the works of death, desolation and tyranny, already begun with circumstances of Cruelty & perfidy scarcely paralleled in the most barbarous ages, and totally unworthy the Head of a civilized nation.

He has constrained our fellow Citizens taken Captive on the high Seas to bear Arms against their Country, to become the executioners of their friends and Brethren, or to fall themselves by their Hands.

He has excited domestic insurrections amongst us, and has endeavoured to bring on the inhabitants of our frontiers, the merciless Indian Savages, whose known rule of warfare, is an undistinguished destruction of all ages, sexes and conditions.

In every stage of these Oppressions We have Petitioned for Redress in the most humble terms: Our repeated Petitions have been answered only by repeated injury. A Prince whose character is thus marked by every act which may define a Tyrant, is unfit to be the ruler of a free people.

Nor have We been wanting in attentions to our Brittish brethren. We have warned them from time to time of attempts by their legislature to extend an unwarrantable jurisdiction over us. We have reminded them of the circumstances of our emigration and settlement here. We have appealed to their native justice and magnanimity, and we have conjured them by the ties of our common kindred to disavow these usurpations, which, would inevitably interrupt our connections and correspondence. They too have been deaf to the voice of justice and of consanguinity. We must, therefore, acquiesce in the necessity, which denounces our Separation, and hold them, as we hold the rest of mankind, Enemies in War, in Peace Friends.

Georgia:	North Carolina:	Maryland:	Pennsylvania:	New York:	New Hampshire:
Button Gwinnet Lyman Hall George Walton	William Hooper Joseph Hewes John Penn **South Carolina:** Edward Rutledge Thomas Heyward Jr. Thomas Lynch, Jr. Arthur Middleton	Samuel Chase William Paca Thomas Stone Charles Carroll of Carrollton **Virginia:** George Wythe Richard Henry Lee Thomas Jefferson Benjamin Harrison Thomas Nelson, Jr. Francis Lightfoot Lee Carter Braxton	Robert Morris Benjamin Rush Benjamin Franklin John Morton George Clymer James Smith George Taylot James Wilson George Ross **Delaware:** Caesar Rodney George Read Thomas McKean	William Floyd Philip Livingston Francis Lewis Lewis Morris **New Jersey:** Richard Stockton John Witherspoon Francis Hopkinson John Hart Abraham Clark	Josiah Bartlett Matthew Thornton William Whipple **Massachusetts:** John Hancock Samuel Adams John Adams Robert Treat Paine Elbridge Gerry **Rhode Island:** Stephen Hopkins William Ellery **Connecticut:** Roger Sherman Samuel Huntington William Williams Oliver Wolcott

We, therefore, the Representatives of the united States of America, in General Congress, Assembled, appealing to the Supreme Judge of the world for the rectitude of our intentions, do, in the Name, and by Authority of the good People of these Colonies, solemnly publish and declare, That these United Colonies are, and of Right ought to be Free and Independent States; that they are Absolved from all Allegiance to the British Crown, and that all political connection between them and the State of Great Britain, is and ought to be totally dissolved; and that as Free and Independent States, they have full Power to levy War, conclude Peace, contract Alliances, establish Commerce, and to do all other Acts and Things which Independent States may of right do. And for the support of this Declaration, with a firm reliance on the protection of divine Providence, we mutually pledge to each other our Lives, our Fortunes and our sacred Honor.

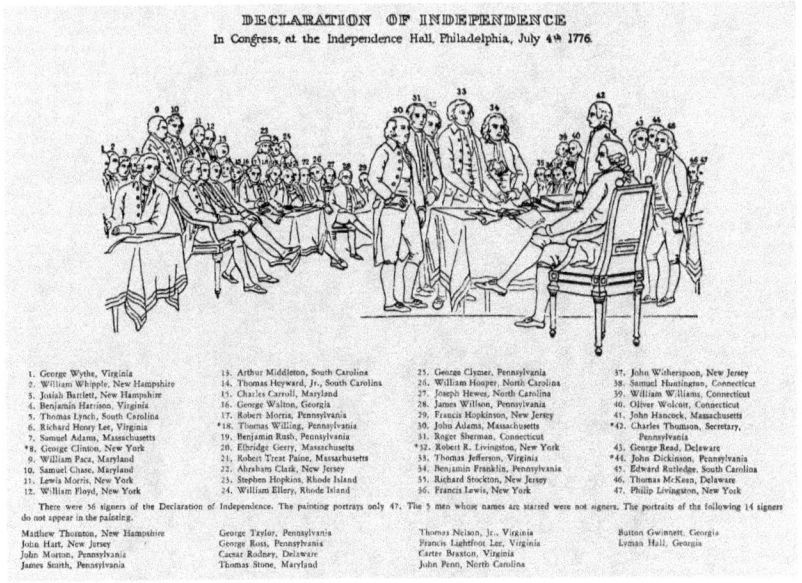

Key to Trumbull, Declaration of Independence. When Trumbull painted this large canvas in 1817-19 he could not locate images for a dozen of the original signatories, but most are here

The Declaration of the Rights of Man and Citizen, 1789

Approved by the National Assembly of France, 26 August 1789

The representatives of the French people, organized as a National Assembly, believing that the ignorance, neglect, or contempt of the rights of man are the sole cause of public calamities and of the corruption of governments, have determined to set forth in a solemn declaration the natural, unalienable, and sacred rights of man, in order that this declaration, being constantly before all the members of the Social body,

The Declaration of the Rights of Man and Citizen, 1789 [Jean-Jacques Le Barbier]

shall remind them continually of their rights and duties; in order that the acts of the legislative power, as well as those of the executive power, may be compared at any moment with the objects and purposes of all political institutions and may thus be more respected, and, lastly, in order that the grievances of the citizens, based hereafter upon simple and incontestable principles, shall tend to the maintenance of the constitution and redound to the happiness of all. Therefore the National Assembly recognizes and proclaims, in the presence and under the auspices of the Supreme Being, the following rights of man and of the citizen:

Articles:

1. Men are born and remain free and equal in rights. Social distinctions may be founded only upon the general good.

2. The aim of all political association is the preservation of the natural and imprescriptible rights of man. These rights are liberty, property, security, and resistance to oppression.

3. The principle of all sovereignty resides essentially in the nation. No body nor individual may exercise any authority which does not proceed directly from the nation.

4. Liberty consists in the freedom to do everything which injures no one else; hence the exercise of the natural rights of each man has no limits except those which assure to the other members of the society the enjoyment of the same rights. These limits can only be determined by law.

5. Law can only prohibit such actions as are hurtful to society. Nothing may be prevented which is not forbidden by law, and no one may be forced to do anything not provided for by law.

6. Law is the expression of the general will. Every citizen has a right to participate personally, or through his representative, in its foundation. It must be the same for all, whether it protects or punishes. All citizens, being equal in the eyes of the law, are equally eligible to all dignities and to all public positions and occupations, according to their abilities, and without distinction except that of their virtues and talents.

7. No person shall be accused, arrested, or imprisoned except in the cases and according to the forms prescribed by law. Any one soliciting, transmitting, executing, or causing to be executed, any arbitrary order, shall be punished. But any citizen summoned or arrested in virtue of the law shall submit without delay, as resistance constitutes an offense.

8. The law shall provide for such punishments only as are strictly and obviously necessary, and no one shall suffer punishment except it be legally inflicted in virtue of a law passed and promulgated before the commission of the offense.

9. As all persons are held innocent until they shall have been declared guilty, if arrest shall be deemed indispensable, all harshness not essential to the securing of the prisoner's person shall be severely repressed by law.

10. No one shall be disquieted on account of his opinions, including his religious views, provided their manifestation does not disturb the public order established by law.

11. The free communication of ideas and opinions is one of the most precious of the rights of man. Every citizen may, accordingly, speak, write, and print with freedom, but shall be responsible for such abuses of this freedom as shall be defined by law.

12. The security of the rights of man and of the citizen requires public military forces. These forces are, therefore, established for the good of all and not for the personal advantage of those to whom they shall be intrusted.

13. A common contribution is essential for the maintenance of the public forces and for the cost of administration. This should be equitably distributed among all the citizens in proportion to their means.

14. All the citizens have a right to decide, either personally or by their representatives, as to the necessity of the public contribution; to grant this freely; to know to what uses it is put; and to fix the proportion, the mode of assessment and of collection and the duration of the taxes.

15. Society has the right to require of every public agent an account of his administration.

16. A society in which the observance of the law is not assured, nor the separation of powers defined, has no constitution at all.

17. Since property is an inviolable and sacred right, no one shall be deprived thereof except where public necessity, legally determined, shall clearly demand it, and then only on condition that the owner shall have been previously and equitably indemnified.

Questions for discussion:

The Enlightenment thinkers produced an entirely new library full of tracts, broadsheets, polemics and books. Here we deal with just two: the American Declaration of Independence (1776) and the French Declaration of the Rights of Man and Citizen (1789). These are the theoretical bases for almost all of the new nations of the modern period, inspiring nationalist movements across Asia and Africa.

How do the American and French manifestoes differ? One speaks of men 'created free'; the other of men 'born free'. How do we explain those differences? Explain the shift from the deo-centric world to the anthro-centric.

Included here are the names of the men who signed the Declaration of Independence. The diversity of the American population in colonial times was not exactly reflected in the list of signatories: what do they have in common as people? For example, only one of them was a Catholic. Note that the Declaration refers to the United Colonies, but lower-case 'u', 'united States of America'.

What do people mean when they say the French Revolution continues to this day? How can it be seen as a more complete revolution than that of the Americans? Why is there arguably no more important event in the entire history of the world?

Both revolutions drew their inspiration from the Enlightenment. What reading of this Enlightenment did the revolutionaries share?

How would an Islamic state or the State of Israel differ in its foundational principles?

Going further:

David Freeman Hawke, *Everyday Life in Early America*, Harper & Row, New York, 1988

Jonathan I. Israel, *Enlightenment Contested: Philosophy, Modernity, and the Emancipation of Man 1670-1752*, Oxford University Press, Oxford, 2006

D. W. Meinig, *The Shaping of America*, vol. 1, *Atlantic America, 1492-1800*, Yale University Press, New Haven CT, 1986

Edmund S. Morgan, *Benjamin Franklin*, Yale University Press, New Haven CT, 2002

Andrew Wheatcroft, *The World Atlas of Revolutions*, Simon & Schuster, New York, 1983

Unit 15:

Enlightened Despotism: Catherine and Friedrich

In 1790, the year after the French Revolution, the Russian writer Alexsander Radishchev published his *Journey from St Petersburg to Moscow*, a catalogue of the problems persisting in Russia despite the supposedly 'enlightened' policies of its ruler, Catherine the Great. He found peasants working on Sundays, libidinous women cheating on their husbands, lazy innkeepers, and rulers who wanted to invade other countries merely on a whim. Catherine read every page of the book and denounced it:

> Aleksandr Radishchev, collegiate councillor [kollezhskii sovetnik] and chevalier of the Order of Saint Vladimdr, has been found guilty of a crime violating his oath and the duties of a subject, by the publication of a book entitled *A Journey from Saint Petersburg to Moscow*, filled with the most harmful reasonings which disturb the public tranquillity, lessen the respect due the authorities, strive to arouse among the people resentment against authority and against their superiors, and filled, finally, with insulting and violent expressions against the tsarist dignity and power; he has committed, moreover, a deceitful act by adding, after censorship, many pages to this book, published by his own printing shop, which fact he did freely acknowledge. For this crime he has been sentenced to death by the criminal court of the Saint Petersburg guberniia, and then by our Senate, on the basis of the state laws; and although he deserves this sentence of death by the enormity of his crime and the strict application of the law, as designated above, we, nevertheless, following our principle of tempering justice with mercy ... free him from forfeiting his life and command instead that he be deprived of his rank, the insignia of the Order of Saint Vladimir, and of the dignity of a nobleman, and that he be exiled to Siberia to the frontier settlement of Ilimsk [north of Irkutsk] for a continuous term of ten years.

In this denunciation Radishchev is a 'subject', not a 'citizen', and can be exiled to Siberia. The despots of the Enlightenment retained a power over their subjects that revolutions elsewhere had swept away.

The survival of Absolutist rulers in Russia and Germany would have important consequences in 1917 and 1919. Postponing the revolution of the 1770s meant that the governments of the 1910s would have a greater challenge on their hands, four generations later. The phrase 'Enlightened Despotism' was invented by Frederick II of Prussia, who wrote an essay with this title. He had been educated in Paris and had come to accept the advice of Voltaire and Enlightenment ideas. Some historians doubt that he actually had the political skill to introduce the reforms, but his name appears on the list of the Enlightened Despots (Table 15.1).

Here we deal with those Absolutist rulers who broadly accepted the import of the Enlightenment and went about reforming their societies in accordance with the rational principles of the 'philosophes'. The Enlightenment intellectuals, such as Voltaire, were of course naturally quite flattered by this development. But were they defrauded? Were these despots in fact using reform as a mechanism to increase their power over their subjects? The Danish example of Enlightened Despotism has been re-worked as a film in 2012.[20]

What follows is a list of the Absolutist rulers to whom the label has been attached (in chronological order).

---

20 Nikolaj Arcel, dir. *En kongelig affære* (*A Royal Affair*), 137 min., 2012, starring Alicia Vikander, Mads Mikkelsen, and Mikkel Boe Følsgaard. The story was first told in Victor Saville, dir., *The Dictator*, 1935.

Table 15.1: A roll-call of Enlightened Despots, 1643-1839

Louis XIV of France	1643-1715	
Frederick the Great of Prussia	1740-1786	Invented the term 'Enlightened Despotism'
Maria Theresa of Austria	1740-1780	
Sebastião José de Carvalho e Melo, Marquis of Pombal, Minister of the Kingdom of Portugal	1750-1777	
Carlos III of Spain	1759-1788	
Catherine II of Russia	1762-1796	Ascended the throne when her husband Peter III was assassinated
Joseph II, Holy Roman Emperor of Austria	1765-1790	
Maria Carolina of Austria, Queen of Naples	1768-1814	Abandoned her Enlightenment principles with the onset of the French Revolution; turned Naples into a police state
Gustav III of Sweden	1771-1792	Patron of the arts. Reformer. Seized power to restore the monarchy, supported King Louis XVI during the French Revolution, was assassinated by his opponents in the nobility
Napoleon I of France	1804-1815	
Frederick VI of Denmark	1808-1839	Abolished serfdom as Regent in 1788

Absolutism was not a uniform phenomenon. Absolutism in the East was quite different. Here there was little urban development and independence for the cities and towns. Although Sweden, along with Denmark, was a mixture of the West and the East, in the East there was a complete contrast with the West. The Swedish invasions of Poland in the Thirty Years War prevented the development of an Absolutist state in that part of Eastern Europe.

Serfdom was consolidated, not removed – at much the same time as Absolutism was established here, in Prussia (East Germany), Russia and Bohemia (Austria). How does the serf differ from other kinds of peasant? The word 'serf' derives from the Latin word 'servus', meaning a slave, but serfs were not slaves in the classic sense: they were peasants tied to a particular lord's 'bondage'. Serfs could work their own land, but they also worked for the local lord on his farms, in his forests or down in his mines. They agreed to this 'bondage' (in a ceremony involving putting their head into his outstretched hands) for many reasons – perhaps a bad crop, or being threatened by brigands, or some natural catastrophe. In return the lord provided his protection and led his people in times of war. Over time therefore the nobility came to control larger populations and territories. The nobles counted among their assets these 'souls', a term the Romans would never have contemplated for their slaves. Serfdom became more widespread in the East at much the same time as it was disappearing from the West.

Indeed, serfdom was in retreat in Western Europe in the high middle ages. Elizabeth formally abolished serfdom in England in 1574; it was ended in 1789 in France with the Revolution, but had already become less common over the preceding centuries. Nonetheless, serfdom became a dominant economic form in the East around this time. It was yet another example of how feudalism could not produce the unified international economic system later accomplished by industrial capitalism.

In Eastern European new dynastic rulers emerged. There were three new monarchies in the East – the Hohenzollern, the Habsburg and the Romanov dynasties. They used similar strategies of rule. They suppressed the towns, reducing their independence. They enserfed the peasantry (tying them to manors). And they abolished the Estates (the assemblies of the principal categories of society). These changes led to an alliance between these monarchs and the local aristocracies, because their class interests were jointly served by these developments.

So the social structure of Eastern Europe took on a particular form. Eastern Absolutism was even more concerned with the assembly of large military structures than their Western equivalents – these forces covered very large territories. An early casualty was Poland -- Russia, Prussia and Austria divided up Poland among themselves. The absence of a merchant class in Eastern Europe meant that the sale of offices, so prevalent in the West, hardly existed there at all. And, again uniquely, serfdom extended into the cities.

These differences were also reflected in land ownership patterns in the East. The Germano-Roman fusion which had produced classic feudalism in Western Europe was not relevant to Eastern Europe. 'Allodial' title to land prevailed over 'feudal'. Allodial title to land is the opposite of feudal – there is no vassalage or implied connection to a lordly power. Thus Napoleon's legal code made French property allodial when he abolished feudal ties. Allodial estates outnumbered the fiefs in the East; so the monarchy and the aristocracy were hardly in conflict at all – as in the West, this was particularly true of the eighteenth century. Serfs might be tied to the lord, but the peasant was not.

'Enlightened Despotism' characterised the rule of Frederick II, Catherine II, and Joseph II. Features of this despotism included: the official toleration of religious refugees; the start or development of public education; military conscription; Absolutist mercantilism and protectionism; and economic reform.

Naturally, the 'philosophes' welcomed these reforms, but were ignorant of the underlying reality that these Absolutist regimes would survive the end of serfdom. Prussia ended serfdom only after its defeat by Napoleon in 1811 at Jena. Russia likewise held onto serfdom until its Crimean defeat in 1861. More significantly, the regimes continued to exist unchallenged – were the 'philosophes' fooled? Were they beguiled into thinking that their ideas might really change the world?

Eastern European despots

We turn first to the Kingdom of Prussia, ruled 1701-1867 by the Hohenzollern dynasty.

Table 15.2: Prussian monarchs, 1701-1797

Friedrich I (Frederick I)	1701–13
Friedrich Wilhelm I (Frederick William I)	1713–40
Friedrich II, der Grosse (Frederick II, the Great)	1740–86
Friedrich Wilhelm II (Frederick William II)	1786–97

The Hohenzollern lands were assembled across Eastern Europe. The Hohenzollern house was itself of dubious origins. The dynasty was created in the 1400s by the enforced enserfment of peasants in East Prussia. The house gradually acquired separate disconnected portions of territory, which became in turn an embryonic fraction of modern Germany.

The Hohenzollerns learned how to rule by circumstance. The Swedish invasion of northern Germany had taught the Prussians the importance of war and the methods of taxation used by the invaders. In due course the Hohenzollerns created a Treasury and a Commissariat – the latter was the means by which large numbers of Huguenot refugees from France and other immigrants were settled. In short, it was a bureaucracy staffed by military aristocrats.

Frederick II (1712-86) was a musician and philosopher who reacted against the traditional military aggressiveness of his father and the Prussian Junker class. There is debate among historians, however, whether he really introduced significant new reforms, or merely continued those of his father and grandfather. He proved his worth as the king with the successful annexation of Silesia.

Meanwhile, with no local monarchy, the Polish nobility introduced a succession of foreigners to the throne, but none had sources of income

Frederick the Great, who coined the phrase 'Enlightened Despotism'

inside the country. The Polish nobility failed to produce an Absolutist State and Poland disappeared off the map of early modern Europe.

Further south, the Habsburgs had their successes, and their limits. The Habsburg line ruled longer than other European monarchy, for seven centuries until the Great War of 1914-18. (Of course, the Swiss were able to resist the Hapsburg Empire because of their unique combination of mountainside villages out of the reach of the lords, and the valley towns set up to take advantage of the trade between the Italian peninsula and Western Europe.)

In Russia, a series of rulers dominated, beginning with the Muscovite Princes (1462-1598), notably Ivan III, the Great, and Ivan IV, the Terrible. Then followed the Romanoff Czars (1613-1917), including Michael

Ivan the Terrible

(Mikhail) Romanoff, Peter (Pyotr) I, the Great, Catherine (Yekaterina) I, Peter (Pyotr) II, Elizabeth (Yelisaveta) Petrovna, Catherine (Yekaterina) II, the Great, Paul (Pavel), Alexander (Aleksandr) I, Nicholas (Nikolai) I, Alexander (Aleksandr) II, Alexander (Aleksandr) III, and Nicholas (Nikolai) II.

Ivan, who became the first Romanov, decreed that Russian landowners were required to provide military service and a prescribed number of their peasants to support him in war. In Russia land became the basis of war service: two-thirds of the members of each noble family were required to enlist in the military.

Slavery continued in Russia, against the odds. The only realistic response available to the peasantry was flight – Russia was depopulated as a consequence. One of these groups who fled was the Cossacks, choosing to live a semi-nomadic equestrian life in the lands between

Like Theodora and other powerful women before and after her, Russia's Catherine the Great inspired many unflattering stories about her private life

Russia and Poland. The Cossacks instigated the 1648 peasant revolution against the Polish elite. Then followed a series of peasant revolts across the 1600s and 1700s, all originating in these borderlands, involving a wide range of peasants and Cossacks.

Catherine the Great came to power in Russia unexpectedly in 1762 with the assassination of her husband, and proved to be an inspiring leader in her own right.[21] She put Russia at the centre of international relations. Although she kept the serfs in their position, she liberalised many other aspects of Russian life. She installed a boyfriend on the throne in Poland. Catherine in many ways personified the Absolutist woman, with her legendary penchant for male lovers. She can reasonably

---

21 Zoé Oldenbourg, *Catherine the Great*, trans Anne Carter, The Reprint Society, London, 1967 [1965].

claim to be the foundress of modern Russia, but her despotic ways mean she will always be understood in quite ambivalent ways.

The House of Islam

How did the Ottoman Empire resemble other Absolutist powers of the East Europe and how did it differ? The Seljuk arrival in Anatolia [Unit 6] has been likened to the occupation of the late Roman Empire by the German tribes. Their adoption of Islam and the continuation of their warrior tradition produced the Ottoman formula.

This formula needs to be understood historically. The Seljuk Turks had seized parts of the Balkans even before they captured Constantinople

Suleiman I, The Magnificent

in 1453. Their income was considerable: Suleiman I enjoyed double the revenue of Charles V. Marx (wrongly) believed that there was no private property in the Ottoman Empire. The Ottoman formula was based on a division between 'ruling institution' and 'Muslim institution'. Despite all the alarmist predictions in the West, the Ottoman Empire survived until 1923, with the creation of the Republic of Turkey.

Indeed, the Ottoman rulers welcomed local diversity and custom. The allegiance of the citizens was to their religious grouping – there were eventually 17 recognised millets across the Empire, providing both cultural tolerance and local control.

Recruits to the 'ruling institution' had to be outside the power of the ulama – loyal not to the 'Muslim institution', but to the Sultan, yet converted to Islam. It was this contradictory aspect of Ottoman hegemony that gave the Empire its strength – closer to the Eastern Absolutist model than to the Western.

Table 15.3: Western versus Eastern Absolutism

Western Europe	Eastern Europe	Ottoman Empire
Army raised when necessary	Army and the State interwoven	Ghazi tradition critical to the Ottoman State
Late feudal Bureaucracy	Effective bureaucracy	Meritocratic bureaucracy
Taxation used to fund wars	Centralised taxation extremely efficient	Taxation devolved to 'the notables'
Mercantilist trade	Mercantilist and protectionist	Protectionist
Diplomacy a major tool of the State	Russia under Catherine a key international player	Empire establishing embassies
Schools for the elite	Public education introduced	Each millet able to build its own schools
Latin Christendom	Orthodox Christianity	Islamic, multi-faith

It is possible now to set out in tabular form (Table 15.3) some of the critical differences across the institutions of the Absolutist State. If we use these institutions (the army, the bureaucracy, etc.) as understood in the scholarly literature to be the sites of Absolutist power, it is readily obvious that the Ottoman Empire was much closer to the Eastern Absolutist model than to that of the West.

Turning next to the empires of India and China, this framework proves useful once more in thinking about the style government typical of the Mughals and the Mandarins.

Primary Source:

Jonathan Swift, *A Modest Proposal*

A MODEST PROPOSAL FOR

Preventing the children of poor people in **Ireland,** *from being a Burden to their Parents, or the Country; and for making them beneficial to the Publick.*

DUBLIN: Written in the Year 1729

It is a melancholly Object to those, who walk through this great Town, or travel in the Country, when they see the *Streets*, the *Roads* and *Cabbin-doors* crowded with *Beggars* of the Female Sex, followed by three, four, or six Children, *all in Rags*, and importuning every Passenger for an Alms. These *Mothers*, instead of being able to work for their honest Livelyhood, are forced to employ all their Time in stroling to beg Sustenance for their *helpless Infants*; who, as they grow up, either turn *Thieves* for want of Work, or leave their *dear Native Country, to fight for the Pretender* [Catholic monarch] *in* Spain, or sell themselves to the *Barbadoes* [emigrate to the New World].

I THINK it is agreed by all Parties, that this prodigious Number of Children in the Arms, or on the Backs, or at the *Heels* of their *Mothers*, and frequently of their *Fathers*, is *in the present deplorable State of the Kingdom*, a very great additional Grievance; and therefore, whoever could find out a fair, cheap and easy Method of making these Children sound and useful Members of the Commonwealth, would deserve so well of the Publick, as to have his Statue set up for a Preserver of the Nation.

BUT my Intention is very far from being confined to provide only for the Children of *professed Beggars*: It is of a much greater Extent, and shall take in the whole Number of Infants at a certain Age, who are born of Parents, in effect as little able to support them, as those who demand our Charity in the Streets.

As to my own Part, having turned my Thoughts for many Years, upon this important Subject, and maturely weighed the several *Schemes of other Projectors* [social planners], I have always found them grossly mistaken in their Computation. It is true, a Child, *just dropt from its Dam* [animal mother], may be supported by her Milk, for a Solar Year with little other Nourishment; at most not above the Value of two Shillings, which the Mother may certainly get, or the Value in *Scraps*, by her lawful Occupation of *Begging*; And it is exactly at one Year old, that I propose to provide for them in such a Manner, as, instead of being a Charge upon their *Parents*, or the *Parish*, or *wanting Food and Raiment* [clothing] for the rest of their Lives, they shall, on the contrary, contribute to the Feeding, and partly to the Cloathing of many Thousands.

THERE is likewise another great Advantage in my *Scheme*, that it will prevent those *voluntary Abortions*, and that horrid Practice of Women *murdering their Bastard Children*; alas! too frequent among us; sacrificing the *poor innocent Babes*, I doubt, more to avoid the Expence than the Shame; which would move Tears and Pity in the most Savage and inhuman Breast.

THE Number of Souls in *Ireland* being usually reckoned one Million and a half; of these I calculate there may be about Two hundred Thousand Couple whose Wives are Breeders; from which Number I subtract thirty thousand Couples, who are able to maintain their own Children; although I apprehend there cannot be so many, under the present Distresses of the Kingdom; but this being granted, there will remain an Hundred and Seventy Thousand Breeders. I again subtract Fifty Thousand, for those Women who miscarry, or whose Children die by Accident or Disease within the Year. There only remain an Hundred and Twenty Thousand Children of poor Parents, annually born. The Question therefore is, How this Number shall be reared, and provided for? Which, as I have already said, under the present Situation of Affairs, is utterly impossible by all the Methods hitherto proposed: For we can *neither employ them in handicraft or agriculture*; we neither build Houses, (I mean in the Country)

Jonathan Swift advertises O'Malley's restaurant

nor cultivate Land: they can very seldom pick up a Livelyhood by Stealing till they arrive at six Years old; except where they are of towardly Parts; although, I confess, they learn the Rudiments much earlier; during which Time, they can, however, be properly looked upon only as *Probationers*; As I have been informed by a principal Gentleman in the county of *Cavan*, who protested to me, that he never knew above one or two instances under the Age of six, even in a Part of the Kingdom *so renowned for the quickest Proficiency in that Art.*

I AM assured by our Merchants, that a Boy or a Girl before twelve Years old, is no saleable Commodity; and even when they come to this Age, they will not yield above Three Pounds, or Three Pounds and half a Crown at most, on the Exchange; which cannot turn to Account either to the Parents or the Kingdom, the Charge of Nutriments and Rags, having been at least four Times that Value.

I SHALL now therefore humbly propose my own Thoughts; which I hope will not be liable to the least Objection.

I HAVE been assured by a very knowing *American* of my Acquaintance in *London*, that a young healthy Child, well nursed, is, at a Year old, a most delicious, nourishing and wholesome Food; whether *Stewed*, *Roasted*, *Baked*, or *Boiled*; and, I make no doubt, that it will equally serve in a *Fricasie*, or a *Ragoust*.

I DO therefore humbly offer it to *publick Consideration*, that of the Hundred and Twenty Thousand Children, already computed, Twenty thousand may be reserved for Breed, whereof only one Fourth Part to be Males; which is more than we allow to *Sheep*, *black Cattle*, or *Swine*, and my reason is, that these Children are seldom the Fruits of Marriage, *a Circumstance not much regarded by our Savages*; therefore, *one Male* will be sufficient to serve *four Females*. That the remaining Hundred thousand may, at a Year old, be offered in Sale to the *Persons of Quality and Fortune*, through the Kingdom, always advising the Mother to let them suck plentifully in the last Month, so as to render them plump, and fat for a good Table. A child will make two Dishes at an Entertainment for Friends; and when the Family dines alone, the fore or hind Quarter will make a reasonable Dish; and seasoned with a little Pepper or Salt, will be very good Boiled on the fourth Day, especially in *Winter*.

I HAVE reckoned upon a Medium, that a Child just born will weigh Twelve Pounds; and in a solar Year, if tolerably nursed, encreaseth to twenty eight Pounds.

I GRANT this Food will be somewhat dear, and therefore very proper for Landlords; who, as they have already devoured most of the Parents, seem to have the best Title to the Children.

INFANTS Flesh will be in Season throughout the Year; but more plentiful in *March*, and a little before and after: For we are told by a grave Author [Rabelais], an eminent *French Physician*, that *Fish being a prolifick*

Dyet, there are more Children born in *Roman Catholick Countries* about Nine Months after *Lent*, than at any other Season: Therefore reckoning a Year after *Lent*, the Markets will be more glutted than usual; because the Number of *Popish Infants*, is, at least, three to one in this kingdom: and therefore it will have one other Collateral Advantage, by lessening the Number of Papists [Catholics] among us.

I HAVE already computed the Charge of nursing a Beggar's Child (in which List I reckon all *Cottagers*, *Labourers*, and Four fifths of the *Farmers*) to be about two Shillings per Annum, Rags included; and I believe, no Gentleman would repine to [complain about] give Ten Shillings for the *Carcase of a good fat Child*, which, as I have said, will make four Dishes of excellent nutritive Meat, when he hath only some particular Friend, or his own Family, to dine with him. Thus the Squire will learn to be a good Landlord, and grow popular among his Tenants; the Mother will have Eight Shillings net Profit, and be fit for Work till she produceth another Child.

THOSE who are more thrifty (*as I must confess the Times require*) may flay the Carcase; the Skin of which, artificially dressed, will make admirable *Gloves for Ladies*, and *Summer Boots for fine Gentlemen*.

As to our City of *Dublin*, Shambles [slaughterhouses] may be appointed for this Purpose, in the most convenient Parts of it, and Butchers we may be assured will not be wanting; although I rather recommend buying the Children alive, and dressing them hot from the Knife, as we do *roasting Pigs*.

A VERY worthy Person, a true Lover of his Country, and whose Virtues I highly esteem, was lately pleased, in discoursing on this Matter, to offer a Refinement upon my Scheme. He said, that many Gentlemen of this Kingdom, having of late destroyed their Deer; he conceived, that the Want of Venison might be well supplied by the Bodies of young Lads and Maidens, not exceeding fourteen Years of Age, nor under twelve; so great a Number of both Sexes in every County being now ready to starve, for Want of Work and Service: And these to be disposed of by their parents, if alive, or otherwise by their nearest Relations. But with due Deference to so excellent a Friend, and so deserving a Patriot, I cannot be altogether in his Sentiments; for as to the Males, my *American Acquaintance* assured me from frequent Experience, that their Flesh was generally tough and lean, like that of our School-boys, by continual Exercise, and their Taste disagreeable; and to fatten them would not answer the Charge. Then as to the Females, it would, I think, with humble Submission, *be a loss to the Publick*, because they soon would become breeders themselves: And besides, it is not improbable, that some scrupulous People might be apt to censure such a Practice, (although indeed very unjustly) as a little bordering upon Cruelty, which, I confess, hath always been with me the strongest Objection against any Project, how well soever intended.

BUT in order to justify my Friend; he confessed, that this Expedient was put into his Head by the famous *Salmanaazor*, a native of the island *Formosa* [Taiwan], who came from thence to *London*, above twenty Years ago, and in Conversation told my Friend, that in his Country, when any young Person happened to be put to Death, the Executioner sold the Carcase to *Persons of Quality*, as a prime Dainty; and that, in his Time, the Body of a plump Girl of fifteen, who was crucified for an Attempt to poison the Emperor, was sold to his Imperial *Majesty's prime Minister of State*, and other great *Mandarins* of the Court in *Joints from the Gibbet* [the gallows], at Four hundred Crowns. Neither indeed can I deny, that if the same Use were made of several plump young girls in this Town, who, without one single Groat [a four pence coin] to their Fortunes, cannot stir Abroad without a Chair [a sedan], and appear at a *Play-house* [the theatre] and *Assemblies* in foreign Fineries [clothes] which they never will pay for; the Kingdom would not be the worse.

SOME Persons of a desponding Spirit are in great Concern about that vast Number of poor People, who are Aged, Diseased, or Maimed; and I have been desired to employ my Thoughts what Course may be taken, to ease the Nation of so grievous an Incumbrance. But I am not in the least Pain upon that Matter, because it is very well known, that they are every Day *dying*, and *rotting*, by *Cold* and *Famine*, and *Filth*, and *Vermin*, as fast as can be reasonably expected. And as to the young Labourers, they are now in almost as hopeful a Condition: They cannot get Work, and consequently pine away for Want of Nourishment, to a Degree, that if at any Time they are accidentally hired to common Labour, they have not Strength to perform it; and thus the Country, and themselves, are in a fair Way of being soon delivered from the Evils to come.

I HAVE too long digressed; and therefore shall return to my Subject. I think the Advantages by the Proposal which I have made, are obvious, and many, as well as of the highest Importance.

FOR, *First*, as I have already observed, it would greatly lessen *the Number of Papists*, with whom we are Yearly over-run; being the principal Breeders of the Nation, as well as our most dangerous Enemies, and who stay at home on Purpose with a Design *to deliver the Kingdom to the Pretender*, hoping to take their Advantage by the absence of *so many good Protestants*, who have chosen rather to leave their Country, than stay at home, and pay Tythes against their Conscience to an idolatrous *Episcopal Curate*.

SECONDLY, The poorer Tenants will have something valuable of their own, which by Law may be made liable to Distress [arrest for debt], and help to pay their Landlord's Rent; their Corn and Cattle being already seized, and *Money a Thing unknown*.

THIRDLY, Whereas the Maintenance of an Hundred Thousand Children, from two Years old, and upwards, cannot be computed at less than ten Shillings a piece *per Annum*, the Nation's Stock will be thereby encreased Fifty Thousand Pounds *per Annum*, besides the Profit of a new Dish, introduced to the Tables of all Gentlemen of Fortune in the Kingdom, who have any Refinement in Taste; And the Money will circulate among ourselves, the Goods being entirely of our own Growth and Manufacture.

FOURTHLY, The constant Breeders, besides the gain of Eight Shillings *Sterling per Annum* by the Sale of their Children, will be rid of the Charge of maintaining them after the first Year.

FIFTHLY, This Food would likewise bring great *Custom to Taverns*, where the Vintners will certainly be so prudent, as to procure the best receipts [recipes] for dressing it to Perfection; and consequently have their Houses frequented by all the *fine Gentlemen*, who justly value themselves upon their Knowledge in good Eating; and a skilful Cook, who understands how to oblige his Guests, will contrive to make it as expensive as they please.

SIXTHLY, This would be a great Inducement to Marriage, which all wise Nations have either encouraged by Rewards, or enforced by Laws and Penalties. It would encrease the Care and Tenderness of Mothers towards their Children, when they were sure of a Settlement for Life, to the poor Babes, provided in some Sort by the Publick, to their annual Profit instead of Expence. We should soon see an honest Emulation among the married Women, *which of them could bring the fattest Child to the Market*. Men would become as *fond* of their *Wives*, during the Time of their Pregnancy, as they are now of their *Mares* in Foal, their *Cows* in Calf, or *Sows* when they are ready to farrow; nor offer to Beat or Kick them (as is too *frequent* a Practice) for fear of a Miscarriage.

MANY other Advantages might be enumerated. For instance, the Addition of some Thousand carcases in our Exportation of barrelled Beef: The Propagation of *Swines Flesh*, and Improvement in the Art of making good *Bacon*; so much wanted among us by the great Destruction of *Pigs*, too frequent at our Tables, which are no way comparable in Taste or Magnificence to a well-grown, fat yearling Child; which, roasted whole, will make a considerable Figure at a *Lord Mayor's Feast*, or any other publick Entertainment. But this, and many others, I omit; being studious of Brevity.

SUPPOSING that one Thousand Families in this City, would be constant Customers for Infants Flesh; besides others who might have it at *merry Meetings*, particularly at *Weddings* and *Christenings*, I compute that *Dublin* would take off, annually, about Twenty Thousand Carcases; and the rest of the Kingdom (where probably they will be sold somewhat cheaper) the remaining Eighty Thousand.

I CAN think of no one Objection, that will possibly be raised against this proposal; unless it should be urged, that the Number of People will be thereby much lessened in the Kingdom. This I freely own [admit], and it was indeed one principal Design in offering it to the World. I desire the Reader will observe, that I calculate my Remedy *for this one individual Kingdom of IRELAND, and for no other that ever was, is, or, I think, ever can be upon Earth.* Therefore, let no man talk to me of other Expedients: *Of taxing our Absentees at five Shillings a pound: Of using neither Cloaths, nor Household Furniture, except what is of our own Growth and Manufacture: Of utterly rejecting the Materials and Instruments that promote foreign Luxury: Of curing the Expensiveness of Pride, Vanity, Idleness, and Gaming in our Women: Of introducing a Vein of Parsimony, Prudence and Temperance: Of learning to love our Country, wherein we differ even from LAPLANDERS, and the Inhabitants of TOPINAMBOO* [a district in Brazil]: *Of quitting our Animosities and Factions, nor acting any longer like the Jews, who were murdering one another at the very moment their City was taken* [a reference to the fall of Jerusalem in 70 CE]: *Of being a little cautious not to sell our Country and Consciences for nothing: Of teaching Landlords to have, at least, one Degree of Mercy towards their Tenants. Lastly, Of putting a Spirit of Honesty, Industry, and Skill into our Shop-keepers; who, if a Resolution could now be taken to buy only our native Goods, would immediately unite to cheat and exact* [impose] *upon us in the Price, the Measure, and the Goodness; nor could ever yet be brought to make one fair Proposal of just Dealing, though often and earnestly invited to it.*

THEREFORE I repeat, let no Man talk to me of these and the like Expedients, till he hath, at least, some Glimpse of Hope, that there will ever be some hearty and sincere Attempt to put *them into Practice.*

BUT, as to my self; having been wearied out for many Years with offering vain, idle, visionary Thoughts; and at length utterly despairing of Success, I fortunately fell upon this Proposal; which, as it is wholly new, so it hath something *solid* and *real*, of no Expence and little Trouble, full in our own Power; and whereby we can incur no Danger in *disobliging* ENGLAND: For this Kind of Commodity will not bear Exportation;

the Flesh being of too tender a Consistence, to admit a long Continuance in Salt, *although, perhaps, I could name a Country, which would be glad to eat up our whole Nation without it.*

AFTER all, I am not so violently bent upon my own Opinion, as to reject any Offer proposed by wise Men, which shall be found equally innocent, cheap, easy, and effectual. But before something of that Kind shall be advanced, in Contradiction to my Scheme, and offering a better; I desire the Author or Authors, will be pleased maturely to consider two Points. *First*, As Things now stand, how they will be able to find Food and Raiment, for a Hundred Thousand useless Mouths and Backs? And *secondly*, There being a round Million of Creatures in human Figure, throughout this Kingdom; whose whole Subsistence, put into a common Stock, would leave them in Debt two Millions of Pounds *Sterling*; adding those, who are Beggars by Profession, to the Bulk of Farmers, Cottagers and Labourers, with their Wives and Children, who are Beggars in Effect; I desire those Politicians, who dislike my Overture, and may perhaps be so bold to attempt an Answer, that they will first ask the Parents of these Mortals, Whether they would not, at this Day, think it a great Happiness to have been sold for Food at a year Old, in the manner I prescribe; and thereby have avoided such a perpetual Scene of Misfortunes, as they have since gone through; by the *Oppression of Landlords*; the Impossibility of paying Rent, without Money or Trade; the Want of common Sustenance, with neither House nor Cloaths to cover them from Inclemencies of Weather; and the most inevitable Prospect of intailing the like, or greater Miseries, upon their Breed for ever.

I PROFESS, in the sincerity of my Heart, that I have not the least personal Interest, in endeavouring to promote this necessary Work; having no other Motive than the *publick Good of my Country, by advancing our Trade, providing for Infants, relieving the Poor, and giving some Pleasure to the Rich.* I have no Children, by which I can propose to get a single Penny; the youngest being nine Years old, and my Wife past child-bearing.

Questions for discussion:

As political debates became more complex, shades of argument began to appear. Swift's justly famous *Modest Proposal* remains to this day the definitive example of political satire.

In the 1720s there were many schemes to improve social conditions in England through the use of supposedly rational plans that were of a limited value in correcting the ills of the day. In an era before the rights of citizens were enunciated, and before the subjugation of the Irish by the English was understood to be a political problem, Swift stands out as a surprisingly modern thinker. He is profoundly critical of schemes that deal with complex problems such as the Irish Question in simplistic terms.

Swift's satire is based on Roman principles of satire, as laid down by Juvenal and Tertullian, which prescribed that the arguments of one's opponents should be turned on their head. He draws us into his logic and then takes us to conclusions that we do not immediately find repugnant. He uses images of food that are part of the everyday husbandry of animals and applies them to baby humans, with devastating effect.

Jonathan Swift

There are two voices in this pamphlet. One has been called 'The Proposer' – 'delinquent and lunatic' – who makes the case that we should invite young destitute women to sell their one-year-olds as food for the rich. The other is Swift himself – 'angry but fugitive' (not really an Author as such).

Can you detect these two voices? What is their rhetorical function in the essay? (In other words, how do they advance Swift's argument?) And how do they relate to Absolutism as a form of government? (This is a tricky problem!)

How does his rhetoric compare to the language used on *Masterchef* today?

Going further:

Perry Anderson, *Lineages of the Absolutist State*, Verso, London, 1979 [1974]

Jonathan I. Israel, *Enlightenment Contested: Philosophy, Modernity, and the Emancipation of Man 1670-1752*, Oxford University Press, Oxford, 2006

Zoé Oldenbourg, *Catherine the Great*, trans Anne Carter, The Reprint Society, London, 1967 [1965]

Unit 16

Mandarins and Mughals

The Baburnama begins with the following words:

> In the province of Fergana, in the year 1494, when I was twelve years old, I became king.

This was the opening to his famous memoir, the first in the Islamic world, written for his grandson Akbar, a book that would later be fully illustrated. This was an empire written into existence by monarchs who understood the world in the first person. Yet Eastern Absolutism had its own qualities which distinguished it from the Absolutism of the West.

India and China after the Mongols

In early-modern China and India, Absolutist rulers were successful in directing large populations numbering in the tens of millions. Following the end of the Mongol rule, these populations began to increase again and people's general standards of living began to rise. It was still not clear that East Asian, South Asian and Middle Eastern economies would be eclipsed by Europe in the modern period.

As we saw [Unit 15], Western Absolutism differed from the Absolutism prevalent in the East. The Eastern model of Absolutism through which we could understand Eastern Europe and the Ottoman Empire can be applied to understanding India and China in the early modern period. Western scholars have often been astonished by the sheer cultural diversity and tolerance of Mughal India, and by the efficiency of the Chinese mandarins. But neither feature should be puzzling if we reflect on the model of Eastern Absolutism we have developed: India and China are in fact good examples of the Eastern Absolutist model operating in an Asian context.

Babur and the Mughals

The origins of Mughal India can be traced to one man: Babur. A brilliant military commander, and in fact a descendant of the fabled general Timur, Babur came from Afghanistan and took over India in the Islamic cause. In so doing, he established an entirely new State.

By 1530 the Muslim rule of India was established, following the invasion led by Babur. His grandson was Akbar the Great (ruling 1556-1605) who completed the conquest of the entire subcontinent, created a powerful bureaucracy (despite his own illiteracy), and introduced a policy of religious toleration that allowed the Hindu majority to continue their practices, and the other religions, including Christianity, to flourish in what remained a Muslim-dominated empire.

Babur reading

Akbar the Great, with Jodha, one of his three dozen wives

The Mughal Empire ran from 1526 to 1858. It included Babur, 1526-1530, its founder; Humayun, who ruled 1530-1539, and was restored 1555-1556; Akbar ('the Great'), 1556-1605; Jahāngīr, 1605-1627; Shah Jahan, 1628-1658; and Aurangzeb, 1658-1707. Later emperors led India with diminished power and then found themselves under the control of the British.

Akbar was illiterate because he grew up away from his father, owing to a Pashtun rebellion. He was proclaimed 'Shahanshah' (Persian for 'King of Kings').

Several of Akbar's 36 wives were daughters of Hindu Rajputs, given to him as part of matrimonial alliances, opening the court to Hindus and helping cross-faith understanding.

The Departments of State created under Akbar proved to be long-lasting. The Revenue department, led by a 'diwan' (a 'wazir', chief minister), included the operation of the land tax. The Military and Intelligence Department was headed by the 'mir bakshi' (lieutenant-general). The Imperial household, including the court, royal bodyguard

Akbar's new capital, Fatehpur Sikri, a model of Mughal city-building

and harem, was run by the 'mir saman'. There was a separate judiciary, under a chief 'qazi'. This structure was a mixture of Indian and Persian administrative traditions.

Akbar devised his own taxation regime. Each plot of cultivatable land was measured by imperial revenue officials with bamboo sticks joined by iron rings; they assessed its productivity and taxed it accordingly at one-fifth, payable in cash. Akbar later (in 1580) introduced the 'dahsala' system of one-third of the crop, assessed over the previous ten years, with remission for flood or other natural emergencies.

The peasants kept their inherited land as long as they paid this tax and were encouraged to improve productivity through loans from local 'zamindars' (aristocrats).

Akbar also reformed the military. The 'mansabdari' system divided the officers into 33 ranks ('mansabs'), each with increasingly larger numbers of men and horses they needed to maintain for the purpose of fighting. The top ranks were reserved for princes, with lower ranks for the nobles who would seek promotion in this system, relying on recommendations to the emperor made by the 'mir bakshi'. The Mughal military were the best paid in their day. Akbar succeeded in consolidating Mughal rule across most of the subcontinent, adapting this 'mansabdari' system for his civil servants also.

In his memoirs, Jahāngīr explains how he directed the vast empire he had inherited from his father Akbar in 1605. *The Memoirs of Jahāngīr* are important because, like *The Baburnama* of Babur, the Absolutist ruler directs the course of history by his individual actions. Setting up the Chain of Justice at Agra was, Jahāngīr claims, his very first action. He then explained his legislative program of reforming the internal trading system of his empire.

But there are important aspects of Mughal life that he takes for granted, and we need to turn to other sources to understand them. One of these is the court itself that surrounded the emperor and the role of women in that intense royal household. The royal women each lived in their own 'zenana', a closed section of the palace reserved for each princess. The princesses competed with each other with their adornment, their singing and dancing entertainments, and their political intrigues at the court. Eunuchs supervised the zenana, assisted by strong slave women from Kashmir or Uzbekistan armed with bows and arrows. Drugs were rife. Intoxicants included 'afeem' (opium) and 'bhang' (cannabis).[22]

The Mughal empire became distinguished for its creative expression. In painting, Mughal miniatures fused Persian and Hindu traditions. These miniature artworks employed the Hindu perspective and the strong narratives typical of Persian culture. In urban design, Akbar built a beautiful new capital at Fatehpur Sikri. Today it is a ghost town, but in its day was regarded as one of the great Muslim cities. This palace-city included a major library of 24,000 volumes. Architecture was another accomplishment of the Mughals. The fifth Mughal emperor, Shah Jahan

---

[22] A recent novel depicting this life in fictional form is *Shadow Princess*, by Indu Sundaresan (Atria, New York, 2010).

was responsible for the Pearl Mosque, much of the Red Fort, Jama Mosque, and sections of the Lahore Fort.

But his Taj Mahal is, for most critics, the most beautiful building in the world. It is an interesting mix of Muslim, Hindu and Persian styles, reflecting the cosmopolitan nature of the Mughal Empire. It was built in grief by Shah Jahan in honour of his third wife, Mumtaz Mahal, who died during her fourteenth pregnancy. Both the emperor and his favourite wife are buried in the building's crypt; Jahan was imprisoned by his son Aurangzeb when he took power, dying eight years later. To build, the Taj Mahal required two decades (1632-1653) and 20 000 craftsmen. (It is a wonderful myth that these men were disfigured to prevent them working on anything so magnificent again.) The Taj Mahal comprises four minarets used to call the faithful, a dome topped by a moon, extensive gardens and its own river.

Towards the end of the Mughal period, India became the so-called 'jewel in the British crown', the centrepiece of their growing empire. The death of Aurangzeb in 1707 saw a gradual reversal of Mughal fortunes. In 1603 the British East India Company had been given commercial access to the Empire, trading in tea and cotton. During the 1670s the French East India Company began in rivalry. The British secured their grip on India with military force, particularly following Robert Clive's victory at the Battle of Plassey, 1757. Faced with Russian territorial interest in the subcontinent, the British engaged in a long series of skirmishes with this rival from 1824 that was nicknamed 'the Great Game'. In 1857 the Mutineers who rose up against the British restored the Mughals briefly, but it was an illusory moment.

The Mughal heritage is significant. They provided the first centralised government of the subcontinent. They encouraged education, whether in the form of madrasas for Muslims or open-air Brahmin-led schools. Under the Mughals, the Urdu language replaced the Hindu Sanskrit. They established the earliest secondary industries in India, such as shipbuilding, and new trading routes across Eurasia. Under them the

Sikh religion flourished, as a blend of Islam and Hinduism. The material inheritance they bequeathed included Mughal art, architecture and landscape gardening. Under them, there was an advance in technologies (such as the volley gun, and seamless metal globes).

The Ming and Qing dynasties in China

The Ming ('luminous') dynasty came to power following a rebellion during the Mongol occupation. Under the Ming China began to recover. The Ming Empire chose to remain a terrestrial power, despite the naval successes of Admiral Zheng He [Unit 11]. Under Zhu Yuanzhang (ruling as Hongwu, 1368-1398) and his son Yongle (1402-1424), this dynasty restored China and its population began to grow again as a result, reaching 150 million by 1600. This increased population demanded better agriculture, leading to the development of rice cultivation in the south.

The role of the Mandarins was critical to this success. The stability and fairness of government was a major factor in this population growth. Confucianism provided a unifying element in their training and administration. The Chinese civil service continued to be meritocratic, open to all who passed the gruelling entrance examination. Administrative handbooks developed to assist the Mandarins in their exercise of State power. For instance, the *Washing Away of the Wrongs* (1247) remained the basic text for coronial inquiries.[23]

Trade with the Europeans returned. The Ming dynasty began to trade in ceramics with Europeans, and possession of a Ming vase became a marker of bourgeois taste in London and Paris. The Ming vase was judged superior to European porcelain for its durability and craftsmanship.

In choosing the name 'Ming' as their title, this dynasty managed to fuse two elements of Chinese history – traditional Confucian values and

---

23 Today there is some nostalgia for this period. *Witness to a Prosecution*, a Hong Kong TV series (1999-2000) recreates the life and times of Song Ci, the original author of *The Washing Away of the Wrongs*.

the philosophical triumph of light over the darkness of the preceding government.[24]

In the 1600s, Manchu invaders from Manchuria created the new Qing dynasty (pronounced Ching), which lasted until 1911. In 1670 a Qing emperor, Kangxi, issued a famous decree which was designed to be read aloud in every hamlet across the vast country. Kangxi was hard-working and diligent, determined not to rely too heavily on his mandarins. The purpose of this edict was to reassure all levels of society, but in particular the bureaucracy, that the Manchu court supported Confucian values.

The Manchu rulers kept their own informants in all parts of the empire to provide parallel, confidential reports on what was going on. Nine-tenths of Chinese continued to live in villages, and these villages, so long as they paid their taxes, were given considerable autonomy.

The binding agent in this vast empire was the extended family, stretching back in time to one's ancestors and forward to the generations ahead. Confucian values of family loyalty and hierarchy were espoused, although in reality men could openly keep concubines and male sons were always preferred to daughters. Foot-binding was designed to make women more attractive and to keep them indoors. The mother-in-law played a central role in socialising the new bride, often within an arranged marriage, into her new husband's home.

The Qing dynasty began to decline in the nineteenth century under pressure from the Europeans. The British East India Company began to import opium into China during the late 1700s as an item for trade. The Chinese official Lin Zexu attempted to restrict these imports, leading to the Opium Wars (1839-42) and a one-sided naval war with the British. The Taiping Rebellion of 1840s and 1850s reflected a corroded State, especially in the south. The Late Qing reforms of 1870s and 1880s attempted to modernise the Qing State, but China lost Vietnam to the French in 1884 and was defeated in Korea by the Japanese, 1894-95. The Boxer Rebellion of 1900 was crushed.

---

24 John W. Dardess, 'The transformations of messianic revolt and the founding of the Ming Dynasty', *The Journal of Asian Studies*, vol. 29, no. 3, May 1979, pp. 539-58.

The British in India and in China

In both India and China, the local empires became the object of British interest as it expanded its empire in the wake of the loss of the American colonies. The British rule of India provided a legislative template for much of the British Empire. Hong Kong was excised from China for use as a British enclave until 1992. There were similar patterns elsewhere, including Britain's reaction to the Urabi Revolt in Egypt in 1882, and other British colonisations in Africa.

The significance of Eastern Absolutism

Many textbooks describe these Eastern Absolutist States chronologically before the Enlightenment and the British Industrial Revolution. However, it is important to recognise that Absolutism as part of the late feudal economic structure generated its own particular cultural and industrial achievements. Mughal attainments in art and architecture moved outside of traditional Islamic representations, while Ming pottery exemplified a 'commercial' revolution, not an 'industrial' revolution of the British kind.

'The Chinese puzzle' can be explained using the framework of Eastern Absolutism. There were new and large urban populations throughout China, just as there were in the Ottoman Empire. China had financially sophisticated merchant elites. Trade with the Europeans produced a market for finished products. China had stable political and judicial systems. It could show technological innovations (paper and gunpowder are the two best-known). Yet the traditional Confucian attitude to merchants persisted; the venerable wisdom of scholars commanded more respect than the entrepreneurial culture of the commercial elites.

There has been considerable historical debate about why Chinese civilisation did not produce the kind of economic breakthrough associated with the West. However, we need to look for commonalities across all the Eastern Absolutist regimes. What did East Europe, the Ottoman Empire, Mughal India and Ming/Qing China have in common? There were three obvious features. With a labour force in abundance, there was no pressure to automate their factories. Each had a militarised economy and State, closely interwoven. And each enjoyed harmonious class relationships.

In short, they remained pre-capitalist, but departed from the classic feudalism of Western Europe.

The Revolutions in France and Britain

Late feudalism produced Absolutism, an assembly of power in the control of powerful monarchs across Europe and Asia. Some monarchs were forcibly removed: from England temporarily, from the American colonies, and, most spectacularly, from France. These latter cases continued to inspire national independence movements well into the twentieth century. Monarchs survived in Eastern Europe, the Ottoman Empire, Mughal India and Ming/Qing China, thanks to a form of rule we can call Eastern Absolutism.

The British Revolution, better known as the Industrial Revolution, led directly to the events of 1848, the development of nationalism and the Paris Commune. As the new capitalist economies expanded, they embarked on a global colonialism, including the 'Scramble for Africa', and their imperial rivalries set the context for the Great War and the emergence of Bolshevism in Russia.

Primary sources:

The Memoirs of Jahāngīr and Kangxi's *Sacred Edict*

The Memoirs of Jahāngīr

After my accession, the first order that I gave was for the fastening up of the Chain of Justice, so that if those engaged in the administration of justice should delay or practise hypocrisy in the matter of those seeking justice, the oppressed might come to this chain and shake it so that its noise might attract attention. Its fashion was this: I ordered them to make a chain of pure gold, 30 gaz in length and containing 60 bells. Its weight was 4 Indian maunds, equal to 42 'Irāqī maunds. One end of it they made fast to the battlements of the Shāh Burj of the fort at Agra

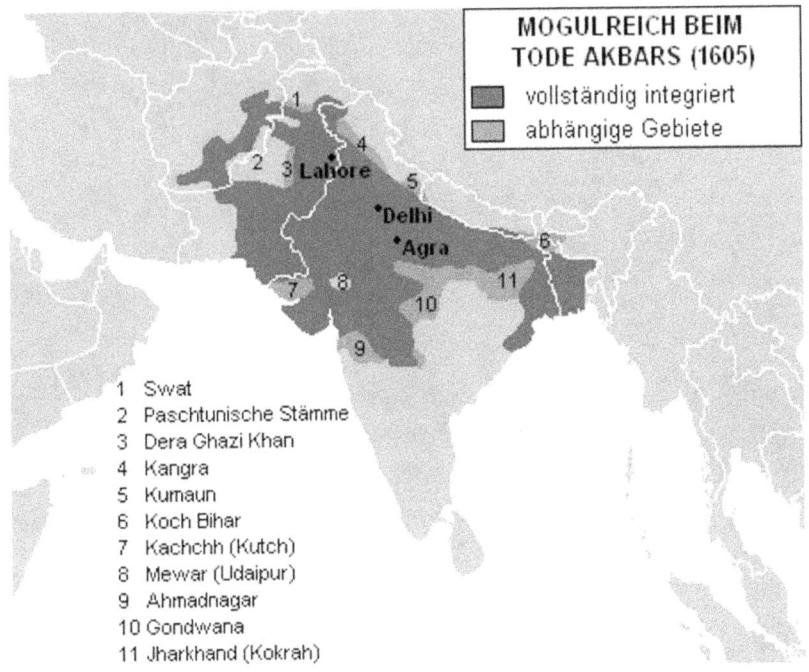

MOGULREICH BEIM TODE AKBARS (1605)
- vollständig integriert
- abhängige Gebiete

1 Swat
2 Paschtunische Stämme
3 Dera Ghazi Khan
4 Kangra
5 Kumaun
6 Koch Bihar
7 Kachchh (Kutch)
8 Mewar (Udaipur)
9 Ahmadnagar
10 Gondwana
11 Jharkhand (Kokrah)

The Mughal Empire as conquered by Akbar, 1605

Jahāngīr

and the other to a stone post fixed on the bank of the river. I also gave twelve orders to be observed as rules of conduct (dastūru-l-'amal) in all my dominions:

(1) Forbidding the levy of cesses under the names of tamghā and mīr baṣrī (river tolls), and other burdens which the jāgīrdārs (landowners) of every province and district had imposed for their own profit.

(2) On roads where thefts and robberies took place, which roads might be at a little distance from habitations, the jāgīrdārs of the neighbourhood should build sarāʾīs (public rest-houses), mosques, and

dig wells, which might stimulate population, and people might settle down in those sarāʾīs. If these should be near a khāliṣa estate (under direct State management), the administrator (mutaṣaddī) of that place should execute the work.

(3) The bales of merchants should not be opened on the roads without informing them and obtaining their leave.

(4) In my dominions if anyone, whether unbeliever or Musalman, should die, his property and effects should be left for his heirs, and no one should interfere with them. If he should have no heir, they should appoint inspectors and separate guardians to guard the property, so that its value might be expended in lawful expenditure, such as the building of mosques and sarāʾīs, the repair of broken bridges, and the digging of tanks and wells.

(5) They should not make wine or rice-spirit (darbahra) or any kind of intoxicating drug, or sell them; although I myself drink wine, and from the age of 18 years up till now, when I am 38, have persisted in it. When I first took a liking to drinking I sometimes took as much as twenty cups of double-distilled spirit; when by degrees it acquired a great influence over me I endeavoured to lessen the quantity, and in the period of seven years I have brought myself from fifteen cups to five or six. My times for drinking were varied; sometimes when three or four sidereal hours of the day remained I would begin to drink, and sometimes at night and partly by day. This went on till I was 30 years old. After that I took to drinking always at night. Now I drink only to digest my food.

(6) They should not take possession of any person's house.

(7) I forbade the cutting off the nose or ears of any person, and I myself made a vow by the throne of God that I would not blemish anyone by this punishment.

(8) I gave an order that the officials of the Crown lands and the jāgīrdārs should not forcibly take the lands of ryots (peasants) and cultivate them on their own account.

(9) A government collector or a jāgīrdār should not without permission intermarry with the people of the pargana (district) in which he might be.

(10) They should found hospitals in the great cities, and appoint physicians for the healing of the sick; whatever the expenditure might be, should be given from the *khāliṣa* (government-directed) establishment.

(11) In accordance with the regulations of my revered father, I ordered that each year from the 18th of Rabīʿu-l-awwal, which is my birthday, for a number of days corresponding to the years of my life, they should not slaughter animals (for food). Two days in each week were also forbidden, one of them Thursday, the day of my accession, and the other Sunday, the day of my father's birth. He held this day in great esteem on this account, and because it was dedicated to the Sun, and also because it was the day on which the Creation began. Therefore it was one of the days on which there was no killing in his dominions.

(12) I gave a general order that the offices and jāgīrs (revenue-producing lands) of my father's servants should remain as they were. Later, the manṣabs (ranks or offices) were increased according to each one's circumstances by not less than 20 per cent to 300 or 400 per cent. The subsistence money of the aḥadīs (imperial domestic servants) was increased by 50 per cent, and I raised the pay of all domestics by 20 per cent. I increased the allowances of all the veiled ladies of my father's harem from 20 per cent to 100 per cent, according to their condition and relationship. By one stroke of the pen I confirmed the subsistence lands of the holders of aimas (charity lands) within the dominions, who form the army of prayer, according to the deeds in their possession. I gave an order to Mīrān Ṣadr Jahān, who is one of the genuine Sayyids of India, and who for a long time held the high office of ṣadr (ecclesiastical officer) under my father, that he should every day produce before me deserving people (worthy of charity). I released all criminals who had been confined and imprisoned for a long time in the forts and prisons.

At a propitious hour I ordered that they should coin gold and silver of different weights. To each coin I gave a separate name, viz., to the muhr of 100 tola, that of nūr-shāhī; to that of 50 tola, that of nūr-sulānī; to that of 20 tola, nūr-daulat; to that of 10 tola, nūr-karam; to that of 5 tola, nūr-mihr; and to that of 1 tola, nūr-jahānī. The half of this I called nūrānī, and the quarter, rawājī. With regard to the silver coins (sikkas) I gave to the coin of 100 tola the name of kaukab-i-ālīʿ (star of horoscope); to that of 50 tola, the name of kaukab-i-iqbāl (star of fortune); to that of 20 tola, the name of kaukab-i-murād (star of desire); to that of 10 tola, the name of kaukab-i-bakht (star of good luck); to that of 5 tola, the name of kaukab-i-saʿd (star of auspiciousness); to that of 1 tola, the name of jahāngīrī. The half jahāngīrī I called sulānī; the quarter, niārī (showering money); the dime, khair-i-qabūl (the acceptable). Copper, also, I coined in the same proportions, and gave each division a particular name. I ordered that on the gold muhr of 100, 50, 20, and 10 *tola* the following verse by Āṣaf Khān should be impressed – namely, on the obverse was this couplet:

> "Fate›s pen wrote on the coin in letters of light,
> The Shāh Nūru-d-dīn Jahāngīr";

and between the lines of the verse the Creed (Kalima) was impressed. On the reverse was this couplet, in which the date of coinage was signified:

> "Through this coin is the world brightened as by the sun,
> And the date thereof is 'Sun of Dominion' (Āftāb-i-Mamlakat)."

Between the lines of the verse, the mint, the Hijra year, and the regnal year were impressed. On the nūr-jahānī, which is in the place of the ordinary gold muhr and exceeds it in weight by 20 per cent (as 12 to 10), is impressed this couplet of the Amīru-l-umarā:

> "Shāh Nūru-d-dīn Jahāngīr ibn Akbar Pādshāh
> Made gold›s face bright with the sheen of sun and moon."

Accordingly, a hemistich was impressed on each face, and also the mint, and the Hijra and regnal year. The jahāngīrī sikka, also, which is greater in weight by 20 per cent, was reckoned as equal to a rupee, its weight being fixed in the same manner as that of the nūr-jahānī (each was a tola in weight, but one was in gold and the other was in silver). The weight of a tola is 2 1/2 miqāls of Persia and Tūrān (central Asia).

It would not be good to give all the versified chronograms which were made for my accession. I therefore content myself with the one which Maktūb Khān, the superintendent of the library and picture gallery, and one of my old servants, composed:

> "The second lord of conjunction, Shāhinshāh Jahāngīr,
> With justice and equity sat on the throne of happiness.
> Prosperity, Good Fortune, Wealth, Dignity, and Victory,
> With loins girt in his service, stood rejoicing before him.
> It became the date of the accession when Prosperity
> Placed his head at the feet of the Ṣāḥib-Qirān-i-ānī."

To my son Khusrau a lakh of rupees was presented that he might build up for himself the house of Mun'im Khān, the (former) Khānkhānān, outside the fort. The administration and government of the Panjab was bestowed on Sa'īd Khān, who was one of the confidential nobles and connected with my father by marriage. His origin was from the Moghul tribe, and his ancestors were in the service of my forefathers. At the time of his taking leave, as it was said that his eunuchs oppressed and tyrannised over the weak and the poor, I sent a message to him that my justice would not put up with oppression from anyone, and that in the scales of equity neither smallness nor greatness was regarded. If after this any cruelty or harshness should be observed on the part of his people, he would receive punishment without favour.

Again, having previously bestowed on Shaikh Farīd Bukhārī, who had been Mīr Bakhshī in my father's service, a dress of honour, a jewelled sword, a jewelled inkstand and pen, I confirmed him in the same post, and in order to exalt him I said to him, "I regard thee as Ṣāḥibu-s-saif-wa-l-qalam" ("Captain Sword and Captain Pen"). Muqīm, to whom my father had given at the end of his reign the title of Wazīr Khān and the viziership of his dominions, I selected for the same title, rank, and service. I also gave Khwājagī Fatḥu-llah a dress of honour, and made him a bakhshi, as formerly. 'Abdu-r-Razzāq Ma'mūrī, although when I was prince he had left my service without cause or reason and had gone over to my father, I made bakhshi as formerly, and I gave him a dress of honour. To Amīnu-d-daula, who when I was prince had the post of bakhshi, and without my leave had run away and taken service with my revered father, not looking to his offences I gave the office of Ātish-i-begī (Head of the Artillery), which he had held under my father. I left all those who were in possession of posts, both inside and outside, in the positions which they had with my father. Sharīf Khān had lived with me from his early years. When I was prince I had given him the title of khān, and when I left Allahabad to wait upon my honoured father I presented him with a drum and the tūmān-togh (standard of yāk tails). I had also promoted him to the rank of 2500 and given him the government of the province of Bihar. I gave him complete control over the province, and sent him off there. On the 4th of Rajab, being fifteen days after my accession, he waited upon me. I was exceedingly pleased at his coming, for his connection with me is such that I look upon him as a brother, a son, a friend, and a companion. As I had perfect confidence in his friendship, intelligence, learning, and acquaintance with affairs, having made him Grand Vizier, I promoted him to the rank of 5000 with 5000 horse and the lofty title of Amīru-l-umarā, to which no title of my servants is superior. Though his position might have warranted a higher rank, he himself represented to me that until some notable service on his part had become perceptible to me he would not accept a higher grade than that mentioned (5000).

As the reality of the loyalty of my father's servants had not yet become apparent, and certain faults and errors and unbecoming intentions which were not approved at the throne of the Creator or pleasing to His creatures had shown themselves, they of themselves became ashamed. Though on the day of my accession I had forgiven all offences and determined with myself that I would exact no retribution for past deeds, yet on account of the suspicion that had been aroused in my mind about them I considered the Amīru-l-umarā my guardian and protector; although God Almighty is the guardian of all His servants, and is especially so of kings, because their existence is the cause of the contentment of the world. His father, 'Abdu-ṣ-Ṣamad, who in the art of painting had no equal in the age, had obtained from the late king (Jannat-āshyānī) Humāyūn the title of Shīrīn-qalam (Sweet pen), and in his council had attained a great dignity and was on intimate terms with him (the king). He was one of the chief men of Shīrāz. My honoured father, on account of his former services, paid him great honour and reverence. I made Raja Mān Singh – who was one of the greatest and most trusted noblemen of my father, and had obtained alliances with this illustrious family, inasmuch as his aunt had been in my father's house (i.e. was his wife), and I had married his sister, and Khusrau and his sister Sulānu-n-nisā Begam, the latter of whom is my eldest child, were born of her – as before, ruler of the province of Bengal. Though as in consequence of certain of his acts he had no expectation of this favour towards himself, I dignified him with a *chārqab* (vest without sleeves) as a robe of honour, a jewelled sword, and one of my own horses, and sent him off to his province, which is a place of (or can keep up) 50 000 horse. His father was Raja Bhagwān Dās. His grandfather, Raja Bihārī Mal, was the first of the Kachwāha Rājpūts to have the honour of entering my father's service, and he excelled his tribe in truth and sincerity of friendship, and in the quality of valour. After my accession, when all the nobles with their retinues presented themselves at my palace, it came into my mind that I should send this body of retainers under my son, Sultan Parwīz, to make a holy war against the Rānā, who was one of evil deeds, and a foul infidel of the country of Hindustan, and in my father's time had had troops sent constantly against him, but had not been driven off. In a fortunate hour I invested my said son with gorgeous robes of honour, a jewelled waist – sword, a jewelled waist-dagger, and a rosary of pearls intermixed with rubies of great price of the value of 72 000 rupees, 'Irāq and Turkmān horses and famous elephants, and dismissed him. About 20 000 horsemen with nobles and chief leaders were appointed to this service. The first was Āṣaf Khān, who in my father's time was one of his confidential servants, and for a long time had been confirmed in the post of bakhshi and afterwards became dīwān ba istiqlāl (Chancellor with full powers); him I advanced from the rank of an Amīr to that of Vizier, and promoting him from the command of 2500 horse to that of 5000 made him guardian to Parwīz. Having honoured him with a robe of honour, jewelled waist-sword, a horse and an elephant, I ordered that all the manṣabdārs (commanders), small and great, should not depart from such orders as he thought proper to give them. I made 'Abdu-r-Razzāq Ma'mūrī his bakhshi and Mukhtār Beg, Āṣaf Khān's paternal uncle, diwan to Parwīz. I also presented to Raja Jagannāth, son of Raja Bihārī Mal, who had the rank of 5000, a robe of honour and a jewelled waist-sword.

Again, I gave Rānā Shankar, cousin of the Rānā – to whom my father had given the title of Rānā, proposing to send him with Khusrau against the Rānā, but at that time he (Akbar) became a shanqar (a falcon, i.e. he died) – a robe of honour and a jewelled sword, and sent him with him.

I presented Mādho Singh, brother's son of Raja Mān Singh, and Rāwal Sāl Darbārī with flags, from this consideration, that they were always present at Court and belonged to the Sekhāwaṭ Rājpūts, and were confidential servants of my father. Each received also the rank of 3,000.

I promoted Shaikh Ruknu-d-dīn the Afghan, to whom when I was prince I had given the title of Shīr Khān, from the grade of 500 to that of 3500. Shīr Khān is the head of his clan and a very valiant man. He lost his arm by the sword in service against the Uzbegs. 'Abdu-r-Raḥman, son of Shaikh Abu-l-fazl, Maha Singh, grandson of Rāja Mān Singh, Zāhid Khān, son of Ṣādiq Khān, Wazīr Jamīl, and Qarā Khān Turkmān were exalted to the rank of 2000; all these obtained robes of honour and horses, and were dismissed. Manohar also obtained leave to join the expedition. He is of the tribe of the Sekhāwaṭ Kachhwāhas, and on him in his young days my father bestowed many favours. He had learned the Persian language, and, although from him up to Adam the power of understanding cannot be attributed to any one of his tribe, he is not without intelligence. He makes Persian verses, and the following is one of his couplets:

> "The object of shade in Creation is this
> That no one place his foot on the light of my Lord, the Sun."

A rhino hunt illustrating the *Baburnama*

If the details were to be described of all the commanders and servants appointed by me, with the conditions and connections and rank of each, it would be a long business. Many of my immediate attendants and personal followers and nobles› sons, house-born ones (khānazādān) and zealous Rajputs, petitioned to accompany this expedition. A thousand ahadis, the meaning of which is single ones, were also appointed. In short, a force was collected together such that if reliance on the Friend (God) were vouchsafed, it could have embarked on enmity and conflict with any one of the monarchs of power.

> "Soldiers came up from all sides,
> Seizing life from heroes of the world in battle;
> They had no fear of death from the sharp sword,
> No terror of water and no flight from fire;
> In valour singular, in vigour a crowd,
> Anvils in endurance, rocks in attack."

When I was prince I had entrusted, in consequence of my extreme confidence in him, my own ūzuk seal to the Amīru-l-umarā (Sharīf), but when he was sent off to the province of Bihar I made it over to Parwīz. Now that Parwīz went off against the Rānā, I made it over, according to the former arrangement, to the Amīru-l-umarā.

Kangxi's *Sacred Edict*

Kangxi's *Sacred Edict* (1670) was read out aloud in villages across China:

Esteem most highly filial piety and brotherly submission, in order to give due importance to the social relations.

Behave with generosity toward your kindred, in order to illustrate harmony and benignity.

Cultivate peace and concord in your neighbourhoods, in order to prevent quarrels and litigations.

Recognise the importance of husbandry and the culture of the mulberry tree, in order to ensure a sufficiency of clothing and food.

Show that you prize moderation and economy, in order to prevent the lavish waste of your means.

Give weight to colleges and schools, in order to make correct the practice of the scholar.

Extirpate strange principles, in order to exalt the correct doctrine.

Lecture on the laws, in order to warn the ignorant and obstinate.

Elucidate propriety and yielding courtesy, in order to make manners and customs good.

Modern portrait of Emperor Kangxi

Labour diligently at your proper callings, in order to stabilise the will of the people.

Instruct sons and younger brothers, in order to prevent them from doing what is wrong.

Put a stop to false accusations, in order to preserve the honest and good.

Warn against sheltering deserters, in order to avoid being involved in their punishment.

Fully remit your taxes, in order to avoid being pressed for payment.

Unite in hundreds and tithing, in order to put an end to thefts and robbery.

Remove enmity and anger, in order to show the importance due to the person and life.

Questions for discussion:

What are the values implicit or stated by these two men, Jahāngīr and Kangxi?

Where do these values come from philosophically?

To what extent are they values we would expect from all Absolutist rulers?

How would a monarch of Western Europe have described his or her achievements?

What factors, especially of an economic or political kind, are neglected in these accounts?

Going further:

William Dalrymple, *The Last Mughal: The Fall of a Dynasty, Delhi, 1857*, Bloomsbury, London, 2006

John W. Dardess, 'The transformations of messianic revolt and the founding of the Ming Dynasty', *The Journal of Asian Studies*, vol. 29, no. 3, May 1979, pp. 539-58

John F Richards, *The Mughal Empire*, Cambridge University Press, 1993

Units 17-20: The British revolution

The British revolution was the Industrial Revolution, dating from 1780 to about 1830. It was the first economic modernisation, and its effects were as profound in the economic sphere as the French Revolution had proved in the world of politics. It ushered in the mode of production known as capitalism, which would have long lasting effects into the nineteenth and twentieth centuries.

Unit 17

The Industrial Revolution

> And did those feet in ancient time
> Walk upon England's mountains green:
> And was the holy Lamb of God,
> On England's pleasant pastures seen!
>
> And did the Countenance Divine,
> Shine forth upon our clouded hills?
> And was Jerusalem builded here,
> Among these dark Satanic Mills?
>
> Bring me my Bow of burning gold;
> Bring me my Arrows of desire:
> Bring me my Spear: O clouds unfold!
> Bring me my Chariot of fire!
>
> I will not cease from Mental Fight,
> Nor shall my Sword sleep in my hand:
> Till we have built Jerusalem,
> In England's green & pleasant Land.

Events such as the opening ceremony for the 2012 London Olympics see this anthem performed. Serving as Britain's unofficial anthem, William Blake's *Jerusalem* (1804) imagines a life before the Industrial Revolution, and is also used on Royal occasions. These are quite different purposes, which invites the question: how are these two themes connected?

The British Industrial Revolution was deeply significant. The political movements that emerged out of the chaos of the Industrial Revolution were passionately anthro-centric. The Conservatives were horrified by the French Revolution and sought a leadership role for the new urban bourgeoisie previously held by the landed aristocracy. Liberalism traced its origins to the Whigs of the Glorious Revolution who had constrained the monarchy and its illusions of divine right. Socialism later emerged as a genuine third alternative.

Now the West made a sustained productivity leap. The Industrial Revolution was really confined to only two industries – iron and textiles. Elsewhere the gains were in improved productivity, especially in farming. A key factor was that Britain controlled all its economic institutions – drawing from American slavery and Irish agriculture. As a consequence of this Industrial Revolution, the West moved decisively ahead of East Asia and the Islamic world in economic terms.

What had changed in the Western Absolutist State to help us understand this revolution? Firstly, mercantilism was under attack from the American colonists (1776-1783), and philosophically from Adam Smith (the Scottish Enlightenment); this was less of an issue in the East, which relied less on maritime imperialism. Secondly, the Napoleonic wars (1799-1815) saw improvements in the military forces of Western Europe. And, as we have already stressed [in Unit 8], the Western Absolutist State had given the urban merchant elites more space to develop than their Eastern counterparts.

Albion Flour Mills, Bankside, London, 1786: The inspiration for William Blake's 'dark Satanic mills'

Three major changes of the modern period were closely linked to the British Industrial Revolution. The end of Absolutist governments was legitimated by the French Revolution, but had been already modified in Britain by the Glorious Revolution of 1688. There was the geopolitical rise to power of the North Atlantic, especially Britain and America. And there was the development of the factory system – the phenomenon usually termed the Industrial Revolution. Britain was the place where these changes first came together.

British historians regard their Industrial Revolution as one of their nation's greatest achievements – hence its appearance as a vignette in the opening ceremony of the 2012 London Games. These historians emphasise the abundant existence of iron and coal in Britain, as well as the easy access by water to all parts of the island. They stress that the British population, thanks to an improved diet, increased from 6.5 million in 1750 to 9 million by 1801, providing a local labour force to be employed by the factory owners. They write about the development of scientific academies for those who were not yet entitled to enrol in British universities. Patents rise from dozen a year to 250 annually by 1825. There was greater accessibility to capital in a trading nation, with a developed financial sector (which had been lacking in the earlier empires of the Spanish and the Portuguese). And no doubt Britain had improved transport, with canals and roads, and then rail.

Three important technological improvements are emphasised in the traditional accounts of the Industrial Revolution. One was the mechanisation of the textile industry. The first mechanised cotton looms were in private houses; as these looms became larger, stand-alone factories became necessary. Manchester had only two cotton factories in 1782, but 52 in 1802. Coal, once valued merely for heating, was now used for making iron and steel. Coal production trebled during the eighteenth century, and then increased by another twenty-fold during the twentieth century. Steam was the third improvement. Steam engines were used for pumping Cornish mines by Thomas Newcomen; they were then adapted by James Watt for use in Matthew Boulton's Birmingham factory.

Peasants into proletarians

What was the human impact of these technological changes? Putting it briefly, the peasant triangle of land-labour-family was thoroughly transformed by the process of industrialisation, and by the metamorphosis of the peasantry into the proletariat.

In the case of land, the first factories were built alongside fast-running rivers in the British countryside. Very soon the Industrial Revolution became an urban phenomenon and the proletariat lost their connection to land. The land was 'enclosed' when agriculture was commercialised and the commons were taken. The old peasant ideal of self-sufficiency was replaced by a new urban household budget with income from various sources, including female piecework at home.

One of the eight scenes from William Hogarth's *A Rake's Progress*, printed in 1735 [Sir John Soane's Museum, London]

The second angle of the triangle, labour, was also changed. Human labour was mimicked by the machinery of the Industrial Revolution – many of the old skills were lost as people moved into factory work and their bodies were employed differently. The Spinning Jenny was a good example of how human dexterity was emulated by the new technologies of the Industrial Revolution. The back-breaking work in the fields was replaced by the more routinised work of the factories. They were called 'factory hands' as if to signify this new emphasis on manual dexterity. 'Industrial time' replaced 'peasant time' – people lost control over the timing of their work.

The third corner of the old peasant triangle was family. The authority of the peasant father was replaced by the control of the factory foreman. Family and kin was replaced by 'neighbourhood', as proletarians settled into their new urban lives. The village square was replaced by the neighbourhood local or the urban parkland or the sporting club as a place to gather and make new friends.

We can vividly see the transformation of Welsh peasants into proletarians from an unusual source. Francis Crawshay was an unusual capitalist, and a reluctant one, who inherited an ironworks in Hirwaun, Wales. In the late 1830s he commissioned portraits of sixteen of his workers -- the result is that we are bequeathed images of workers, atypically for this period, and at the very moment when Welsh peasants were being transformed into industrial proletarians.[25] All the images are of men, so they have lost any sense of connection to their kinfolk; instead they now report as individuals to Crawshay. Each man is described by his name and occupation. Only one of them carries a tool of trade. Their occupations are a mix of the old peasantry and the new proletariat.

From nearby Cornwall a half-century later we get an arresting image of proletarian women, by a female artist of the day, Emily Mary Osborn.

---

25 These images are in the National Museum, Cardiff. See Peter Lord, *Francis Crawshay Workers' Portraits*, University of Wales, 1996, and his *The Visual Culture of Wales: Industrial Society*, 2000. The factory itself features in a portrait of iron and tin works, by W Pascoe, pencil and wash, 1850, and the Tinplate works at Treforest, near Pontypridd.

The Bal Maidens, 1883, is fetching portrait of three Cornish ore diggers dressed not in their workaday wear, but instead in pretty dresses that seem to belie their social class. Their innocence masks the grim reality of a Cornwall undergoing both industrialisation and depopulation.

When rural peasants became urban proletarians, their politics would also change. To understand this change, we need to consider class theory, the conceptual basis of social class. When it mobilises, a 'class-in-itself' (the class as a hostage to history) becomes a 'class-for-itself' (the class as an agent of history). Accordingly, History as told by the ruling class ('history-from-above') can become 'History-from-below', an account told by the peasants and proletarians themselves.

People were pushed off the land by the mechanisation of agriculture. The British population moved away from agriculture. 1867 was the last year in which as many people lived in English countryside as in towns. The working class (the proletariat) made itself in this process. In E.P. Thompson's *The Making of the English Working Class* (1963) there is a famous quote: 'The English working class was present at its own making', a radical statement that resonated for subsequent generations of historians.[26] By now the bourgeoisie was clearly the dominant class vis-à-vis the landed aristocracy – they defined themselves in relation to the new urban proletariat.

Notions of time were changing. The new pocket watch became a symbol of 'industrial time'. In the tavern scene from Hogarth's *The Rake's Progress*, what most interests the thieving prostitute is Tom Rakewell's pocket watch, which she passes to an accomplice.[27] The 1700s saw so

---

26 On Thompson and the other British Marxist historians, drawn to study the Industrial Revolution, see Harvey. J. Kaye, *The British Marxist Historians*, Macmillan, Basingstoke, UK, 1995 [1984], and Harvey J. Kaye and Keith McClelland, eds, *E. P. Thompson: Critical Perspectives*, Temple University Press, Philadelphia, 1990.

27 John Styles, 'Time piece: Working men and watches', *History Today*, January 2008, pp. 44-50.

much change in the everyday lives of the British that it has become a very popular field for British historians.[28]

The British Industrial Revolution and World History

This significant moment in World History can be understood in two quite different ways. This Industrial Revolution was either delayed by feudalism, or else it was a natural next step from late feudalism.[29] The origin of capitalism is sometimes seen as the removal of feudal blockages that were holding back a 'natural' tendency in humans to be profit-maximising – to 'truck, barter, and exchange', as Adam Smith put it. This assumption is contained even within Marxist accounts – we will also see it in *The Communist Manifesto* – but it needs to be questioned. It is allied to the idea that commercial societies existed within cities and only needed to be freed of feudal constraints for the capitalist industrial revolution to take place. However, if feudalism is seen as the creative synthesis that emerged with the fusion of the primitive communism of the German tribes and the slave economy of imperial Rome, then feudalism represents a necessary and important next step in human history.

Late feudalism bears some resemblance to the river valley cultures like ancient Egypt – they successfully competed against the weaker rival states, just as the Eastern European, Ottoman Empire, Mughal India and Ming/Ching dynasties achieved a relative success in their own time. The anthro-centric era, beginning with the Enlightenment prevailing across Europe and North America, no doubt contributed to this change, either directly in terms of what is often called the Scientific Revolution or indirectly in terms of creating the space in which the Industrial Revolution could take place.

But it is the particular combination of a reformed Absolutist state

---

28 Penelope J. Corfield, 'British history: The exploding galaxy', *Journal for Eighteenth-Century Studies*, vol. 34, 2011, pp. 517-26.
29 Ellen Meiksins Wood, *The Origin of Capitalism: A Longer View*, Verso, London, 2002.

in Britain and its Industrial Revolution of a century later that demands attention. The question of 'why Britain?' ignores another possibility – that Britain was forced to adopt the industrial revolution because it lacked certain advantages held by the Eastern Absolutist states, such as a large ready labour force. So, was Western success in producing the first Industrial Revolution a reflection of their cultural differences with the Muslim, Hindu and Confucian leaders?

We need to discard Eurocentric assumptions to get to an answer to this question, which we called 'the Chinese puzzle'.[30] The Middle East, south Asia and China were clearly ahead of Europe in technology, state-building and military-naval capacity. The merchant class in Europe was undoubtedly more politically powerful than their counterparts in the Eastern Absolutist regimes. They and the guilds constituted a powerful group within the city-states of Western Europe. They were able to leverage advantages from the city-states, such as reduced transport costs, that aided long-term capital accumulation. They also enjoyed privileges attached to the notion of 'citizenship' within these city-states. Citizenship before the French Revolution was a commodity that could be purchased, so ex-Byzantine merchants purchased it in Italy's northern cities. Only the propertied could buy citizenship. There was usually a pecking order, but with the fall of Byzantium in 1453 there were many Greeks, Jews and others who wanted to settle in Venice or Genoa, and used proof of residency, local intermarriage or business or professional interests to claim citizenship. (For instance, Jews in Venice living in the ghetto were often doctors.) The urban elites began purchasing land from the surrounding areas; peasants got work in the cities as a result. The rural overlords in Western Europe were far more cash-strapped than their counterparts in the Eastern Absolutist regimes.

The merchant elites in the West also controlled the thinking that went on at the time of the Industrial Revolution: the bourgeoisie mobilised

---

30 Eric H. Mielants, *The Origins of Capitalism and the "Rise of the West"*, Temple University Press, Philadelphia PA, 2007.

itself around the new ideas of the economists of the day (then called 'political economists' but lacking in what we would today think of as politics), like Adam Smith. Smith wrote about the 'invisible hand'. Self-interested individuals, according to Smith, are 'led by an invisible hand to promote an end which [is] no part of [their] intention': this is the market, at the heart of capitalist thinking. Some historians have wondered whether Smith's hand might be a reference to divinity, that is, God's hand, since Smith was writing at the end of the deo-centric period. R.H. Tawney understood Smith's metaphor in these terms. 'The existing order, except insofar as the short-sighted enactments of Governments interfered with it, was the natural order, and the order established by nature was the order established by God.... [As expressed by the poet Alexander Pope:] Thus God and Nature formed the general frame, And bade self-love and social be the same.' 'But where did this leave Christian charity?', Tawney wanted to know. That 'self-love and the social be the same' carried important implications. Arguments against being too charitable to the working class did not come from Adam Smith (in *Wealth of Nations*) even though he became the iconic thinker for the bourgeoisie – in fact he knew perfectly well the social effects of a laissez faire economy. Arguments against charity came instead from Thomas Malthus (population growth would mean the condition of the masses could not be ameliorated); from David Ricardo (his Iron Law of Wages dictated that wages must be remain lower than profits for the economy to succeed, and taxes should be kept low); and from Jeremy Bentham (his concept of the greatest happiness for the greatest number rationalised the prospect of an unemployed minority).[31] Interestingly, Malthus was proven wrong when nutrition levels did improve, thanks to the Columbian Exchange.

The global consequences of the Industrial Revolution were profound. It had the most important transforming effect on society since the

---

31 Bentham gave instructions in his Will that he was to be mummified and kept on display at the University of London, where he presides to this day.

discovery of agriculture in prehistoric times. In the first stage of this revolution, from roughly 1780 to 1830, it remained British, focused on cotton mills (factories) that produced cheap clothing. In the second phase, from 1830 to 1870, it spread to France, Germany and the United States, producing a railway boom across the globe, and in the third stage, from 1890 onwards, it spread to Russia and Japan, with developments based on electricity, oil, and the motor car. In each case inventions took place at the core and then spread to the periphery. This became the model for industrial innovation. (The post-industrial model, characteristic of the early twenty-first century, would, in contrast, be multiply-centred, as discussed in Unit 24.)

This global development included the Australian colonies. The Australian goldrushes of the 1850s were a shot in the arm for European industrial capitalism, as Marx noted with rue. 'Marvellous Melbourne' grew from 270 000 inhabitants in 1880 to 470 000 in 1890. The colonies were needed as integral part of system, providing both raw materials and ready markets. Australia was populated by technicians who represented this Industrial Revolution at the periphery of an expanding British empire.

The literary and artistic consequences and reflections on the Industrial Revolution were also considerable. The Industrial Revolution inspired writers and artists in diverse ways. Poets such as Blake and Matthew Arnold attacked its effects on English society. Painters depicted a changed landscape. The novel emerged as a major new genre, perhaps giving people the opportunity to read to themselves for the first time in human history. (Until now, most people read aloud.) Interestingly, theatre was slower to take up the issues, and then film in the twentieth century (in movies such as Charlie Chaplin's *Modern Times*).

One of the more famous poems written in the direct aftermath of the Industrial Revolution was Matthew Arnold's 'Dover Beach', written in 1867. It laments the passing of a simpler, pre-industrial England:

The sea is calm to-night.
The tide is full, the moon lies fair
Upon the straits; on the French coast the light
Gleams and is gone; the cliffs of England stand;
Glimmering and vast, out in the tranquil bay.
Come to the window, sweet is the night-air!
Only, from the long line of spray
Where the sea meets the moon-blanched land,

Listen! you hear the grating roar
Of pebbles which the waves draw back, and fling,
At their return, up the high strand,
Begin, and cease, and then again begin,

With tremulous cadence slow, and bring
The eternal note of sadness in.

Sophocles long ago
Heard it on the Aegean, and it brought
Into his mind the turbid ebb and flow
Of human misery; we
Find also in the sound a thought,
Hearing it by this distant northern sea.

The Sea of Faith
Was once, too, at the full, and round earth's shore
Lay like the folds of a bright girdle furled.
But now I only hear
Its melancholy, long, withdrawing roar,

Retreating, to the breath
Of the night-wind, down the vast edges drear
And naked shingles of the world.

Ah, love, let us be true
To one another! for the world, which seems

> To lie before us like a land of dreams,
> So various, so beautiful, so new,
> Hath really neither joy, nor love, nor light,
> Nor certitude, nor peace, nor help for pain;
> And we are here as on a darkling plain
> Swept with confused alarms of struggle and flight,
> Where ignorant armies clash by night.

Some have said that this one poem gives a succinct summary of world history up to 1867, the very year when the number of Britons living as urban dwellers finally equaled those still leading rural lives. The 'Sea of Faith' is a reference back to the deo-centric period of world history. The 'ignorant armies' are the two new social classes produced by the Industrial Revolution (the bourgeoisie, the proletariat) which the conservative Arnold saw as equally reprehensible in their political conflict.

These 'ignorant armies' (the class struggle) are well described in the English novels of the day. Charles Dickens, in *Hard Times* (1854), describes the industrial Coketown. Elizabeth Gaskell, in *North and South* (1855) evokes a cotton mill in the North of England. Other powerful novels of this period include Benjamin Disraeli, *Sybil* (1845), and George Eliot, *Felix Holt* (1866). The Victorian novel is a great resource for historians. The novel already existed, but became very popular among the newly literate English working class, as evidenced by the rise of the Mechanics Institutes. Literacy rates were steadily improving in the English-speaking world.

Whatever benefits this Industrial Revolution might have brought to British people came to a crash in the decade known as 'the Hungry 'Forties'. The condition of the working class in Britain began to deteriorate in the 1840s. Cities like London and Dublin had grown faster than it was possible for the authorities to provide reasonable urban amenities. Many aspects of pre-industrial Britain survived until that decade, so the pre-modern world was still within living memory. The 1840s was called the Hungry 'Forties because the full effects of the Industrial Revolution were now being felt. With this came the rise of organised labour. After the failure of the middle-class 1848 Revolution, the writings of Marx and Engels were becoming more influential. The decade is best reflected in the Irish Famine, which saw that country's population emigrate in huge numbers to English cities, to the United States, and to the Australian colonies.

Yet Britain avoided a French Revolution, with the introduction of gradual change to its political system. 1832 saw the First Reform Bill, the first overhaul of the parliamentary system, including a wider vote and electorates for the industrial North that had not been previously represented. Further reform bills, extending the male franchise, were enacted in 1867 and 1884. The secret ballot was introduced in 1872. Nonetheless, it was only in 1918 that all British men got the vote, and not until 1928 did all women enjoy enfranchisement. Curiously, many of these parliamentary reforms were in fact devised in other countries, such as the secret ballot in the colony of Victoria.[32]

Liberalism and parliamentary democracy developed first in the Western Absolutist states and their colonies. On the Continent, the political reverberations continued throughout the nineteenth century, especially in 1848 and the Paris Commune. Nationalism emerged to fragment the dream of a unified working class across language barriers. Capitalism created imperialism, and this helped improve the condition of the metropolitan working classes, and foster the racialism of Social Darwinism. We cannot underplay the long-term effects of European colonialism. The Great War of 1914 and the Russian Revolution of 1917 would follow with remorseless logic.

---

32 John Markoff, 'Where and when was democracy invented?', *Comparative Studies in Society and History*, vol. 41, no. 4, October 1999, pp. 660-90.

Mechanics Institutes, such as this one in Ballarat, Victoria, helped improve literacy rates

Memorial to the Irish Famine, Dublin

Primary sources:

Thomas Spence, *The Real Rights of Man*, and Thomas Paine, *Agrarian Justice*

Thomas Spence, *The Real Rights of Man*, 1775

A lecture read at The Philosophical Society in Newcastle on November 8th, 1775, for Printing of which the Society did the Author the Honour to expel him.

Mr President, -- It being my turn to lecture, I beg to give some thoughts on this important question, viz.: -- Whether mankind in society reap all the advantages from their natural and equal rights of property in land and liberty, which in that state they possibly may and ought to expect? And as I hope you, Mr President and the good company here, are sincere friends to truth, I am under no apprehensions of giving offence by defending her cause with freedom.

That property in land and liberty among men in a state of nature ought to be equal, few, one would be fain to hope, would be foolish enough to deny. Therefore, taking this to be granted, the country of any people, in a native state, is properly their common, in which each of them has an equal property, with free liberty to sustain himself and family with the animals, fruits and other products thereof. Thus such a people reap jointly the whole advantages of their country, or neighbourhood, without having their right in so doing called in question by any, not even by the most selfish and corrupt. For upon what must they live if not upon the productions of the country in which they reside? Surely, to deny them that right is in effect denying them a right to live. Well, methinks some are now ready to say, but is it lawful, reasonable and just, for this people to sell, or make a present even, of the whole of their country, or common, to whom they will, to be held by them and their heirs for ever?

To this I answer, if their posterity require no grosser materials to live and move upon than air, it would certainly be very ill-natured to dispute their right of parting, for what of their own, their posterity would never have occasion for; but if their posterity cannot live but as grossly as they do, the same gross materials must be left them to live upon. For the right to deprive anything of the means of living, supposes a right to deprive it of life; and this right ancestors are not supposed to have over their posterity.

Hence it is plain that the land or earth, in any country or neighbourhood, with everything in or on the same, or pertaining thereto, belongs at all times to the living inhabitants of the said country or neighbourhood in an equal manner. For, as I said before, there is no living but on land and its productions, consequently, what we cannot live without we have the same property in as our lives.

Now as society ought properly to be nothing but a mutual agreement among the inhabitants of a country to maintain the natural rights and privileges of one another against all opposers, whether foreign or domestic, it would lead one to expect to find those rights and privileges no further infringed upon among men pretending to be in that state,

The English Radical, Thomas Spence (1750-1814)

than necessity absolutely required. I say again, it would lead one to think so. But I am afraid whoever does will be mightily mistaken. However, as the truth here is of much importance to be known, let it be boldly fought out; in order to which it may not be improper to trace the present method of holding land among men in society from its original.

If we look back to the origin of the present nations, we shall see that the land, with all its appurtenances, was claimed by a few, and divided among themselves, in as assured a manner as if they had manufactured it and it had been the work of their own hands; and by being unquestioned, or not called to an account for such usurpations and unjust claims, they fell into a habit of thinking, or, which is the same thing to the rest of mankind, of acting as if the earth was made for or by them, and did not scruple to call it their own property, which they might dispose of without regard to any other living creature in the universe. Accordingly they did so; and no man, more than any other creature, could claim a right to so much as a blade of grass, or a nut or an acorn, a fish or a fowl, or any natural production whatever, though to save his life, without the permission of the pretended proprietor; and not a foot of land, water, rock or heath but was claimed by one or other of those lords; so that all things, men as well as other creatures who lived, were obliged to owe their lives to some or other's property, consequently they like the creatures were claimed, and, certainly as properly as the wood herbs, etc., that were nourished by the soil. And so we find, that whether they lived, multiplied, worked or fought, it was all for their respective lords; and they, God bless them, most graciously accented of all as their due. For by granting the means of life, they granted the life itself; and of course, they thought they had a right to all the services and advantages that the life or death of the creatures they gave life to could yield.

Thus the title of gods seems suitable enough to such great beings; nor is it to be wondered at that no services could be thought too great by poor dependent needy wretches to such mightly and all-sufficient lords, in whom they seemed to live and move and have their being. Thus were the first landholders usurpers and tyrants; and all who have since possessed their lands, have done so by right of inheritance, purchase, etc., from them; and the present proprietors, like their predecessors, are proud to own it; and like them, too, they exclude all others from the least pretence to their respective properties. And any one of them still can, by laws of their own making, oblige every living creature to remove off his property (which, to the great distress of mankind, is too often put in execution); so of consequence were all the landholders to be of one mind, and determined to take their properties into their own hands, all the rest of mankind might go to heaven if they would, for there would be no place found for them here. Thus men may not live in any part of this world, not even where they are born, but as strangers, and by the permission of the pretender to the property thereof; which permission is, for the most part, paid extravagantly for, though many people are so straitened to pay the present demands, that it is believed if they hold on, there will be few to grant the favour to. And those land-makers, as we shall call them, justify all this by the practice of other manufacturers, who take all they can get for the products of their hands; and because that everyone ought to live by his business as well as he can, and consequently so ought the land-makers. Now, having before supposed it both proved and allowed, that mankind have as equal and just a property in land as they have in liberty, air, or the light and heat of the sun, and having also considered upon what hard conditions they enjoy those common gifts of nature, it is plain they are far from reaping all the advantages from them which they may and ought to expect.

But lest it should be said that a system whereby they may reap more advantages consistent with the nature of society cannot be proposed, I will attempt to show the outlines of such a plan.

Let it be supposed, then, that the whole people in some country, after much reasoning and deliberation, should conclude that every man has an equal property in the land in the neighbourhood where he resides. They therefore resolve that if they live in society together, it shall only be with a view that everyone may reap all the benefits from their natural rights and privileges possible.

Therefore a day appointed on which the inhabitants of each parish meet, in their respective parishes, to take their long-lost rights into possession, and to form themselves into corporations. So then each parish becomes a corporation, and all men who are inhabitants become members or burghers. The land, with all that appertains to it, is in every parish made the property of the corporation or parish, with as ample power to let, repair, or alter all or any part thereof as a lord of the manor enjoys over his lands, houses, etc,; but the power of alienating the least morsel, in any manner, from the parish either at this or any time hereafter is denied. For it is solemnly agreed to, by the whole nation, that a parish that shall either sell or give away any part of its landed property, shall be looked upon with as much horror and detestation, and used by them as if they had sold all their children to be slaves, or massacred them with their own hands. Thus are there no more nor other lands in the whole country than the parishes; and each of them is sovereign lord of its own territories.

Then you may behold the rent which the people have paid into the parish treasuries, employed by each parish in paying the Government its share of the sum which the Parliament or National Congress at any time grants; in maintaining and relieving its own poor, and people out of work; in paying the necessary officers their salaries; in building, repairing, and adorning its houses, bridges, and other structures; in making and maintaining convenient and delightful streets, highways, and passages both for foot and carriages; in making and maintaining canals and other conveniences for trade and navigation; in planting and taking in waste grounds; in providing and keeping up a magazine of ammunition, and all sorts of arms sufficient for all its inhabitants in case of danger from enemies; in premiums for the encouragement of agriculture, or anything else thought worthy of encouragement; and, in a word, in doing whatever the people think proper; and not, as formerly, to support and spread luxury, pride, and all manner of vice. As for corruption in elections, it has now no being or effect among them; all affairs to be determined by voting, either in a full meeting of a parish, its committees, or in the house of representatives, are done by balloting, so that votings or elections among them occasion no animosities, for none need to let another know for which side he votes; all that can be done, therefore, in order to gain a majority of votes for anything, is to make it appear in the best light possibly by speaking or writing. Among them Government does not meddle in every trifle; but on the contrary, allows each parish the power of putting the laws in force in all cases, and does not interfere but when they act manifestly to the prejudice of society and the rights and liberties of mankind, as established in their glorious constitution and laws. For the judgment of a parish may be as much depended upon as that of a House of Lords, because they have as little to fear from speaking or voting according to truth as they.

A certain number of neighbouring parishes, as those in a town or county, have each an equal vote in the election of persons to represent them in Parliament, Senate, or Congress; and each of them pays equally towards their maintenance. They are chosen thus: all the candidates are proposed in every parish on the same day, when the election by balloting immediately proceeds in all the parishes at once, to prevent too great a concourse at one place; and they who are found to have a majority, on a proper survey of the several poll-books, are acknowledged to be their representatives.

A man by dwelling a whole year in any parish, becomes a parishioner or member of its corporation; and retains that privilege till he lives a full year in some other, when he becomes a member in that parish, and immediately loses all his right to the former for ever, unless he choose to go back and recover it by dwelling again a full year there. Thus none can be a member of two parishes at once, and yet a man is always member of one though he move ever so oft.

If in any parish should be dwelling strangers from foreign nations, or people from distant countries who by sickness or other casualties should become so necessitous as to require relief before they have acquired a settlement by dwelling a full year therein; then this parish, as if it were their proper settlement, immediately takes them under its humane protection, and the expenses thus incurred by any parish in providing those not properly their own poor being taken account of, is discounted by the Exchequer out of the first payment made to the State. Thus poor strangers, being the poor of the State, are not looked upon with an envious eye lest they should become burthensome, – neither are the poor harassed about in the extremity of distress, and perhaps in a dying condition, to justify the litigiousness of the parishes.

All the men in every parish, at times of their own choosing, repair together to a field for that purpose, with their officers, arms, banners, and all sorts of martial music, in order to learn or retain the complete art of war; there they become soldiers. Yet not to molest their neighbours unprovoked, but to be able to defend what none have a right to dispute their title to the enjoyment of; and woe be to them who occasion them to do this, they would use them worse than highwaymen or pirates if they got them in their power.

There is no army kept in pay among them in times of peace, as all have property alike to defend, they are alike ready to run to arms when their country is in danger; and when an army is to be sent abroad, it is soon raised, of ready trained soldiers, either as volunteers or by casting lots in each parish for so many men.

Besides, as each man has a vote in all the affairs of his parish, and for his own sake must wish well to the public, the land is let in very small farms, which makes employment for a greater number of hands, and makes more victualling of all kinds be raised.

There are no tolls or taxes of any kind paid among them by native or foreigner, but the aforesaid rent which every person pays to the parish, according to the quantity, quality, and conveniences of the land, housing, etc., which he occupies in it. The government, poor, roads, etc. etc., as said before, are all maintained by the parishes with the rent; on which account all wares, manufactures, allowable trade employments or actions are entirely duty free. Freedom to do anything whatever cannot there be bought; a thing is either entirely prohibited, as theft or murder; or entirely free to everyone without tax or price, and the rents are still not so high, notwithstanding all that is done with them, as they were formerly for only the maintenance of a few haughty, unthankful landlords. For the government, which may be said to be the greatest mouth, having neither excisemen, customhouse men, collectors, army, pensioners, bribery, nor such like ruination vermin to maintain, is soon satisfied, and moreover there are no more persons employed in offices, either about the government or parishes, than are absolutely necessary; and their salaries are but just sufficient to maintain them suitably to their offices. And, as to the other charges, they are but trifles, and might be increased or diminished at pleasure.

But though the rent, which includes all public burden, were obliged to be somewhat raised, what then? All nations have a devouring landed interest to support besides those necessary expenses of the public; and they might be raised very high indeed before their burden would be as heavy as that of their neighbours, who pay rent and taxes too. And it surely would be the same for a person in any country to pay for instance an increase of rent if required, as to pay the same sum by little and little on everything he gets. It would certainly save him a great deal of trouble and inconvenience and Government much expense.

But what makes this prospect yet more glowing is that after this empire of right and reason is thus established, it will stand for ever. Force and corruption attempting its downfall shall equally be baffled, and all other nations, struck with wonder and admiration at its happiness and stability, shall follow the example; and thus the whole earth shall at last be happy and live like brethren.

Thomas Paine, *Agrarian Justice*, 1797

To the Legislature and the Executive Directory of the French Republic

To preserve the benefits of what is called civilized life, and to remedy at the same time the evil which it has produced, ought to be considered as one of the first objects of reformed legislation.

Whether that state that is proudly, perhaps erroneously, called civilization, has most promoted or most injured the general happiness of man is a question that may be strongly contested. On one side, the spectator is dazzled by splendid appearances; on the other, he is shocked by extremes of wretchedness; both of which it has erected. The most affluent and the most miserable of the human race are to be found in the countries that are called civilized.

Revolutionary on both sides of the Atlantic, Thomas Paine (1737-1809)

To understand what the state of society ought to be, it is necessary to have some idea of the natural and primitive state of man; such as it is at this day among the Indians of North America. There is not, in that state, any of those spectacles of human misery which poverty and want present to our eyes in all the towns and streets in Europe.

Poverty, therefore, is a thing created by that which is called civilized life. It exists not in the natural state. On the other hand, the natural state is without those advantages which flow from agriculture, arts, science and manufactures.

The life of an Indian is a continual holiday, compared with the poor of Europe; and, on the other hand it appears to be abject when compared to the rich. Civilization, therefore, or that which is so-called, has operated two ways: to make one part of society more affluent, and the other more wretched, than would have been the lot of either in a natural state.

It is always possible to go from the natural to the civilized state, but it is never possible to go from the civilized to the natural state. The reason is that man in a natural state, subsisting by hunting, requires ten times the quantity of land to range over to procure himself sustenance, than would support him in a civilized state, where the earth is cultivated.

When, therefore, a country becomes populous by the additional aids of cultivation, art and science, there is a necessity of preserving things in that state; because without it there cannot be sustenance for more, perhaps, than a tenth part of its inhabitants. The thing, therefore, now to be done is to remedy the evils and preserve the benefits that have arisen to society by passing from the natural to that which is called the civilized state.

In taking the matter upon this ground, the first principle of civilization ought to have been, and ought still to be, that the condition of every person born into the world, after a state of civilization commences, ought not to be worse than if he had been born before that period.

But the fact is that the condition of millions, in every country in Europe, is far worse than if they had been born before civilization begin, had been born among the Indians of North America at the present. I will shew how this fact has happened.

It is a position not to be controverted that the earth, in its natural, uncultivated state was, and ever would have continued to be, the common property of the human race. In that state every man would have been born to property. He would have been a joint life proprietor with rest in the property of the soil, and in all its natural productions, vegetable and animal.

But the earth in its natural state, as before said, is capable of supporting but a small number of inhabitants compared with what it is capable of doing in a cultivated state. And as it is impossible to separate the improvement made by cultivation from the earth itself, upon which that improvement is made, the idea of landed property arose from that parable connection; but it is nevertheless true, that it is the value of the improvement, only, and not the earth itself, that is individual property.

Every proprietor, therefore, of cultivated lands, owes to the community a ground-rent (for I know of no better term to express the idea) for the land which he holds; and it is from this ground-rent that the fund proposed in this plan is to issue.

It is deducible, as well from the nature of the thing as from all the stories transmitted to us, that the idea of landed property commenced with cultivation, and that there was no such thing, as landed property before that time. It could not exist in the first state of man, that of hunters. It did not exist in the second state, that of shepherds: neither Abraham, Isaac, Jacob, nor Job, so far as the history of the Bible may credited in probable things, were owners of land.

Their property consisted, as is always enumerated in flocks and herds, they travelled with them from place to place. The frequent contentions at that time about the use of a well in the dry country of Arabia, where those people lived, also show that there was no landed property. It was not admitted that land could be claimed as property.

There could be no such thing as landed property originally. Man did not make the earth, and, though he had a natural right to occupy it, he had no right to locate as his property in perpetuity any part of it; neither did the Creator of the earth open a land-office, from whence the first title-deeds should issue. Whence then, arose the idea of landed property? I answer as before, that when cultivation began the idea of landed property began with it, from the impossibility of separating the improvement made by cultivation from the earth itself, upon which that improvement was made.

The value of the improvement so far exceeded the value of the natural earth, at that time, as to absorb it; till, in the end, the common right of all became confounded into the cultivated right of the individual. But there are, nevertheless, distinct species of rights, and will continue to be, so long as the earth endures.

It is only by tracing things to their origin that we can gain rightful ideas of them, and it is by gaining such ideas that we, discover the boundary that divides right from wrong, and teaches every man to know his own. I have entitled this tract "Agrarian Justice" to distinguish it from "Agrarian Law."

Nothing could be more unjust than agrarian law in a country improved by cultivation; for though every man, as an inhabitant of the earth, is a joint proprietor of it in its natural state, it does not follow that he is a joint proprietor of cultivated earth. The additional value made by cultivation, after the system was admitted, became the property of those who did it, or who inherited it from them, or who purchased it. It had originally no owner. While, therefore, I advocate the right, and interest myself in the hard case of all those who have been thrown out of their natural inheritance by the introduction of the system of landed property, I equally defend the right of the possessor to the part which is his.

Cultivation is at least one of the greatest natural improvements ever made by human invention. It has given to created earth a tenfold value. But the landed monopoly that began with it has produced the greatest evil. It has dispossessed more than half the inhabitants of every nation of their natural inheritance, without providing for them, as ought to have been done, an indemnification for that loss, and has thereby created a species of poverty and wretchedness that did not exist before.

In advocating the case of the persons thus dispossessed, it is a right, and not a charity, that I am pleading for. But it is that kind of right which, being neglected at first, could not be brought forward afterwards till heaven had opened the way by a revolution in the system of government. Let us then do honour to revolutions by justice, and give currency to their principles by blessings.

Having thus in a few words, opened the merits of the case, I shall now proceed to the plan I have to propose, which is,

To create a national fund, out of which there shall be paid to every person, when arrived at the age of twenty-one years, the sum of fifteen pounds sterling, as a compensation in part, for the loss of his or her natural inheritance, by the introduction of the system of landed property:

And also, the sum of ten pounds per annum, during life, to every person now living, of the age of fifty years, and to all others as they shall arrive at that age.

MEANS BY WHICH THE FUND IS TO BE CREATED

I have already established the principle, namely, that the earth, in its natural uncultivated state was, and ever would have continued to be, the common property of the human race; that in that state, every person would have been born to property; and that the system of landed property, by its inseparable connection with cultivation, and with what is called civilized life, has absorbed the property of all those whom it dispossessed, without providing, as ought to have been done, an indemnification for that loss.

The fault, however, is not in the present possessors. No complaint is tended, or ought to be alleged against them, unless they adopt the crime by opposing justice. The fault is in the system, and it has stolen perceptibly upon the world, aided afterwards by the agrarian law of the sword. But the fault can be made to reform itself by successive generations; and without diminishing or deranging the property of any of present possessors, the operation of the fund can yet commence, and in full activity, the first year of its establishment, or soon after, as I shall show.

It is proposed that the payments, as already stated, be made to every person, rich or poor. It is best to make it so, to prevent invidious distinctions. It is also right it should be so, because it is in lieu of the natural inheritance, which, as a right, belongs to every man, over and above property he may have created, or inherited from those who did. Such persons as do not choose to receive it can throw it into the common fund.

Taking it then for granted that no person ought to be in a worse condition when born under what is called a state of civilization, than he would have been had he been born in a state of nature, and that civilization ought to have made, and ought still to make, provision for that purpose, it can only be done by subtracting from property a portion equal in value to the natural inheritance it has absorbed.

Various methods may be proposed for this purpose, but that which appears to be the best (not only because it will operate without deranging any present possessors, or without interfering with the collection of taxes or emprunts necessary for the purposes of government and the Revolution, but because it will be the least troublesome and the most effectual, and also because the subtraction will be made at a time that best admits it) is at the moment that property is passing by the death of one person to the possession of another. In this case, the bequeather gives nothing: the receiver pays nothing. The only matter to him is that the monopoly of natural inheritance, to which there never was a right, begins to cease in his person. A generous man would not wish it to continue, and a just man will rejoice to see it abolished.

MEANS FOR CARRYING THE PROPOSED PLAN INTO EXECUTION, AND TO RENDER IT AT THE SAME TIME CONDUCIVE TO THE PUBLIC INTEREST

Each canton shall elect in its primary assemblies, three persons, as commissioners for that canton, who shall take cognizance, and keep a register of all matters happening in that canton, conformable to the charter that shall be established by law for carrying this plan into execution.

Questions for discussion:

Even before Marx, there were numerous critics of the decisive changes wrought to European society by the Industrial Revolution. Two of the more original were Spence and Paine, who proposed quite fundamental overhauls of British society. In their writings we can discern the beginnings of the Marxist tradition of social and economic critique. In hindsight, we can also see the limitations of their thinking.

Thomas Spence was an English Radical: he was born in poverty, died in poverty, and was often sent to prison. Here he outlines his Spence Plan.

Thomas Paine (often described simply as Tom Paine) was another English Radical. He emigrated to the American colonies and defended both the American Revolution and the French Revolution. His work was so admired by the French that, even though he spoke no French, they voted him into their parliament! Rather than his earlier works on the rights of man, we are reading a later work, *Agrarian Justice*, 1797, as its arguments are a precursor to modern debates about national taxation.

How do the views of these Radicals differ from those of the neo-classical economists?

In what ways do they make similar assumptions to the economists about the nature of the changes through which Britain was going?

What are the elements of their critique which will be adopted by the Marxists later in the nineteenth century?

Going further:

Penelope J. Corfield, 'British history: The exploding galaxy', *Journal for Eighteenth-Century Studies*, vol. 34, 2011, pp. 517–26

Harvey. J. Kaye, *The British Marxist Historians*, Macmillan, Basingstoke, UK, 1995 [1984]

Harvey J. Kaye and Keith McClelland, eds, *E. P. Thompson: Critical Perspectives*, Temple University Press, Philadelphia, 1990

Pat Hudson, *The Industrial Revolution*, E. Arnold, New York, 1992

David S. Landes, *The Unbound Prometheus*, Cambridge University Press, London, 1969

John Markoff, 'Where and when was democracy invented?', *Comparative Studies in Society and History*, vol. 41, no. 4, October 1999, pp. 660–90

Eric H. Mielants, *The Origins of Capitalism and the "Rise of the West"*, Temple University Press, Philadelphia PA, 2007

Charles More, *The Industrial Age: Economy and Society in Britain, 1750–1995*, Longman, London, second edition, 1997

W.W. Rostow, The *Stages of Economic Growth: A Non-Communist Manifesto*, Cambridge University Press, Cambridge UK, second edition, 1971

John Styles, 'Time piece: Working men and watches', *History Today*, January 2008, pp. 44-50

R.H. Tawney, *Religion and the Rise of Capitalism*, Penguin, Harmondsworth UK, 1938

Ellen Meiksins Wood, *The Origin of Capitalism: A Longer View*, Verso, London, 2002

Unit 18

1848, Nationalism and the Commune

> Stand up, damned of the Earth
> Stand up, prisoners of hunger
> Reason thunders in its volcano
> This is the eruption of the end
> Of the past let us make a clean slate
> Enslaved masses, stand up, stand up
> The world is about to change its foundation
> We are nothing, let us be all
> This is the final struggle
> Let us group together, and tomorrow
> The Internationale
> Will be the human race

'The Internationale' was written in 1871 as a rallying cry for the new social movement that emerged in the nineteenth century. Across the course of the nineteenth century the new social class, the proletariat, was defined by the industrial revolution as a 'class-in-itself' (with nothing but its labour power to sell, its objective definition), but by century's end it had become a 'class-for-itself' (with clearly defined group objectives, giving it a subjective reality). This process is sometimes called a 'mobilisation'. How and why did the European working class mobilise itself? And, equally important, how did it become so nationalistic, so entangled in differences in language and national culture?

Critics of the Industrial Revolution

The English Radicals [Unit 17], especially Thomas Paine (1737-1809) and Thomas Spence (1750-1814) were early critics of the changes through which Britain was undergoing: both understood that the land belonged to all and that a land tax on the propertied should be used to support the poor, or all land should belong to the parishes and profits from rents go to public institutions; neither foresaw the dislocation that would make their plans unworkable.

A powerful symbol of the Industrial Revolution was the Albion Flour Mills, Bankside, in the middle of London. Land in Southwark was purchased by Samuel Wyatt in 1784; here in 1786 he built the Albion Mills, equipped with a rotary steam-powered flour-mill (its engine was manufactured by Boulton & Watt, its grinding gears by John Rennie). This was London's first great factory, producing six thousand bushels of flour per week. Regarded as a wonder of the modern world, it became London's symbol for the new industrial revolution and attracted into Lambeth low-wage country labour and exposed them to the deprivations of urban poverty as this once-green river bank became an inner-city slum. Moreover, the cheap flour bankrupted the less efficient local millers, so when the Albion Mills were destroyed by fire in 1791, Luddite arsonists were suspected, and the other millers openly celebrated. The Luddites represented the first political reaction to the Industrial Revolution.

A more sophisticated reaction came during the Hungry 'Forties. Work had lost its 'charm' in the process of mechanisation. The early factory owners worked their employees with very long hours: there were no limits. This was a new process, with no understanding of the physical effects of these long hours on working-class people and their children. Children were able to use the new machinery, so were pressed into full-time service sooner than had been the case on the peasant's property.

The formal political processes remained indifferent to these changes. Parliaments took little or no interest in the factories. The parliamentarians belonged to shifting interest groups, and were not yet members of stable political parties. Although the Whigs (liberals) and Tories (conservatives) were the nominal parties, local issues and self-interest often dictated voting preferences.[33] Broadsheets were stuck onto the walls of London

---

33 Lewis Namier, *The Structure of Politics at the Accession of George III*, MacMillan, London, 1957.

The 1848 Revolution erupted along the spine of Continental Europe

coffee shops around 1800 (people then read them out loud). This was the origin of modern newspapers and the 'imagined community' that subscribed to them.[34] The newspapers reported the debates in parliament and connected the previously elite world of politics to a broader community that was becoming increasingly literate.

The Chartists, the first evidence of working-class mobilisation, campaigned from 1838 to 1850 for six straightforward demands: '(1) A vote for every man twenty-one years of age, of sound mind, and not undergoing punishment for crime; (2) The secret ballot, to protect the elector in the exercise of his vote; (3) No property qualification for members of parliament, thus enabling the constituencies to return the man of their choice, be he rich or poor; (4) Payment of Members, thus enabling an honest tradesman, working man, or other person, to serve

---

34 Benedict Anderson, *Imagined Communities*, Verso, London, 1991.

a constituency, when taken from his business to attend to the interests of the Country; (5) Equal constituencies, securing the same amount of representation for the same number of electors, instead of allowing small constituencies to swamp the votes of large ones; and (6) Annual parliaments, thus presenting the most effectual check to bribery and intimidation, since though a constituency might be bought once in seven years (even with the ballot), no purse could buy a constituency (under a system of universal suffrage) in each ensuing twelve-month; and since members, when elected for a year only, would not be able to defy and betray their constituents as now.'

The Chartists left an important legacy. They demonstrated that ordinary working-class people could indeed mobilise themselves around issues of common concern, meeting in mass assemblies. The Chartist demands were rejected by the British parliament, because there were insufficient numbers in the parliament (six representatives) to make a difference. But all their demands, except annual parliaments, were adopted during the 1850s in the British colonies, especially in the Australian Colony of Victoria, and by 1918 in Britain itself.

Meanwhile more dramatic demands were being made across the English Channel, with the 1848 Revolution. The so-called 'Springtime of the peoples' erupted over much of Europe, but was mostly centred in the Eastern Absolutist regimes. It was a revolution without much of an agenda, except 'land' and 'freedom', but its real value was to show that the mob could exercise real power in the streets of European cities. In 1848, the 'Year of Revolutions', Governments fell right across Europe under middle-class pressure, but only temporarily – the kings who fled their capitals soon returned to their thrones. The liberals became conservative. In the end they feared the workers; they feared raw working-class power (and were haunted by memories of the Terror in revolutionary Paris). When it came to committing to a proletarian revolution, these liberals felt they had more to fear from that quarter than from the aristocracy and vested interests, and so they put down working-class risings brutally.

This was the context in which the new political creed of socialism developed. The first socialists included some of those factory owners who imagined that some workers would benefit from these new developments. Thus so-called 'Early Socialism' was quite idealistic – it was a reaction to the unchecked, feral capitalism of the Industrial Revolution. Robert Owen, a Scottish factory owner, created a model industrial community; however, few followed him. Early Socialism was aimed at the new middle class rather than at the workers, who were assumed to be passive victims of history, rather than agents of change.

Socialism is a social theory – or policy – which aims at securing the ownership and control of the means of production (capital, factories, mines, land) by the community as a whole, the benefits (profits) being distributed among all. To succeed, it needed a stronger theorist than the early English Radicals.

Meanwhile Italy was undergoing its Unification, the 'Risorgimento'. During the heyday of Western Absolutism, the city-states of north Italy remained stubbornly independent. The state-building project undertaken elsewhere was blocked here by the interests of the local merchant elites.[35] The 1860 revolution in Italy was begun from above, by the wealthier Northerners. Garibaldi was a professional revolutionary who had learned the craft in Latin America when younger. When he landed at Sicily, before the battle of Calatafimi, on 15 May 1860, Giuseppe Garibaldi famously declared, 'Qui si fa l'Italia o si muore' ('Here we make Italy – or die!') Significantly, he was leading an invasion: his attack on Italy followed the same path to be taken by the Allies in World War Two, 1943. Garibaldi and his red-shirts took Italy with surprising ease, but the military success did not change the divided nature of the peninsula. 1943 was the year Italy was finally unified – the Risorgimento was merely the take-over

---

35 Ludivine-Julie Olard, 'Venice-Babylon: Foreigners and citizens in the Renaissance period (14th-16th Centuries), in Steven G. Ellis and Luďa Klusáková, eds, *Imagining Frontiers, Contesting Identities*, Pisa University Press, Pisa, 2007, pp. 155-74; Sidney Tarrow, 'From comparative historical analysis to "Local Theory": The Italian city-state route to the modern state', *Theory and Society*, vol. 33, no. 3/4 (June-August 2004), pp. 443-71.

of the peninsula by the Northerners. The new so-called 'Italian' was as much an artificial creation as Pinocchio, the point made by the Tuscan journalist Carlo Lorenzini (1826-1890), writing under the nom de plume, Carlo Collodi, in his famous satire which became a children's classic.

Urban change in Paris

Paris had achieved prominence as the seedbed of the French Revolution. It continued in the nineteenth and twentieth centuries to be the city most likely to foment change (in 1848; 1871; 1968). Paris was equally important as a source of new and creative ideas about city-building (notably, the use of boulevards and parklands; the underground Metro; shopping arcades). It was the setting for the largest urban redesign in history, beginning after the 1848 Revolution, during the Second Empire under Napoleon III. In the field of painting, French impressionism derives

Édouard Manet's last painting, *A Bar at the Folies-Bergère*, depicting a barmaid named Suzon [Collection of the Courtauld Institute of Art]

much of its energy from these major changes occurring in the fabric of people's lives. Édouard Manet's *Rue Mosnier* depicts a street being torn up to make for the new Paris. His masterwork, *A Bar at the Folies-Bergère*, 1881-82, shows us a city whose inhabitants can hardly recognise each other in these uncertain times.

Paris was re-designed in the 1860s by Baron Georges-Eugène Haussmann. Haussmann replaced the jumble of tiny streets that typified the old revolutionary city with elegant boulevards, buildings that were constructed in proportion to street width, lines of trees and other street decoration, and a uniformity of street paving. The Haussmann building code still governs modern Paris with its limit of five storeys. The re-design of Paris inspired many other cities worldwide, and cities vied to be known as the Paris of their region. Beirut called itself the Paris of the Levant, while Buenos Aires claimed the coveted title for South America.

The new Paris was designed to be counter-revolutionary. Haussmann designed the boulevards to be too wide for barricades and to allow cannon fire from military forces that would be brought into the capital by train.

It was all to no avail, as it was followed soon after by the Paris Commune, 1871, a left-wing revolt after the French surrender to Germany, in the Franco-Prussian War (1870-71). The communards seized the city using artillery purchased by public donation, and survived by self-sufficiency, even eating the animals from the zoo.

The Paris Commune became a model for socialist uprisings, criticised by later revolutionaries (particularly Stalin) for not plundering the city treasury when they had the chance. It was put down brutally. The Commune meant more in symbolic terms than in actual results.

Elsewhere developments occurred which suggested that merely having a parliament did not guarantee a democracy. Parliaments had been created in the feudal period, but had declined in power during the Absolutist period; they now returned with the development of the franchise. In Germany, under Otto von Bismarck (1871-1890), all men

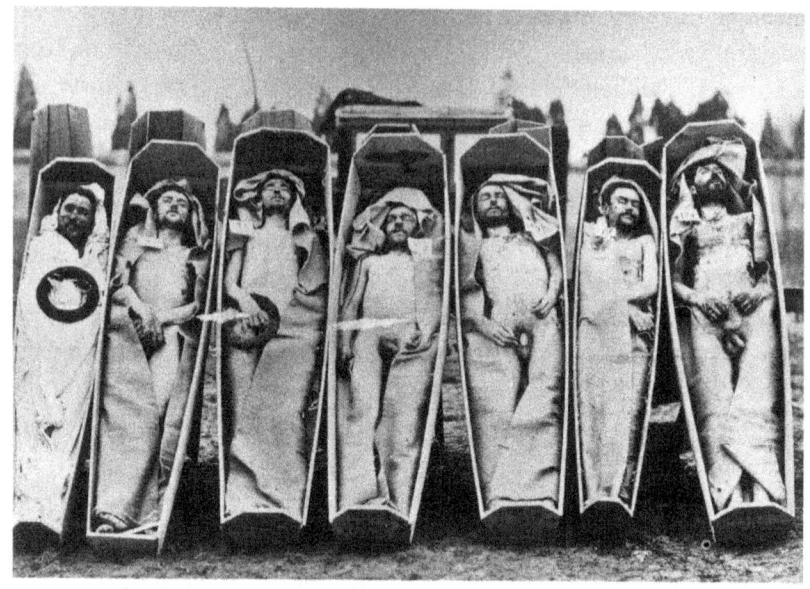

Bodies of Paris Communards [André-Adolphe-Eugène Disdéri]

had the vote, but the upper house checked the lower house, with much power still residing with the Kaiser (Emperor).

Karl Marx: Life and legacy

One of the most astute observers of these developments was Karl Marx. Marx, a journalist, wrote well and included graphical information in his analysis of contemporary problems, giving his work an immediacy that propelled his ideas into the reading public.

Marx was born in Germany in 1818 to wealthy Jewish parents, and was later aided by another bourgeois heretic, Frederick Engels. The fact his parents were Jewish might be less important that the fact that his father was a product of the Enlightenment, a progressive in his day. Marx studied at Bonn and at Berlin, practised as a journalist in Cologne, and moved to Paris in 1843 – he was thus, for an historian's point of view, an eyewitness to history. He was then based in London most of his life after

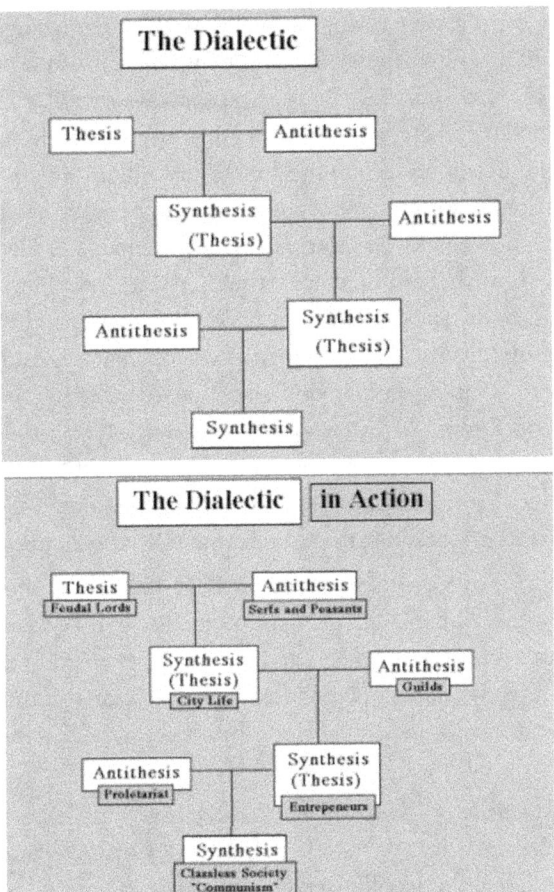

The dialectic, as theorised by Hegel and adopted by Marx

exile from Paris in 1849. Above all else, he was a witty and trenchant critic of the industrial revolution and the changes it had wrought in European society. He never travelled outside Europe, so he relied on what he could read in the British Library to understand developments across the globe, and he wrote prodigiously. For example, his references to the Australian colonies fill an entire book.[36]

---

36 Henry Mayer, *Marx, Engels and Australia*, Cheshire, Melbourne, 1964.

It is always possible to reinterpret the work of earlier writers, which have different meanings in particular epochs, and this is particularly true of Marx. For some he must be understood as a product of his age.[37] For others he stands forever condemned as the person in whose name many horrific acts were committed in the twentieth century. A recent reinterpretation by Francis Wheen is insightful, because he concentrates on the published works of Marx. His early writings, which are often overlooked, show that although it is true that Marx kept Hegel's dialectic he discarded the mystical mumbo-jumbo.[38] He understood that humans found their identity in the transformation of Nature, and this work was central to defining humankind. In 'Towards a Critique of Hegel's Philosophy of Right: An Introduction' (1843-4) Hegel's universal class is not the bureaucracy, but the proletariat. The word 'proletariat', says Wheen, sounds like a thunderclap.[39] He did not set out to establish the working class as a force in history, but came to that conclusion.

Turning to the Paris manuscripts of 1844 (known as the Economic and Philosophical Manuscripts), it is often noted that Marx sees true Communism as more humanist than crude Communism, but, as Wheen points out, already Marx understands that as capital accumulates, work itself becomes objectified.[40] Surplus product and alienation are key elements of capitalism.

In the *Manifesto of the Communist Party* (1848), the opening section headed by the sentence, 'A spectre is haunting Europe – the spectre of Communism', gives a detailed account of class struggles, but it is often overlooked that Marx and Engels also praise the bourgeoisie for its revolutionary part in moving society forward.[41]

The most quotable part of *The Eighteenth Brumaire of Louis Bonaparte*

---

37 Jonathan Sperber, *Karl Marx: A Nineteenth-Century Life*, W.W. Norton, New York, 2013.
38 Francis Wheen, *Karl Marx*, Fourth Estate, London, 1999, pp. 22-24.
39 Wheen, *Marx*, pp. 57-59, 64.
40 Wheen, *Marx*, pp. 68-75, 227-28.
41 Wheen, *Marx*, pp. 115-22. A section of the *Manifesto* appears in Unit 19, below.

(1851) is that 'History repeats itself – the first time as tragedy, the second time as farce', because Marx likens the French coup of 1851 to Napoleon's coup of 1799.[42]

When we turn to his *Grundrisse der Kritik der Politischen Oekonomie* (Outlines of a Critique of Political Economy) (1857-58, published 1939, translated into English 1971), we are struck by his trenchant critique of both the economist David Ricardo and the anarchist Pierre-Joseph Proudhon, but, Wheen argues, it is more important as the missing link between the Paris Notebooks and *Capital*, setting out a materialist version of human history.[43]

Then came *Capital*, vol. 1 (1867). His great work is based on a complete assimilation of an enormous amount of evidence. But, Wheen argues, it is not merely an economic text, but a work of great satire also.

Finally, there is *The Civil War in France* (1871). Marx argued that the Paris Commune was not a return to the medieval community, but a model for the future. It should be added that he also said that the spirit of the Commune could not be suppressed.[44]

If we view Marx from a nineteenth-century perspective, we can see that he understood more deeply than most of his contemporaries the underlying logic of capitalism. Indeed, he took a world-history perspective. He saw that parliamentary democracy would bring about only limited improvements in people's lives, and he understood that the new labour parties were significant but limited in their capacity for fundamental change.

Marx is still being read in the twenty-first century. If anything, Marx is more relevant than ever. Today the basic issues are the same – surplus value is still true of our lives; private property still creates a sense of alienation. We need to understand the social world as made, not natural. The early Marx, with his attention to Nature is more relevant than ever.

---

42 Wheen, *Marx*, pp. 9, 26, 189, 243, 323.
43 Wheen, *Marx*, pp. 227-29.
44 Wheen, *Marx*, pp. 327-35.

We are all Marxists now, in the strict sense that no historian would now ignore the economics of any given historical situation, however that economic theory is understood. No historian would now ignore the economic base. Sociology would be far more positivist without Marx.

We should read different periods of Marx's work for different purposes. His best history books are *Eighteenth Brumaire* and *The Civil War in France*. His best philosophy is to be found in Early Marx and in the *1844 Mss*. He is at his best in economic theory in *Capital*, vol. 1 and *The German Ideology*.

Nationalism

Just as Marx was still profoundly Eurocentric in his worldview, the Europeans were still divided by language and culture. Working-class mobilisation did little to bridge these gaps. The path to the nation-state was not as uniform as earlier scholars had claimed.[45] Those elements of the old Absolutist State which had now changed [Unit 17] were not able to change back. But in nineteenth-century Europe nation-states were coalescing around the remaining elements. There is a famous saying that a dialect becomes a language when it acquires a flag and an army, even when that process (such as in the case of the Tuscan dialect) took a long time to come to fruition. The view that these nations are ethnic expressions is no longer readily accepted, but it is a compelling view.[46]

Socialism continued to grow, with the expansion and industrialisation of cities. By 1912, the Socialists constituted the biggest political party in Germany. Marxism made them conscious of surfing the wave of history, of being the main agent for social progress. At the same the party organisers knew they also needed to organise, and to relate to

---

45 Sidney Tarrow, 'From comparative historical analysis to "Local Theory": The Italian city-state route to the modern state', *Theory and Society*, vol. 33, no. 3/4 (June-August 2004), pp. 443-71.
46 Anthony D. Smith, *The Ethnic Origins of Nations*, Basil Blackwell, Oxford, 1986.

the workers in each workplace. The disappearance of slavery was one of the more remarkable features of the century. Slaves were, however, replaced by indentured labour, especially workers of Chinese and Indian backgrounds.

Now came new empires. The Portuguese and the Spanish had failed to use their New World wealth productively. The British and the French created global empires from their industrial revolutions. Colonisation was a key feature of this new imperialism. Marx could not see this as clearly as Lenin and the Marxists of the twentieth century. The colonised became the real victims of capitalism when it became imperialist, more so than the metropolitan working classes. By 1935, 85 per cent of the world's entire population was under the control of the European empires (notably the British and French). How had that situation come about? And what did this mean for the mobilisation of the European working class later in the nineteenth century and into the twentieth?

Primary sources:

Adam Smith, *The Wealth of Nations*, 1776; David Ricardo, *On the Principles of Political Economy and Taxation*, 1817; and John Stuart Mill, *Principles of Political Economy*, 1848

Adam Smith, *The Wealth of Nations*

(1776; reprinted in Everyman's Library, M. Dent & Sons, Ltd., London, 1910)

Chapter 1: Of the Division of Labour

The greatest improvement in the productive powers of labour, and the greater part of the skill, dexterity, and judgment with which it is any where directed, or applied, seem to have been the effects of the division of labour.

The effects of the division of labour, in the general business of society, will be more easily understood, by considering in what manner it operates in some particular manufactures. It is commonly supposed to be carried furthest in some very trifling ones; not perhaps that it really is carried further in them than in others of more importance: but in those trifling manufactures which are destined to supply the small wants of but a small number of people, the whole number of workmen must necessarily be small; and those employed in every different branch of the work can often be collected into the same workhouse, and placed at once under the view of the spectator. In those great manufactures, on the contrary, which are destined to supply the great wants of the great body of the people, every different branch of the work employs so great a number of workmen, that it is impossible to collect them all into the same workhouse. We can seldom see more, at one time, than those employed in one single branch. Though in such manufactures, therefore, the work may really be divided into a much greater number of parts, than in those of a more trifling nature, the division is not near so obvious, and has accordingly been much less observed.

Adam Smith (1723-1790)

To take an example, therefore, from a very trifling manufacture; but one in which the division of labour has been very often taken notice of, the trade of the pin-maker; a workman not educated to this business (which the division of labour has rendered a distinct trade), nor acquainted with the use of the machinery employed in it (to the invention of which the same division of labour has probably given occasion), could scarce, perhaps, with his utmost industry, make one pin in a day, and certainly could not make twenty. But in the way in which this business is now carried on, not only the whole work is a peculiar trade, but it is divided into a number of branches, of which the greater part are likewise peculiar trades. One man draws out the wire, another straights it, a third cuts it, a fourth points it, a fifth grinds it at the top for receiving the head; to make the head requires two or three distinct operations; to put it on, is a peculiar business, to whiten the pins is another; it is even a trade by itself to put them into the paper; and the important business of making a pin is, in this manner, divided into about eighteen distinct operations, which, in some manufactories, are all performed by distinct hands, though in others the same man will sometimes perform two or three of them. I have seen a small manufactory of this kind where ten men only were employed, and where some of them consequently performed two or three distinct operations. But though they were very poor, and therefore but indifferently accommodated with the necessary machinery, they could, when they exerted themselves, make among them about twelve pounds of pins in a day. There are in a pound upwards of four thousand pins of a middling size. Those ten persons, therefore, could make among them upwards of forty-eight thousand pins in a day. Each person, therefore, making a tenth part of forty-eight thousand pins, might be considered as making four thousand eight hundred pins in a day. But if they had all wrought separately and independently, and without any of them having been educated to this peculiar business, they certainly could not each of them have made twenty, perhaps not one pin in a day; that is, certainly, not the two hundred and fortieth, perhaps not the four thousand eight hundredth part of what they are at present capable of performing, in consequence of a proper division and combination of their different operations.

In every other art and manufacture, the effects of the division of labour are similar to what they are in this very trifling one; though, in many of them, the labour can neither be so much subdivided, nor reduced to so great a simplicity of operation.

David Ricardo, *On the Principles of Political Economy and Taxation*, 1817

[http://www.econlib.org/library/Ricardo/ricP.html, accessed 3 July 2011]

Chapter 5: Of Wages

Labour, like all other things which are purchased and sold, and which may be increased or diminished in quantity, has its natural and its market price. The natural price of labour is that price which is necessary to enable the labourers, one with another, to subsist and to perpetuate their race, without either increase or diminution.

The power of the labourer to support himself, and the family which may be necessary to keep up the number of labourers, does not depend on the quantity of money which he may receive for wages, but on the quantity of food, necessaries, and conveniences become essential to him from habit, which that money will purchase. The natural price of labour, therefore, depends on the price of the food, necessaries, and

David Ricardo (1772-1823)

conveniences required for the support of the labourer and his family. With a rise in the price of food and necessaries, the natural price of labour will rise; with the fall in their price, the natural price of labour will fall.

With the progress of society the natural price of labour has always a tendency to rise, because one of the principal commodities by which its natural price is regulated, has a tendency to become dearer, from the greater difficulty of producing it. As, however, the improvements in agriculture, the discovery of new markets, whence provisions may be imported, may for a time counteract the tendency to a rise in the price of necessaries, and may even occasion their natural price to fall, so will the same causes produce the correspondent effects on the natural price of labour.

The natural price of all commodities, excepting raw produce and labour, has a tendency to fall, in the progress of wealth and population; for though, on one hand, they are enhanced in real value, from the rise in the natural price of the raw material of which they are made, this is more than counterbalanced by the improvements in machinery, by the better division and distribution of labour, and by the increasing skill, both in science and art, of the producers.

The market price of labour is the price which is really paid for it, from the natural operation of the proportion of the supply to the demand; labour is dear when it is scarce, and cheap when it is plentiful. However much the market price of labour may deviate from its natural price, it has, like commodities, a tendency to conform to it.

It is when the market price of labour exceeds its natural price, that the condition of the labourer is flourishing and happy, that he has it in his power to command a greater proportion of the necessaries and enjoyments of life, and therefore to rear a healthy and numerous family. When, however, by the encouragement which high wages give to the increase of population, the number of labourers is increased, wages again fall to their natural price, and indeed from a re-action sometimes fall below it.

When the market price of labour is below its natural price, the condition of the labourers is most wretched: then poverty deprives them of those comforts which custom renders absolute necessaries. It is only after their privations have reduced their number, or the demand for labour has increased, that the market price of labour will rise to its natural price, and that the labourer will have the moderate comforts which the natural rate of wages will afford.

Notwithstanding the tendency of wages to conform to their natural rate, their market rate may, in an improving society, for an indefinite period, be constantly above it; for no sooner may the impulse, which an increased capital gives to a new demand for labour be obeyed, than another increase of capital may produce the same effect; and thus, if the increase of capital be gradual and constant, the demand for labour may give a continued stimulus to an increase of people.

Capital is that part of the wealth of a country which is employed in production, and consists of food, clothing, tools, raw materials, machinery, &c. necessary to give effect to labour.

Capital may increase in quantity at the same time that its value rises. An addition may be made to the food and clothing of a country, at the same time that more labour may be required to produce the additional quantity than before; in that case not only the quantity, but the value of capital will rise.

Or capital may increase without its value increasing, and even while its value is actually diminishing; not only may an addition be made to the food and clothing of a country, but the addition may be made by the aid of machinery, without any increase, and even with an absolute diminution in the proportional quantity of labour required to produce them. The quantity of capital may increase, while neither the whole together, nor any part of it singly, will have a greater value than before, but may actually have a less.

In the first case, the natural price of labour, which always depends on the price of food, clothing, and other necessaries, will rise; in the second, it will remain stationary, or fall; but in both cases the market rate of wages will rise, for in proportion to the increase of capital will be the increase in the demand for labour; in proportion to the work to be done will be the demand for those who are to do it.

In both cases too the market price of labour will rise above its natural price; and in both cases it will have a tendency to conform to its natural price, but in the first case this agreement will be most speedily effected. The situation of the labourer will be improved, but not much improved; for the increased price of food and necessaries will absorb a large portion of his increased wages; consequently a small supply of labour, or a trifling increase in the population, will soon reduce the market price to the then increased natural price of labour.

In the second case, the condition of the labourer will be very greatly improved; he will receive increased money wages, without having to pay any increased price, and perhaps even a diminished price for the commodities which he and his family consume; and it will not be till after a great addition has been made to the population, that the market price of labour will again sink to its then low and reduced natural price.

Thus, then, with every improvement of society, with every increase in its capital, the market wages of labour will rise; but the permanence of their rise will depend on the question, whether the natural price of labour has also risen; and this again will depend on the rise in the natural price of those necessaries on which the wages of labour are expended.

It is not to be understood that the natural price of labour, estimated even in food and necessaries, is absolutely fixed and constant. It varies at different times in the same country, and very materially differs in different countries. It essentially depends on the habits and customs of the people. An English labourer would consider his wages under their natural rate, and too scanty to support a family, if they enabled him to purchase no other food than potatoes, and to live in no better habitation than a mud cabin; yet these moderate demands of nature are often deemed sufficient in countries where "man's life is cheap", and his wants easily satisfied. Many of the conveniences now enjoyed in an English cottage, would have been thought luxuries at an earlier period of our history.

From manufactured commodities always falling, and raw produce always rising, with the progress of society, such a disproportion in their relative value is at length created, that in rich countries a labourer, by the sacrifice of a very small quantity only of his food, is able to provide liberally for all his other wants.

Independently of the variations in the value of money, which necessarily affect money wages, but which we have here supposed to have no operation, as we have considered money to be uniformly of the same value, it appears then that wages are subject to a rise or fall from two causes:

1st. The supply and demand of labourers.

2dly. The price of the commodities on which the wages of labour are expended.

In different stages of society, the accumulation of capital, or of the means of employing labour, is more or less rapid, and must in all cases depend on the productive powers of labour. The productive powers of labour are generally greatest when there is an abundance of fertile land: at such periods accumulation is often so rapid, that labourers cannot be supplied with the same rapidity as capital.

It has been calculated, that under favourable circumstances population may be doubled in twenty-five years; but under the same favourable circumstances, the whole capital of a country might possibly be doubled in a shorter period. In that case, wages during the whole period would have a tendency to rise, because the demand for labour would increase still faster than the supply.

In new settlements, where the arts and knowledge of countries far advanced in refinement are introduced, it is probable that capital has a tendency to increase faster than mankind: and if the deficiency of labourers were not supplied by more populous countries, this tendency would very much raise the price of labour. In proportion as these countries become populous, and land of a worse quality is taken into cultivation, the tendency to an increase of capital diminishes; for the surplus produce remaining, after satisfying the wants of the existing population, must necessarily be in proportion to the facility of production, viz. to the smaller number of persons employed in production. Although, then, it is probable, that under the most favourable circumstances, the power of production is still greater than that of population, it will not long continue so; for the land being limited in quantity, and differing in quality, with every increased portion of capital employed on it, there will be a decreased rate of production, whilst the power of population continues always the same.

In those countries where there is abundance of fertile land, but where, from the ignorance, indolence, and barbarism of the inhabitants, they are exposed to all the evils of want and famine, and where it has been said that population presses against the means of subsistence, a very different remedy should be applied from that which is necessary in long settled countries, where, from the diminishing rate of the supply of raw produce, all the evils of a crowded population are experienced. In the one case, the evil proceeds from bad government, from the insecurity of property, and from a want of education in all ranks of the people. To be made happier they require only to be better governed and instructed, as the augmentation of capital, beyond the augmentation of people, would be the inevitable result. No increase in the population can be too great, as the powers of production are still greater. In the other case, the population increases faster than the funds required for its support. Every exertion of industry, unless accompanied by a diminished rate of increase in the population, will add to the evil, for production cannot keep pace with it.

With a population pressing against the means of subsistence, the only remedies are either a reduction of people, or a more rapid accumulation of capital. In rich countries, where all the fertile land is already cultivated, the latter remedy is neither very practicable nor very desirable, because its effect would be, if pushed very far, to render all classes equally poor. But in poor countries, where there are abundant means of production in store, from fertile land not yet brought into cultivation, it is the only safe and efficacious means of removing the evil, particularly as its effect would be to elevate all classes of the people.

The friends of humanity cannot but wish that in all countries the labouring classes should have a taste for comforts and enjoyments, and that they should be stimulated by all legal means in their exertions to procure them. There cannot be a better security against a superabundant population. In those countries, where the labouring classes have the fewest wants, and are contented with the cheapest food, the people are exposed to the greatest vicissitudes and miseries. They have no place of refuge from calamity; they cannot seek safety in a lower station; they are already so low, that they can fall no lower. On any deficiency of the chief article of their subsistence, there are few substitutes of which they can avail themselves, and dearth to them is attended with almost all the evils of famine.

In the natural advance of society, the wages of labour will have a tendency to fall, as far as they are regulated by supply and demand; for the supply of labourers will continue to increase at the same rate, whilst the demand for them will increase at a slower rate. If, for instance, wages were regulated by a yearly increase of capital, at the rate of 2 per cent, they would fall when it accumulated only at the rate of $1\frac{1}{2}$ per cent. They would fall still lower when it increased only at the rate of 1, or $\frac{1}{2}$ per cent, and would continue to do so until the capital became stationary, when wages also would become stationary, and be only sufficient to keep up the numbers of the actual population. I say that, under these circumstances, wages would fall, if they were regulated only by the supply and demand of labourers; but we must not forget, that wages are also regulated by the prices of the commodities on which they are expended.

As population increases, these necessaries will be constantly rising in price, because more labour will be necessary to produce them. If, then, the money wages of labour should fall, whilst every commodity on which the wages of labour were expended rose, the labourer would be doubly affected, and would be soon totally deprived of subsistence. Instead, therefore, of the money wages of labour falling, they would rise; but they would not rise sufficiently to enable the labourer to purchase as many comforts and necessaries as he did before the rise in the price of those commodities. If his annual wages were before £24, or six quarters of corn when the price was £4 per quarter, he would probably receive only the value of five quarters when corn rose to £5 per quarter. But five quarters would cost £25; he would therefore receive an addition in his money wages, though with that addition he would be unable to furnish himself with the same quantity of corn and other commodities, which he had before consumed in his family.

Notwithstanding, then, that the labourer would be really worse paid, yet this increase in his wages would necessarily diminish the profits of the manufacturer; for his goods would sell at no higher price, and yet the expense of producing them would be increased. This, however, will be considered in our examination into the principles which regulate profits.

It appears, then, that the same cause which raises rent, namely, the increasing difficulty of providing an additional quantity of food with the same proportional quantity of labour, will also raise wages; and therefore if money be of an unvarying value, both rent and wages will have a tendency to rise with the progress of wealth and population.

But there is this essential difference between the rise of rent and the rise of wages. The rise in the money value of rent is accompanied by an increased share of the produce; not only is the landlord's money rent greater, but his corn rent also; he will have more corn, and each defined measure of that corn will exchange for a greater quantity of all other goods which have not been raised in value. The fate of the labourer will be less happy; he will receive more money wages, it is true, but his corn wages will be reduced; and not only his command of corn, but his general condition will be deteriorated, by his finding it more difficult to maintain the market rate of wages above their natural rate. While the price of corn rises 10 per cent, wages will always rise less than 10 per cent, but rent will always rise more; the condition of the labourer will generally decline, and that of the landlord will always be improved.

When wheat was at £4 per quarter, suppose the labourer's wages to be £24 per annum, or the value of six quarters of wheat, and suppose half his wages to be expended on wheat, and the other half, or £12, on other things. He would receive

£24 14*s*.	} when wheat was at	{	£4 4*s*. 8*d*.	} or the value of	{	5.83 qrs.
£25 10*s*.			£4 10*s*.			5.66 qrs.
£26 8*s*.			£4 16*s*.			5.50 qrs.
£27 8*s*. 6*d*.			£5 2*s*. 10*d*.			5.33 qrs.

He would receive these wages to enable him to live just as well, and no better, than before; for when corn was at £4 per quarter, he would expend for three quarters of corn, at £4 per quarter

....	£12
and on other things ...	£12
	£24

When wheat was £4 4*s*. 8*d*., three quarters, which he and his family consumed, would cost him

....	£12 14*s*.
other things not altered in price ...	£12
	£24 14*s*.

When at £4 10*s*., three quarters of wheat would cost

....	£13 10*s*.

| and other things ... | £12 |
| | £25 10s. |

When at £4 16s., three quarters of wheat

....	£14 8s.
Other things ...	£12
	£26 8s.

When at £5 2s. 10d. three quarters of wheat would cost

....	£15 8s. 6d.
Other things ...	£12
	£27 8s. 6d.

In proportion as corn became dear, he would receive less corn wages, but his money wages would always increase, whilst his enjoyments, on the above supposition, would be precisely the same. But as other commodities would be raised in price in proportion as raw produce entered into their composition, he would have more to pay for some of them. Although his tea, sugar, soap, candles, and house rent, would probably be no dearer, he would pay more for his bacon, cheese, butter, linen, shoes, and cloth; and therefore, even with the above increase of wages, his situation would be comparatively worse. But it may be said that I have been considering the effect of wages on price, on the supposition that gold, or the metal from which money is made, is the produce of the country in which wages varied; and that the consequences which I have deduced agree little with the actual state of things, because gold is a metal of foreign production. The circumstance, however, of gold being a foreign production, will not invalidate the truth of the argument, because it may be shewn, that whether it were found at home, or were imported from abroad, the effects ultimately and, indeed, immediately would be the same.

When wages rise, it is generally because the increase of wealth and capital have occasioned a new demand for labour, which will, infallibly be attended with an increased production of commodities. To circulate these additional commodities, even at the same prices as before, more money is required, more of this foreign commodity from which money is made, and which can only be obtained by importation. Whenever a commodity is required in greater abundance than before, its relative value rises comparatively with those commodities with which its purchase is made. If more hats were wanted, their price would rise, and more gold would be given for them. If more gold were required, gold would rise, and hats would fall in price, as a greater quantity of hats and of all other things would then be necessary to purchase the same quantity of gold. But in the case supposed, to say that commodities will rise, because wages rise, is to affirm a positive contradiction; for we first say that gold will rise in relative value in consequence of demand, and secondly, that it will fall in relative value because prices will rise, two effects which are totally incompatible with each other. To say that commodities are raised in price, is the same thing as to say that money is lowered in relative value; for it is by commodities that the relative value of gold is estimated. If then all commodities rose in price, gold could not come from abroad to purchase those dear commodities, but it would go from home to be employed with advantage in purchasing the comparatively cheaper foreign commodities. It appears, then, that the rise of wages will not raise the prices of commodities, whether the metal from which money is made be produced at home or in a foreign country. All commodities cannot rise at the same time without an addition to the quantity of money. This addition could not be obtained at home, as we have already shewn; nor could it be imported from abroad. To purchase any additional quantity of gold from abroad, commodities at home must be cheap, not dear. The importation of gold, and a rise in the price of all home-made commodities with which gold is purchased or paid for, are effects absolutely incompatible. The extensive use of paper money does not alter this question, for paper money conforms, or ought to conform, to the value of gold, and therefore its value is influenced by such causes only as influence the value of that metal.

These then are the laws by which wages are regulated, and by which the happiness of far the greatest part of every community is governed. Like all other contracts, wages should be left to the fair and free competition of the market, and should never be controlled by the interference of the legislature.

The clear and direct tendency of the poor laws, is in direct opposition to these obvious principles: it is not, as the legislature benevolently intended, to amend the condition of the poor, but to deteriorate the condition of both poor and rich; instead of making the poor rich, they are calculated to make the rich poor; and whilst the present laws are in force, it is quite in the natural order of things that the fund for the maintenance of the poor should progressively increase, till it has absorbed all the net revenue of the country, or at least so much of it as the state shall leave to us, after satisfying its own never failing demands for the public expenditure.

This pernicious tendency of these laws is no longer a mystery, since it has been fully developed by the able hand of Mr Malthus; and every friend to the poor must ardently wish for their abolition. Unfortunately, however, they have been so long established, and the habits of the poor have been so formed upon their operation, that to eradicate them with safety from our political system, requires the most cautious and skilful management. It is agreed by all who are most friendly to a repeal of these laws, that if it be desirable to prevent the most overwhelming distress to those for whose benefit they were erroneously enacted, their abolition should be effected by the most gradual steps.

It is a truth which admits not a doubt, that the comforts and well-being of the poor cannot be permanently secured without some regard on their part, or some effort on the part of the legislature, to regulate the increase of their numbers, and to render less frequent among them early and improvident marriages. The operation of the system of poor laws has been directly contrary to this. They have rendered restraint superfluous, and have invited imprudence, by offering it a portion of the wages of prudence and industry.

The nature of the evil points out the remedy. By gradually contracting the sphere of the poor laws; by impressing on the poor the value of independence, by teaching them that they must look not to systematic or casual charity, but to their own exertions for support, that prudence and forethought are neither unnecessary nor unprofitable virtues, we shall by degrees approach a sounder and more healthful state.

No scheme for the amendment of the poor laws merits the least attention, which has not their abolition for its ultimate object; and he is the best friend to the poor, and to the cause of humanity, who can point out how this end can be attained with the most security, and at the same time with the least violence. It is not by raising in any manner different from the present, the fund from which the poor are supported, that the evil can be mitigated. It would not only be no improvement, but it would be an aggravation of the distress which we wish to see removed, if the fund were increased in amount, or were levied according to some late proposals, as a general fund from the country at large. The present mode of its collection and application has served to mitigate its pernicious effects. Each parish raises a separate fund for the support of its own poor. Hence it becomes an object of more interest and more practicability to keep the rates low, than if one general fund were raised for the relief of the poor of the whole kingdom. A parish is much more interested in an economical collection of the rate, and a sparing distribution of relief, when the whole saving will be for its own benefit, than if hundreds of other parishes were to partake of it.

It is to this cause, that we must ascribe the fact of the poor laws not having yet absorbed all the net revenue of the country; it is to the rigour with which they are applied, that we are indebted for their not having become overwhelmingly oppressive. If by law every human being wanting support could be sure to obtain it, and obtain it in such a degree as to make life tolerably comfortable, theory would lead us to expect that all other taxes together would be light compared with the single one of poor rates. The principle of gravitation is not more certain than the tendency of such laws to change wealth and power into misery and weakness; to call away the exertions of labour from every object, except that of providing mere subsistence; to confound all intellectual distinction; to busy the mind continually in supplying the body's wants; until at last all classes should be infected with the plague of universal poverty. Happily these laws have been in operation during a period of progressive prosperity, when the funds for the maintenance of labour have regularly increased, and when an increase of population would be naturally called for. But if our progress should become more slow; if we should attain the stationary state, from which I trust we are yet far distant, then will the pernicious nature of these laws become more manifest and alarming; and then, too, will their removal be obstructed by many additional difficulties.

John Stuart Mill, *Principles of Political Economy with some of their Applications to Social Philosophy*, 1848

[ed. William James Ashley, Longmans, Green and Co., London, 7th ed., 1909; http://oll.libertyfund.org/title/101/36225 (accessed on 8 January 2009)]

Chapter II: *Of labour as an agent of production*

§ 1. The labour which terminates in the production of an article fitted for some human use, is either employed directly about the thing, or in previous operations destined to facilitate, perhaps essential to the possibility of, the subsequent ones. In making bread, for example, the labour employed about the thing itself is that of the baker; but the labour of the miller, though employed directly in the production not of bread but of flour, is equally part of the aggregate sum of labour by which the bread is produced; as is also the labour of the sower and of the reaper. Some may think that all these persons ought to be considered as employing their labour directly about the thing; the corn, the flour, and the bread being one substance in three different states. Without disputing about this question of mere language, there is still the ploughman, who prepared the ground for the seed, and whose labour never came in contact with the substance in any of its states; and the plough-maker, whose share in the result was still more remote. All these persons ultimately derive the remuneration of their labour from the bread, or its price: the plough-maker as much as the rest; for since ploughs are of no use except for tilling the soil, no one would make or use ploughs for any other reason than because the increased returns, thereby obtained from the ground, afforded a source from which an adequate equivalent could be assigned for the labour of

John Stuart Mill (1806-1873)

the plough-maker. If the produce is to be used or consumed in the form of bread, it is from the bread that this equivalent must come. The bread must suffice to remunerate all these labourers, and several others; such as the carpenters and bricklayers who erected the farm-buildings; the hedgers and ditchers who made the fences necessary for the protection of the crop; the miners and smelters who extracted or prepared the iron of which the plough and other implements were made. These, however, and the plough-maker, do not depend for their remuneration upon the bread made from the produce of a single harvest, but upon that made from the produce of all the harvests which are successively gathered until the plough, or the buildings and fences, are worn out. We must add yet another kind of labour; that of transporting the produce from the place of its production to the place of its destined use: the labour of carrying the corn to market, and from market to the millers, the flour from the millers to the bakers, and the bread from the bakers to the place of its final consumption. This labour is sometimes very considerable: flour is [1848] transported to England from beyond the Atlantic, corn from the heart of Russia; and in addition to the labourers immediately employed, the waggoners and sailors, there are also costly instruments, such as ships, in the construction of which much labour has been expended: that labour, however, not depending for its whole remuneration upon the bread, but for a part only; ships being usually, during the course of their existence, employed in the transport of many different kinds of commodities.

To estimate, therefore, the labour of which any given commodity is the result, is far from a simple operation. The items in the calculation are very numerous – as it may seem to some persons, infinitely so; for if, as a part of the labour employed in making bread, we count the labour of the blacksmith who made the plough, why not also (it may be asked) the labour of making the tools used by the blacksmith, and the tools used in making those tools, and so back to the origin of things? But after mounting one or two steps in this ascending scale, we come into a region of factions too minute for calculation. Suppose, for instance, that the same plough will last, before being worn out, a dozen years. Only one-twelfth of the labour of making the plough must be placed to the account of each year's harvest. A twelfth part of the labour of making a plough is an appreciable quantity. But the same set of tools, perhaps, suffice to the plough-maker for forging a hundred ploughs, which serve during the twelve years of their existence to prepare the soil of as many different farms. A twelve-hundredth part of the labour of making his tools, is as much, therefore, as has been expended in procuring one year's harvest of a single farm: and when this fraction comes to be further apportioned among the various sacks of corn and loaves of bread, it is seen at once that such quantities are not worth taking into the account for any practical purpose connected with the commodity. It is true that if the tool-maker had not laboured, the corn and bread never would have been produced; but they will not be sold a tenth part of a farthing dearer in consideration of his labour.

Questions for discussion:

The primary sources in Units 18-20 deal with texts as analysis: how do we compare and analyse documents that purport to give an account of historical developments?

Adam Smith, David Ricardo and John Stuart Mill were three of the most persuasive thinkers in dealing with the far-reaching economic changes ushered in by the Industrial Revolution. Mercantilism, or the government control of the economy, was attacked in 1776 not only by the American revolutionaries in their attack on the British monarchy, but also by the Scottish political economist, Adam Smith, who, in *The Wealth of Nations*, sought to show how setting capitalism free (the *laissez-faire* approach) would produce great wealth for more people.

Subsequently, David Ricardo proposed several theories which are still held dear by neo-classical economists, including the idea of 'comparative advantage', which underlies modern ideas of free trade. In the extract we read here, he explains his theory of how wages are determined, and takes issue with his friend, Thomas Malthus, on the issue of how labourers were likely to survive in the new industrial system.

Until now, of course, many labourers had been agricultural workers with limited bargaining power and access to other forms of subsistence through their own farming. Industrial labourers in the new big cities experienced a drop in living standards, so much so that the 1840s in Britain are often called the Hungry 'Forties.

Writing in the 1840s, a generation after Ricardo, John Stuart Mill attempted to locate these economic arguments within a broader philosophical context.

How is the holistic approach of these writers different from the ideas satirised by Jonathan Swift in *A Modest Proposal*?

Why is the economics as propounded by these writers so devoid of political considerations?

What are the images of 'labourers' that emerge through these texts?

Going further:

Benedict Anderson, *Imagined Communities*, Verso, London, 1991

Spiro Kostof, *The City Assembled*, Little, Brown & Co., Boston, 1992

Lewis Namier, *The Structure of Politics at the Accession of George III*, MacMillan, London, 1957 [on-line]

Ludivine-Julie Olard, 'Venice-Babylon: Foreigners and citizens in the Renaissance period (14th – 16th Centuries), in Steven G. Ellis and Luď'a Klusáková, eds, *Imagining Frontiers, Contesting Identities*, Pisa University Press, Pisa, 2007, pp. 155-74 [on-line]

Sidney Tarrow, 'From comparative historical analysis to "Local Theory": The Italian city-state route to the modern state', *Theory and Society*, vol. 33, no. 3/4 (June-August 2004), pp. 443-71

Anthony D. Smith, *The Ethnic Origins of Nations*, Basil Blackwell, Oxford, 1986

Jonathan Sperber, *Karl Marx: A Nineteenth-Century Life*, W.W. Norton, New York, 2013

Andrew Wheatcroft, *The World Atlas of Revolutions*, Simon & Schuster, New York, 1983

Francis Wheen, *Karl Marx*, Fourth Estate, London, 1999

Unit 19
Colonialism and the Scramble for Africa

With his usual trenchant wit, in *Capital*, Vol. 1, Karl Marx poked fun at the inability of Sir Robert Peel's first cousin, Thomas Peel, to succeed in Western Australia:

> Mr Peel, he moans, took him from England to Swan River, West Australia, means of subsistence and of production to the amount of £50,000. Mr. Peel had the foresight to bring with him, besides, 300 persons of the working-class, men, women, and children. Once arrived at his destination, 'Mr Peel was left without a servant to make his bed or fetch him water from the river.' Unhappy Mr Peel who provided for everything except the export of English modes of production to Swan River.

England and France divide the world between them in James Gillray, *The Plumb Pudding*, 1805

Peel and his companions on the long journey to Western Australia in 1829 were part of the colonial age, the expansion of European capitalism into all parts of the world, a process that occupied the hundred years before the outbreak of the Great War in 1914.

Nineteenth-century capitalism was able to transcend its European home ground in ways in which feudalism was mostly not. So capitalism became colonialism, setting up a pattern of global consequences still relevant in the twenty-first century. It was now a world economy. For instance, cotton could be exported from Egypt and India to England to be manufactured, and then sent back to those countries as cotton goods. Rubber was likewise a global industry.[47] This new imperialism generally grew on the back of the Industrial Revolution: earlier empires had not attained this degree of economic unity.

To understand postcolonialism as a political and cultural movement of the twentieth and twenty-first centuries it is necessary to first understand this nineteenth-century colonialism. Postcolonial writing is more important than is often recognised by scholars, given the sheer size of this colonial experience. There are parallels between postcolonial literature and the Victorian novel (including Gaskell, Dickens, and George Eliot) as a comment on the Industrial Revolution.

The making of the European Diaspora

The first global movements of itinerant workers from Africa and Europe to the New World and Australia led to the dramatic population increase in those continents during the nineteenth century. The distribution of surnames across these countries is a reliable guide to this process.[48] 'By

---

47 John Tully, *The Devil's Milk: A Social History of Rubber*, Monthly Review Press, New York, 2011.

48 Frank Thistlethwaite, 'Migration from Europe overseas in the nineteenth and twentieth centuries', XIe Congr. International des Sciences Historiques, *Rapport*, 5, 1960, pp. 32-60.

Tre, Pol and Pen, you shall know the Cornishmen' is an old adage that reflects this fact. These surnames carry parts of the Cornish landscape in them. 'Tre-' means a homestead; 'Ros(e)-' refers to heathland; 'Pol-' means a pond, lake or well; 'Lan-' was a religious enclosure; while 'Pen' was the Cornish word for a hill or headland. 'Pascoe' means 'Easter', while 'Dyer' was a 'thatcher' and 'Helyer' was a 'hunter'. 'Marrak' comes from the Cornish 'marghak', meaning a 'knight' or 'rider'. Surnames derived from animals may indicate making a living from hunting, such as 'Bligh' (from 'Cor.blyth', a wolf) or 'Coon' ('Cor.cun', a hunting dog).

A spatial analysis of surnames around the world shows where Europeans migrated in search of work. For instance, the Pascoe surname reflects the emigration of Cornish men with mining skills following the collapse of the traditional Cornish economy during the Industrial Revolution. In 1881 there were 3393 men with the surname Pascoe living in the United Kingdom; by 2001 there were only 3417, relatively fewer given the increased population of Britain across the twentieth century. In 1880 there were only 556 Pascoes in the United States; by 2011 there were 3328. More significantly, these Pascoes lived in American states with a strong industrial and mining background, such as Michigan (435 in number), California (397) and Pennsylvania (301). They had gone there with their traditional skills. In 2011, another 3014 Pascoes were living in Australia. In other words, there had been more than a threefold increase in the number of Pascoes during the twentieth century, but they were now part of the European Diaspora around the globe.

Each surname thus reflects a cluster of skills appropriate to a part of Europe. The technicians of the Industrial Revolution took their skills and ambitions to the New World and Australia. Clan and village networks operated globally to distribute these workers in specific regions, such as Scandinavian farmers in the American Mid West, Italians in the cities of Eastern USA and Latin America, and East European peasants in New York. The 'industrial' model of innovation produced its own kind of international migration patterns. There were three styles of migration.

One was 'circular' (typified by the 'golondrinas', the Spanish word for 'swallows', who 'flew' between Italy and Argentina and back); another was 'chain' migration (delayed family migration, with the males going ahead), and the third was 'indentured', or 'padrone'-led (made famous by the Corleone family in *Godfather II*). Because Italian modernisation occurred in such an uneven manner, each region had different amounts and types of migration, as well as repatriation.

French and English ambitions

These migrations took place within the boundaries and interests set down by the various European empires. In all, 55 million Europeans emigrated to the USA, Brazil, Argentina, and Canada in the famous 'Atlantic Crossing'. The Italian Empire was small, but Italian emigration was large. The British never saw emigration as a haemorrhage of their people, merely a peopling of the New World and Australia. The displacement of native peoples followed soon afterwards. The French and the British divided up the nineteenth-century world between them, much like the Portuguese and the Spanish of the earlier period [as we saw in Unit 11]. When mapmakers described these empires visually, each colour represented a different empire. The British parts were traditionally shown in pink, the French green. India was conquered before the Industrial Revolution brought technical superiority to British weaponry, and formed the template for its nineteenth- and twentieth-century colonisations. Marx did not anticipate how profoundly the metropolitan proletariat would be compromised in this process, though the emigrants would have to fight for decent living standards.

The empires were not all the same. European empires in the New World were 'settlements', either 'pure' (free), 'plantation' (slave-based) or a mix of the two. The newer empires in Africa, Asia and the Pacific were 'occupations', although Australasia and southern Africa are regarded as exceptions to this rule.[49] Interestingly, America was not fully colonised, even as late as 1800. By the 1930s, 85 per cent of the world's landmass comprised colonies and ex-colonies.

The earlier colonisations were not inevitable, with resistance from the non-European States. But modern colonisation was inevitable, with the increased industrial, military and organisational power of the Europeans. Distance had made the older colonies difficult to govern from the centre. Now improved communication in the modern empires helped centralise imperial power. The older empires were economically illiberal, with mercantilist policies connecting the colonies to the metropole. The new empires had a greater degree of relative economic freedom.

The British and the French empires had more similarities than differences, but the contrasts are worth noting. The British empire was much larger and contained more settlement colonies than the French. The British (and the Russians) did not distinguish between subjects of the Crown and other residents (except in their protectorates). The French (and all other empires) made a clear separation between citizens and subjects.

The French attempted (like the Portuguese, the Americans and the Russians) to incorporate their colonies as dependencies within their empire, while the British (and others) treated their colonies as separate political States. By 1914 the USA and Russia were the only imperial States without a colonial Ministry, while the others (especially the British) attempted to rule their empires from a single building with well-trained bureaucrats (typified by James Stephen). Colonial administrators gradually replaced the middle-men and were incorruptible but paternalistic.

There were profound cultural differences in management style between 'les rosbifs' and 'the frogs'. While the British were typically pragmatic, permissive, austere, believers in the constitutional monarchy

---

49 D.K. Fieldhouse, *The Colonial Empires: A Comparative Study from the Eighteenth Century*, Weidenfeld and Nicholson, London, 1966.

of the Glorious Revolution, and proud of the achievements of the British Empire, the French were more likely to display a leadership style that was theoretical, controlling, flamboyant, showing the continuing influence of the French Revolution and 'Bonapartism', and concerned with national glory, the achievements of the Revolution, authority and order.

British and French leaders differ in their decision-making processes, with the British more inclined to be pragmatic and focused on good communication, while the French make decisions that are better thought through, but imposed in a top-down manner. The body language of French leaders is far more open and direct, while their British counterparts look devious by comparison. In law, the British adhere to common-law traditions that emphasise flexibility, while the French continue to prefer

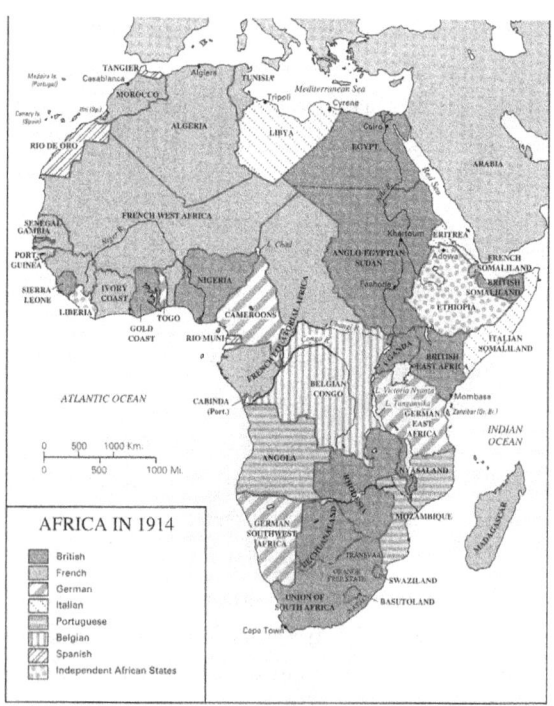

Africa in 1914, mostly colonised

the highly prescriptive nature of Roman Law. The British elite rely on profession for their networks, while the French value their own academic background.[50]

Representative government emerged in the British empire, but not for indigenous peoples. The Enlightenment ideals only slowly came to be applied to all people in the empires: first there was the phase of conquest and destruction, followed by the second phase of social Darwinist trusteeship in the nineteenth century, and the third phase, where the principles of the Enlightenment were applied to all people, was only reached in the 1930s. It was the Second Wold War that fundamentally sped up the process of decolonisation.

The intense rivalry between the French and the British was also reflected in their investment decisions. By 1914, British investment (measured in $m) was concentrated in the USA ($4250m), Canada ($2800m), India ($1850m), Australia ($1700), Argentina ($1550m), the Union of South Africa ($1550m), Brazil ($700m), China ($600m), British East Africa ($600m) and Russia ($550). By comparison, the French had invested $2400m in Russia, and the Germans $400m, investments they would lose in 1917. The French were investing $500m in Egypt, even though it was a British protectorate. Note also how well Australia and Argentina were subsidised, which helps explain why they were so wealthy at this time.

Social Darwinism and new constructions of 'race'

Ideas of racial superiority dominated this era. Charles Darwin's ideas of 'survival of the fittest', expounded in *The Origin of Species* (1859), got taken up and applied to different 'races' of people. Although 'races' such as Caucasian, Negroid etcetera are now regarded as scientifically worthless, they were powerful ideas in their day. Intelligence levels were presumed, and became a justification for occupying lands, such as the Australian continent. 'Natural selection' became a justification for 'progress', and

---

[50] Marshall Young, Oxford Business School, as quoted by Jo Owen in *First*, Second Quarter, 2007, pp. 16-17.

Building the avenue to the Paris Opera, 1877,
an institution copied worldwide [Charles Marville]

White superiority seemed to many people, especially Europeans, to have a scientific basis in fact. Most intellectuals in the nineteenth century, even progressives in their day, now seem utterly racist to the modern sensibility. The insulting term 'ape', still sometimes used by White supremacists to describe people of colour, is a direct reference to this imperialist conquest of Africa and a reference back also to humankind's origins in that continent [Unit 1].

'The Scramble for Africa'

'The Scramble for Africa' refers to the intense partitioning of this continent by the major European powers in the last decades of the nineteenth century. In 1875, only one-tenth of Africa was under European rule; by 1900, only one-tenth was not. The map of Africa showing how it had been colonised by 1914 reveals a pattern of French and British colonisation that runs east-west in the French case and north-south in the British. Britain and France nearly went to war in 1897 over contending claims to the headwaters of the Nile. Britain embarked on two vigorous military campaigns in Africa – in the Sudan, 1885 and 1898, and in South Africa (the Boer War, 1898-1902, a dirty war), both involving Australian troops. Following the Scramble, there was only one independent African nation, Ethiopia.

Colonial cities

In 1882 Britain invaded Egypt to put down the nationalist uprising of Ahmad Urabi and to restore the existing regime (which lasted until 1952). This meant that Cairo was rebuilt in the late nineteenth century by the British under Lord Cromer, following British planning principles and architecture.

In other empires the dominant metaphor reflected the imperial power concerned. A new layer of complexity was added to the city in history, resulting in what has been called the 'baroque city'.[51] This term reflects the new features added to the traditional city around this time. These include: the royal park (exemplified by the Tuileries in Paris), hotels, theatre, pleasure gardens, dance-halls, museums, art galleries, and the zoo. These institutions are emblematic of empire and also show the global circulation of performers and ideas. For example, the Collingwood Football Club in Australia borrowed its distinctive black-and-white guernsey from the travelling American minstrel shows that were popular in 1890s Melbourne. The Melbourne Zoo and its Botanical Gardens were collections and animals and plants that demonstrated its imperial connection in this age of empire. Haussmann's redesign of Paris was copied in many colonial settings, such as Buenos Aires. Beirut was redesigned by the French during the Mandate period to resemble a typical French city.

---

51 Lewis Mumford, *The City in History: Its Origins, Its Transformations, and Its Prospects*, Harcourt, Brace and World, New York, 1961, pp. 436 ff.

Migration and the 'fragment thesis'

In each of these cities and colonies, we can understand the process of colonisation in cultural or ethnic terms, and as fragments of social classes. The new societies are all 'fragments of the larger whole of Europe struck off in the course of the revolution which brought the West into the modern world. For when a part of a European nation is detached from the whole of it, and hurled outward onto new soil, it loses the stimulus to change that the whole provides....'[52]

The Australian colonies are a good example of the 'fragment thesis' in action. British society was never transferred in all its parts and complexities to Australia. The top layer, the landed gentry, did not migrate to the colonies. Families from the minor gentry did, and, without a genuine aristocracy to support them, failed to reproduce what was laughed off as a 'bunyip aristocracy'. The failure of Thomas Peel in Western Australia was one minor instance of this reality. The British bourgeoisie also did not migrate to Australia, even though they invested heavily in its farms and mines. This left a gap in the social order into which the ambitious could hope to insert themselves, and the petit-bourgeois aspirational class has always been a signal aspect of the Australian social structure. Some of these people were remnants of the old British peasantry, now transported as convicts, 'chosen by the best judges in the land', as the old joke has it. Some had become lumpenproletariat, the professional criminals of British cities, and they remained 'the hated stain'. More respectable proletarians from Britain who sought to emigrate were given assisted passage. These included the technicians of the Industrial Revolution [Unit 17]. Thus the lower orders in Australia who made up an important part of the fragment of Britain that settled Australia were far stronger politically than their parents back home, and this helps us understand why democratic forces were more powerful in the colonies [Unit 18]. And then there was that part of the Australian population that had no antecedents in Britain – the Aborigines. They remained

---

52 Louis Hartz, *The Peopling of New Societies*, Harcourt, Brace & World, New York, 1964, p. 3.

marginal because there was no place in White thinking for them. When the Australian constitution was legislated in 1901, they were specifically excluded from the citizenry.

Variations on this fragment thesis can be told for all parts of the imperial world, because no colony perfectly reflected its metropole in its social structure.

Technologies of globalisation

Colonialism produced and was assisted by new technologies of globalisation. For example, undersea cables linked the world for telegrams. This meant that communications from the centre to the periphery were speeded up. The Industrial Revolution had introduced a new time discipline; now, this new discipline of time was globalised. English and French became the world's dominant languages. Weights and measures were regulated within each of their empires. Rules of the road were introduced, again within empires. The French empire drove their carriages on the right, the British on the left.

London took control of the world's measurement of time. Big Ben became a powerful symbol of both the British Empire and of the central role played by London in world time zones. In 1880 Greenwich time (near London) became the official time of Britain. In 1884 the Washington Conference agreed to divide the globe into 24 time zones of 15 degrees each, replacing the local time observed by each city and town. The zone including Greenwich Mean Time (GMT) became the central longitude in this calculation.

Each British city was mapped for postal services, using abbreviations such as W1 (now 3011 in Melbourne), W2 (3012), SE1 (3141), SE2 (3142). In British cities, the tram routes were numbered counter-clockwise. In Melbourne, the No 1 still goes to South Melbourne beach, the No 2 used to go to St Kilda, the No 3 to East St Kilda, and so on.

Another important technology was the military uniform. During the Napoleonic Wars each army wore a distinctive colour in the heat and dust of battle to distinguish friend from foe. During the colonial period, khaki became the British norm, borrowed from India and adapted for fighting in the new terrains of the British Empire. In the colonies June 1 and December 1 were the days the garrisons changed from one season's uniform to the other, which explains why Australia adopted these dates to mark the change of seasons in preference to the traditional equinoxes and solstices.

The postcolonial world

The first signs of decolonisation began in the Philippines in the 1890s (expressed in José Rizal's novel, *Noli Me Tangere*), followed by India (led by Mahatma Gandhi), and then by many others since the end of the Second World War in 1945. These new societies looked to the revolutionary documents of 1776 and 1789 for their inspiration. Some, like the Vietnamese nationalists under Ho Chi Minh, used for their revolutionary warrant both the American Declaration of Independence and also the French Declaration of Rights.

The British and French empires have left a legacy in the cultural and political experiences of the colonised societies since the period of decolonisation. Nationalist literary and media cultures (like Bollywood) developed only slowly and hesitantly as activists and writers removed their colonial blinkers.

As the world's population increased in the nineteenth century, the number of the world's languages actually decreased – this was the cultural impact of imperialism. Classical languages (Greek, Latin) were favoured by the British in their imperial heyday – these had a value superior to those of the colonised languages. Sanskrit had been encouraged by the Muslim invaders of India but it died before the British occupation of India and could not be revived after 1949.[53]

---

53 Sheldon Pollock, 'The death of Sanskrit', *Comparative Studies in Society and History*, vol. 43, 2001, pp. 392-426.

The colonised did not surrender meekly. One-fifth of New Zealand's North Island was not ceded in the Maori Wars by 26 clans who grouped together. Their second leader was King Tawhiao, who ruled a separate kingdom, known as King Country, until 1881.

There is a direct connection between the colonial project of the nineteenth century and the decline of European power in the twentieth. By the 1930s, 85 per cent of the world's landmass comprised colonies and ex-colonies. The most successful colonisers were the British and the French, but the two world wars beginning in 1914 broke apart a peace that had had lasted since 1815. After 1945 Britain and France ceded their imperial role to the Americans and the Russians. Europe declined once more in relative terms. Colonialism on this scale carried within it its own contradiction, for the events of 1914 proved there was the capacity for imperial conflict inherent in the model. Nobody, including the Germans, expected the French and the British could ever become reconciled, as they did in 1904. The Russian empire was also drawn into the conflict, with disastrous results for its ruling class in 1917.

Primary sources:

Karl Marx and Friedrich Engels, *The Communist Manifesto*, 1848, and Émile Zola, *Germinal*, 1885

Karl Marx and Friedrich Engels, *Manifesto of the Communist Party*, 1848

A spectre is haunting Europe – the spectre of communism. All the powers of old Europe have entered into a holy alliance to exorcise this spectre: Pope and Tsar, Metternich and Guizot, French Radicals and German police-spies.

Where is the party in opposition that has not been decried as communistic by its opponents in power? Where is the opposition that has not hurled back the branding reproach of communism, against the more advanced opposition parties, as well as against its reactionary adversaries?

Two things result from this fact:

I. Communism is already acknowledged by all European powers to be itself a power.

II. It is high time that Communists should openly, in the face of the whole world, publish their views, their aims, their tendencies, and meet this nursery tale of the spectre of communism with a manifesto of the party itself.

To this end, Communists of various nationalities have assembled in London and sketched the following manifesto, to be published in the English, French, German, Italian, Flemish and Danish languages.

I -- BOURGEOIS AND PROLETARIANS

The history of all hitherto existing society is the history of class struggles.

Freeman and slave, patrician and plebeian, lord and serf, guild-master and journeyman, in a word, oppressor and oppressed, stood in constant opposition to one another, carried on an uninterrupted, now hidden, now open fight, a fight that each time ended, either in a revolutionary reconstitution of society at large, or in the common ruin of the contending classes.

In the earlier epochs of history, we find almost everywhere a complicated arrangement of society into various orders, a manifold gradation of social rank. In ancient Rome we have patricians, knights, plebians, slaves; in the Middle Ages, feudal lords, vassals, guild-masters,

Frontispiece to *The Communist Manifesto* [mikeely.files.wordpress.com]

journeymen, apprentices, serfs; in almost all of these classes, again, subordinate gradations.

The modern bourgeois society that has sprouted from the ruins of feudal society has not done away with class antagonisms. It has but established new classes, new conditions of oppression, new forms of struggle in place of the old ones.

Our epoch, the epoch of the bourgeoisie, possesses, however, this distinct feature: it has simplified class antagonisms. Society as a whole is more and more splitting up into two great hostile camps, into two great classes directly facing each other -- bourgeoisie and proletariat.

From the serfs of the Middle Ages sprang the chartered burghers of the earliest towns. From these burgesses the first elements of the bourgeoisie were developed.

The discovery of America, the rounding of the Cape, opened up fresh ground for the rising bourgeoisie. The East-Indian and Chinese markets, the colonisation of America, trade with the colonies, the increase in the means of exchange and in commodities generally, gave to commerce, to navigation, to industry, an impulse never before known, and thereby, to the revolutionary element in the tottering feudal society, a rapid development.

The feudal system of industry, in which industrial production was monopolized by closed guilds, now no longer suffices for the growing wants of the new markets. The manufacturing system took its place. The guild-masters were pushed aside by the manufacturing middle class; division of labour between the different corporate guilds vanished in the face of division of labour in each single workshop.

Meantime, the markets kept ever growing, the demand ever rising. Even manufacturers no longer sufficed. Thereupon, steam and machinery revolutionized industrial production. The place of manufacture was taken by the giant, MODERN INDUSTRY; the place of the industrial middle class by industrial millionaires, the leaders of the whole industrial armies, the modern bourgeois.

Modern industry has established the world market, for which the discovery of America paved the way. This market has given an immense development to commerce, to navigation, to communication by land. This development has, in turn, reacted on the extension of industry; and in proportion as industry, commerce, navigation, railways extended, in the same proportion the bourgeoisie developed, increased its capital, and pushed into the background every class handed down from the Middle Ages.

We see, therefore, how the modern bourgeoisie is itself the product of a long course of development, of a series of revolutions in the modes of production and of exchange.

Each step in the development of the bourgeoisie was accompanied by a corresponding political advance in that class. An oppressed class under the sway of the feudal nobility, an armed and self-governing association of medieval commune: here independent urban republic (as in Italy and Germany); there taxable "third estate" of the monarchy (as in France); afterward, in the period of manufacturing proper, serving either the semi-feudal or the absolute monarchy as a counterpoise against the nobility, and, in fact, cornerstone of the great monarchies in general -- the bourgeoisie has at last, since the establishment of Modern Industry and of the world market, conquered for itself, in the modern representative state, exclusive political sway. The executive of the modern state is but a committee for managing the common affairs of the whole bourgeoisie.

The bourgeoisie, historically, has played a most revolutionary part.

The bourgeoisie, wherever it has got the upper hand, has put an end to all feudal, patriarchal, idyllic relations. It has pitilessly torn asunder the motley feudal ties that bound man to his "natural superiors", and has left no other nexus between people than naked self-interest, than callous "cash payment". It has drowned out the most heavenly ecstasies of religious fervour, of chivalrous enthusiasm, of philistine sentimentalism, in the icy water of egotistical calculation. It has resolved personal worth into exchange value, and in place of the numberless indefeasible chartered freedoms, has set up that single, unconscionable freedom -- Free Trade. In one word, for exploitation, veiled by religious and political illusions, it has substituted naked, shameless, direct, brutal exploitation.

The bourgeoisie has stripped of its halo every occupation hitherto honoured and looked up to with reverent awe. It has converted the physician, the lawyer, the priest, the poet, the man of science, into its paid wage labourers.

The bourgeoisie has torn away from the family its sentimental veil, and has reduced the family relation into a mere money relation.

The bourgeoisie has disclosed how it came to pass that the brutal display of vigour in the Middle Ages, which reactionaries so much admire, found its fitting complement in the most slothful indolence. It has been the first to show what man's activity can bring about. It has accomplished wonders far surpassing Egyptian pyramids, Roman aqueducts, and Gothic cathedrals; it has conducted expeditions that put in the shade all former exoduses of nations and crusades.

The bourgeoisie cannot exist without constantly revolutionizing the instruments of production, and thereby the relations of production, and with them the whole relations of society. Conservation of the old modes of production in unaltered form, was, on the contrary, the first condition of existence for all earlier industrial classes. Constant revolutionizing of production, uninterrupted disturbance of all social conditions, everlasting uncertainty and agitation distinguish the bourgeois epoch from all earlier ones. All fixed, fast frozen relations, with their train of ancient and venerable prejudices and opinions, are swept away, all new-formed ones become antiquated before they can ossify. All that is solid melts into air, all that is holy is profaned, and man is at last compelled to face with sober senses his real condition of life and his relations with his kind.

The need of a constantly expanding market for its products chases the bourgeoisie over the entire surface of the globe. It must nestle everywhere, settle everywhere, establish connections everywhere.

The bourgeoisie has, through its exploitation of the world market, given a cosmopolitan character to production and consumption in every country. To the great chagrin of reactionaries, it has drawn from under the feet of industry the national ground on which it stood. All old-established national industries have been destroyed or are daily being destroyed. They are dislodged by new industries, whose introduction becomes a life and death question for all civilized nations, by industries that no longer work up indigenous raw material, but raw material drawn from the remotest zones; industries whose products are consumed, not only at home, but in every quarter of the globe. In place of the old wants, satisfied by the production of the country, we find new wants, requiring for their satisfaction the products of distant lands and climes. In place of the old local and national seclusion and self-sufficiency, we have intercourse in every direction, universal inter-dependence of nations. And as in material, so also in intellectual production. The intellectual creations of individual nations become common property. National one-sidedness and narrow-mindedness become more and more impossible, and from the numerous national and local literatures, there arises a world literature.

The bourgeoisie, by the rapid improvement of all instruments of production, by the immensely facilitated means of communication, draws all, even the most barbarian, nations into civilization. The cheap prices of commodities are the heavy artillery with which it forces the barbarians' intensely obstinate hatred of foreigners to capitulate. It compels all nations, on pain of extinction, to adopt the bourgeois mode of production; it compels them to introduce what it calls civilisation into their midst, i.e., to become bourgeois themselves. In one word, it creates a world after its own image.

The bourgeoisie has subjected the country to the rule of the towns. It has created enormous cities, has greatly increased the urban population as compared with the rural, and has thus rescued a considerable part of the population from the idiocy of rural life. Just as it has made the country dependent on the towns, so it has made barbarian and semi-barbarian countries dependent on the civilized ones, nations of peasants on nations of bourgeois, the East on the West.

The bourgeoisie keeps more and more doing away with the scattered state of the population, of the means of production, and of property. It has agglomerated population, centralized the means of production, and has concentrated property in a few hands. The necessary consequence of this was political centralization. Independent, or but loosely connected provinces, with separate interests, laws, governments, and systems of taxation, became lumped together into one nation, with one government, one code of laws, one national class interest, one frontier, and one customs tariff.

The bourgeoisie, during its rule of scarce one hundred years, has created more massive and more colossal productive forces than have all preceding generations together. Subjection of nature's forces to man, machinery, application of chemistry to industry and agriculture, steam navigation, railways, electric telegraphs, clearing of whole continents for cultivation, canalization or rivers, whole populations conjured out of the ground -- what earlier century had even a presentiment that such productive forces slumbered in the lap of social labour?

We see then: the means of production and of exchange, on whose foundation the bourgeoisie built itself up, were generated in feudal society. At a certain stage in the development of these means of production and of exchange, the conditions under which feudal society produced and exchanged, the feudal organization of agriculture and manufacturing industry, in one word, the feudal relations of property became no longer compatible with the already developed productive forces; they became so many fetters. They had to be burst asunder; they were burst asunder.

Into their place stepped free competition, accompanied by a social and political constitution adapted in it, and the economic and political sway of the bourgeois class.

A similar movement is going on before our own eyes. Modern

bourgeois society, with its relations of production, of exchange and of property, a society that has conjured up such gigantic means of production and of exchange, is like the sorcerer who is no longer able to control the powers of the nether world whom he has called up by his spells. For many a decade past, the history of industry and commerce is but the history of the revolt of modern productive forces against modern conditions of production, against the property relations that are the conditions for the existence of the bourgeois and of its rule. It is enough to mention the commercial crises that, by their periodical return, put the existence of the entire bourgeois society on its trial, each time more threateningly. In these crises, a great part not only of the existing products, but also of the previously created productive forces, are periodically destroyed. In these crises, there breaks out an epidemic that, in all earlier epochs, would have seemed an absurdity -- the epidemic of over-production. Society suddenly finds itself put back into a state of momentary barbarism; it appears as if a famine, a universal war of devastation, had cut off the supply of every means of subsistence; industry and commerce seem to be destroyed. And why? Because there is too much civilization, too much means of subsistence, too much industry, too much commerce. The productive forces at the disposal of society no longer tend to further the development of the conditions of bourgeois property; on the contrary, they have become too powerful for these conditions, by which they are fettered, and so soon as they overcome these fetters, they bring disorder into the whole of bourgeois society, endanger the existence of bourgeois property. The conditions of bourgeois society are too narrow to comprise the wealth created by them. And how does the bourgeoisie get over these crises? On the one hand, by enforced destruction of a mass of productive forces; on the other, by the conquest of new markets, and by the more thorough exploitation of the old ones. That is to say, by paving the way for more extensive and more destructive crises, and by diminishing the means whereby crises are prevented.

The weapons with which the bourgeoisie felled feudalism to the ground are now turned against the bourgeoisie itself.

But not only has the bourgeoisie forged the weapons that bring death to itself; it has also called into existence the men who are to wield those weapons -- the modern working class – the proletarians.

In proportion as the bourgeoisie, i.e., capital, is developed, in the same proportion is the proletariat, the modern working class, developed – a class of labourers, who live only so long as they find work, and who find work only so long as their labour increases capital. These labourers, who must sell themselves piecemeal, are a commodity, like every other article of commerce, and are consequently exposed to all the vicissitudes of competition, to all the fluctuations of the market.

Owing to the extensive use of machinery, and to the division of labour, the work of the proletarians has lost all individual character, and, consequently, all charm for the workman. He becomes an appendage of the machine, and it is only the most simple, most monotonous, and most easily acquired knack, that is required of him. Hence, the cost of production of a workman is restricted, almost entirely, to the means of subsistence that he requires for maintenance, and for the propagation of his race. But the price of a commodity, and therefore also of labour, is equal to its cost of production. In proportion, therefore, as the repulsiveness of the work increases, the wage decreases. What is more, in proportion as the use of machinery and division of labour increases, in the same proportion the burden of toil also increases, whether by prolongation of the working hours, by the increase of the work exacted in a given time, or by increased speed of machinery, etc.

Modern Industry has converted the little workshop of the patriarchal master into the great factory of the industrial capitalist. Masses of labourers, crowded into the factory, are organised like soldiers. As privates of the industrial army, they are placed under the command of a perfect hierarchy of officers and sergeants. Not only are they slaves of the bourgeois class, and of the bourgeois state; they are daily and hourly enslaved by the machine, by the overlooker, and, above all, in the individual bourgeois manufacturer himself. The more openly this despotism proclaims gain to be its end and aim, the more petty, the more hateful and the more embittering it is.

The less the skill and exertion of strength implied in manual labour, in other words, the more modern industry becomes developed, the more is the labour of men superseded by that of women. Differences of age and sex have no longer any distinctive social validity for the working class. All are instruments of labour, more or less expensive to use, according to their age and sex.

No sooner is the exploitation of the labourer by the manufacturer, so far at an end, that he receives his wages in cash, than he is set upon by the other portion of the bourgeoisie, the landlord, the shopkeeper, the pawnbroker, etc.

The lower strata of the middle class – the small tradespeople, shopkeepers, and retired tradesmen generally, the handicraftsmen and peasants – all these sink gradually into the proletariat, partly because their diminutive capital does not suffice for the scale on which Modern Industry is carried on, and is swamped in the competition with the large capitalists, partly because their specialized skill is rendered worthless by new methods of production. Thus, the proletariat is recruited from all classes of the population.

The proletariat goes through various stages of development. With its birth begins its struggle with the bourgeoisie. At first, the contest is carried on by individual labourers, then by the work of people of a factory, then by the operative of one trade, in one locality, against the individual bourgeois who directly exploits them. They direct their attacks not against the bourgeois condition of production, but against the instruments of production themselves; they destroy imported wares that compete with their labour, they smash to pieces machinery, they set factories ablaze, they seek to restore by force the vanished status of the workman of the Middle Ages.

At this stage, the labourers still form an incoherent mass scattered over the whole country, and broken up by their mutual competition. If anywhere they unite to form more compact bodies, this is not yet the consequence of their own active union, but of the union of the bourgeoisie, which class, in order to attain its own political ends, is compelled to set the whole proletariat in motion, and is moreover yet, for a time, able to do so. At this stage, therefore, the proletarians do not fight their enemies, but the enemies of their enemies, the remnants of absolute monarchy, the landowners, the non-industrial bourgeois, the petty bourgeois. Thus, the whole historical movement is concentrated in the hands of the bourgeoisie; every victory so obtained is a victory for the bourgeoisie.

But with the development of industry, the proletariat not only increases in number; it becomes concentrated in greater masses, its strength grows, and it feels that strength more. The various interests and conditions of life within the ranks of the proletariat are more and more equalized, in proportion as machinery obliterates all distinctions of labour, and nearly everywhere reduces wages to the same low level. The growing competition among the bourgeois, and the resulting commercial crises, make the wages of the workers ever more fluctuating. The increasing improvement of machinery, ever more rapidly developing, makes their livelihood more and more precarious; the collisions between individual workmen and individual bourgeois take more and more the character of collisions between two classes. Thereupon, the workers begin to form combinations (trade unions) against the bourgeois; they club together in order to keep up the rate of wages; they found permanent associations in order to make provision beforehand for these occasional revolts. Here and there, the contest breaks out into riots.

Now and then the workers are victorious, but only for a time. The real fruit of their battles lie not in the immediate result, but in the ever expanding union of the workers. This union is helped on by the improved means of communication that are created by Modern Industry, and that place the workers of different localities in contact with one another. It was just this contact that was needed to centralize the numerous local struggles, all of the same character, into one national struggle between classes. But every class struggle is a political struggle. And that union, to attain which the burghers of the Middle Ages, with their miserable highways, required centuries, the modern proletarian, thanks to railways, achieve in a few years.

This organisation of the proletarians into a class, and, consequently, into a political party, is continually being upset again by the competition between the workers themselves. But it ever rises up again, stronger, firmer, mightier. It compels legislative recognition of particular interests of the workers, by taking advantage of the divisions among the bourgeoisie itself. Thus, the Ten-Hours Bill in England was carried.

Altogether, collisions between the classes of the old society further in many ways the course of development of the proletariat. The bourgeoisie finds itself involved in a constant battle. At first with the aristocracy; later on, with those portions of the bourgeoisie itself, whose interests have become antagonistic to the progress of industry; at all time with the bourgeoisie of foreign countries. In all these battles, it sees itself compelled to appeal to the proletariat, to ask for help, and thus to drag it into the political arena. The bourgeoisie itself, therefore, supplies the proletariat with its own elements of political and general education, in other words, it furnishes the proletariat with weapons for fighting the bourgeoisie.

Further, as we have already seen, entire sections of the ruling class are, by the advance of industry, precipitated into the proletariat, or are at least threatened in their conditions of existence. These also supply the proletariat with fresh elements of enlightenment and progress.

Finally, in times when the class struggle nears the decisive hour, the progress of dissolution going on within the ruling class, in fact within the whole range of old society, assumes such a violent, glaring character, that a small section of the ruling class cuts itself a section of the ruling class cuts itself adrift, and joins the revolutionary class, the class that holds the future in its hands. Just as, therefore, at an earlier period, a section of the nobility went over to the bourgeoisie, so now a portion of the bourgeoisie goes over to the proletariat, and in particular, a portion of the bourgeois ideologists, who have raised themselves to the level of comprehending theoretically the historical movement as a whole.

Of all the classes that stand face to face with the bourgeoisie today, the proletariat alone is a genuinely revolutionary class. The other classes decay and finally disappear in the face of Modern Industry; the proletariat is its special and essential product.

The lower middle class, the small manufacturer, the shopkeeper, the artisan, the peasant, all these fight against the bourgeoisie, to save from extinction their existence as fractions of the middle class. They are therefore not revolutionary, but conservative. Nay, more, they are reactionary, for they try to roll back the wheel of history. If, by chance, they are revolutionary, they are only so in view of their impending transfer into the proletariat; they thus defend not their present, but their future interests; they desert their own standpoint to place themselves at that of the proletariat.

The "dangerous class", the social scum, that passively rotting mass thrown off by the lowest layers of the old society, may, here and there, be swept into the movement by a proletarian revolution; its conditions of life, however, prepare it far more for the part of a bribed tool of reactionary intrigue.

In the condition of the proletariat, those of old society at large are already virtually swamped. The proletarian is without property; his relation to his wife and children has no longer anything in common with the bourgeois family relations; modern industry labour, modern subjection to capital, the same in England as in France, in America as in Germany, has stripped him of every trace of national character. Law, morality, religion, are to him so many bourgeois prejudices, behind which lurk in ambush just as many bourgeois interests.

All the preceding classes that got the upper hand sought to fortify their already acquired status by subjecting society at large to their conditions of appropriation. The proletarians cannot become masters of the productive forces of society, except by abolishing their own previous mode of appropriation, and thereby also every other previous mode of appropriation. They have nothing of their own to secure and to fortify; their mission is to destroy all previous securities for, and insurances of, individual property.

All previous historical movements were movements of minorities, or in the interest of minorities. The proletarian movement is the self-conscious, independent movement of the immense majority, in the interest of the immense majority. The proletariat, the lowest stratum of our present society, cannot stir, cannot raise itself up, without the whole superincumbent strata of official society being sprung into the air.

Though not in substance, yet in form, the struggle of the proletariat with the bourgeoisie is at first a national struggle. The proletariat of each country must, of course, first of all settle matters with its own bourgeoisie.

In depicting the most general phases of the development of the proletariat, we traced the more or less veiled civil war, raging within existing society, up to the point where that war breaks out into open revolution, and where the violent overthrow of the bourgeoisie lays the foundation for the sway of the proletariat.

Hitherto, every form of society has been based, as we have already seen, on the antagonism of oppressing and oppressed classes. But in order to oppress a class, certain conditions must be assured to it under which it can, at least, continue its slavish existence. The serf, in the period of serfdom, raised himself to membership in the commune, just as the petty bourgeois, under the yoke of the feudal absolutism, managed to develop into a bourgeois. The modern labourer, on the contrary, instead of rising with the process of industry, sinks deeper and deeper below the conditions of existence of his own class. He becomes a pauper, and pauperism develops more rapidly than population and wealth. And here it becomes evident that the bourgeoisie is unfit any longer to be the ruling class in society, and to impose its conditions of existence upon society as an overriding law. It is unfit to rule because it is incompetent to assure an existence to its slave within his slavery, because it cannot help letting him sink into such a state, that it has to feed him, instead of being fed by him. Society can no longer live under this bourgeoisie, in other words, its existence is no longer compatible with society.

The essential conditions for the existence and for the sway of the bourgeois class is the formation and augmentation of capital; the condition for capital is wage labour. Wage labour rests exclusively on competition between the labourers. The advance of industry, whose involuntary promoter is the bourgeoisie, replaces the isolation of the labourers, due to competition, by the revolutionary combination, due to association. The development of Modern Industry, therefore, cuts from under its feet the very foundation on which the bourgeoisie produces and appropriates products. What the bourgeoisie therefore produces, above all, are its own grave-diggers. Its fall and the victory of the proletariat are equally inevitable.

Karl Marx, *A Contribution to the Critique of Political Economy*, 1859

In the social production of their existence, men inevitably enter into definite relations, which are independent of their will, namely relations of production appropriate to a given stage in the development of their material forces of production. The totality of these relations of production constitutes the economic structure of society, the real foundation, on which arises a legal and political superstructure and to which correspond definite forms of social consciousness. The mode of production of material life conditions the general process of social, political and intellectual life. It is not the consciousness of men that determines their existence, but their social existence that determines their consciousness. At a certain stage of development, the material productive forces of society come into conflict with the existing relations of production or – this merely expresses the same thing in legal terms – with the property relations within the framework of which they have operated hitherto. From forms of development of the productive forces these relations turn into their fetters. Then begins an era of social revolution. The changes in the economic foundation lead sooner or later to the transformation of the whole immense superstructure.

In studying such transformations it is always necessary to distinguish between the material transformation of the economic conditions of production, which can be determined with the precision of natural science, and the legal, political, religious, artistic or philosophic – in short, ideological forms in which men become conscious of this conflict and fight it out. Just as one does not judge an individual by what he thinks about himself, so one cannot judge such a period of transformation by its consciousness, but, on the contrary, this consciousness must be explained from the contradictions of material life, from the conflict existing between the social forces of production and the relations of production. No social order is ever destroyed before all the productive forces for which it is sufficient have been developed, and new superior relations of production never replace older ones before the material conditions for their existence have matured within the framework of the old society.

Mankind thus inevitably sets itself only such tasks as it is able to solve, since closer examination will always show that the problem itself arises only when the material conditions for its solution are already present or at least in the course of formation. In broad outline, the Asiatic, ancient, feudal and modern bourgeois modes of production may be designated as epochs marking progress in the economic development of society. The bourgeois mode of production is the last antagonistic form of the social process of production – antagonistic not in the sense of individual antagonism but of an antagonism that emanates from the individuals' social conditions of existence – but the productive forces developing within bourgeois society create also the material conditions for a solution of this antagonism. The prehistory of human society accordingly closes with this social formation.

Émile Zola, *Germinal*, 1885 (translated by Havelock Ellis)

OVER the open plain, beneath a starless sky as dark and thick as ink, a man walked alone along the highway from Marchiennes to Montsou, a straight paved road ten kilometres in length, intersecting the beetroot-fields. He could not even see the black soil before him, and only felt the immense flat horizon by the gusts of March wind, squalls as strong as on the sea, and frozen from sweeping leagues of marsh and naked earth. No tree could be seen against the sky, and the road unrolled as straight as a pier in the midst of the blinding spray of darkness.

The man had set out from Marchiennes about two o'clock. He walked with long strides, shivering beneath his worn cotton jacket and corduroy breeches. A small parcel tied in a check handkerchief troubled him much, and he pressed it against his side, sometimes with one elbow, sometimes with the other, so that he could slip to the bottom of his pockets both the benumbed hands that bled beneath the lashes of the wind. A single idea occupied his head--the empty head of a workman without work and without lodging--the hope that the cold would be less keen after sunrise. For an hour he went on thus, when on the left, two kilometres from Montsou, he saw red flames, three fires burning in the open air and apparently suspended. At first he hesitated, half afraid. Then he could not resist the painful need to warm his hands for a moment.

The steep road led downwards, and everything disappeared. The man saw on his right a paling, a wall of coarse planks shutting in a line of rails, while a grassy slope rose on the left surmounted by confused gables, a vision of a village with low uniform roofs. He went on some two hundred paces. Suddenly, at a bend in the road, the fires reappeared close to him, though he could not understand how they burnt so high in the dead sky, like smoky moons. But on the level soil another sight had struck him. It was a heavy mass, a low pile of buildings from which rose the silhouette of a factory chimney; occasional gleams appeared from dirty windows, five or six melancholy lanterns were hung outside to frames of blackened wood, which vaguely outlined the profiles of gigantic stages; and from this fantastic apparition, drowned in night and smoke, a single voice arose, the thick, long breathing of a steam escapement that could not be seen.

Then the man recognized a pit. His despair returned. What was the good? There would be no work. Instead of turning towards the buildings he decided at last to ascend the pit bank, on which burnt in iron baskets the three coal fires which gave light and warmth for work. The labourers in the cutting must have been working late; they were still throwing out the useless rubbish. Now he heard the landers push the wagons on the stages. He could distinguish living shadows tipping over the trains or tubs near each fire.

"Good day," he said, approaching one of the baskets. Turning his back to the fire, the carman stood upright. He was an old man, dressed in knitted violet wool with a rabbit-skin cap on his head; while his horse, a great yellow horse, waited with the immobility of stone while they emptied the six trains he drew. The workman employed at the tipping-cradle, a red-haired lean fellow, did not hurry himself; he pressed on the lever with a sleepy hand. And above, the wind grew stronger--an icy north wind--and its great, regular breaths passed by like the strokes of a scythe.

"Good day," replied the old man. There was silence. The man, who felt that he was being looked at suspiciously, at once told his name.

"I am called Étienne Lantier. I am an engine-man. Any work here?"

The flames lit him up. He might be about twenty-one years of age, a very dark, handsome man, who looked strong in spite of his thin limbs.

The carman, thus reassured, shook his head.

"Work for an engine-man? No, no! There were two came yesterday. There's nothing."

A gust cut short their speech. Then Étienne asked, pointing to the sombre pile of buildings at the foot of the platform:

"A pit, isn't it?"

The old man this time could not reply: he was strangled by a violent cough. At last he expectorated, and his expectoration left a black patch on the purple soil.

"Yes, a pit. The Voreux. There! The settlement is quite near."

In his turn, and with extended arm, he pointed out in the night the village of which the young man had vaguely seen the roofs. But the six trams were empty, and he followed them without cracking his whip, his legs stiffened by rheumatism; while the great yellow horse went on of itself, pulling heavily between the rails beneath a new gust which bristled its coat.

Édouard Manet, *Portrait of Émile Zola*, 1868 [Musée d'Orsay]

The Voreux was now emerging from the gloom. Étienne, who forgot himself before the stove, warming his poor bleeding hands, looked round and could see each part of the pit: the shed tarred with siftings, the pit-frame, the vast chamber of the winding machine, the square turret of the exhaustion pump. This pit, piled up in the bottom of a hollow, with its squat brick buildings, raising its chimney like a threatening horn, seemed to him to have the evil air of a gluttonous beast crouching there to devour the earth. While examining it, he thought of himself, of his vagabond existence these eight days he had been seeking work. He saw himself again at his workshop at the railway, delivering a blow at his foreman, driven from Lille, driven from everywhere. On Saturday he had arrived at Marchinnes, where they said that work was to be had at the Forges, and there was nothing, neither at the Forges nor at Sonneville's. He had been obliged to pass the Sunday hidden beneath the wood of a cartwright's yard, from which the watchman had just turned him out at two o'clock in the morning. He had nothing, not a penny, not even a crust; what should he do, wandering along the roads without aim, not knowing where to shelter himself from the wind? Yes, it was certainly a pit; the occasional lanterns lighted up the square; a door, suddenly opened, had enabled him to catch sight of the furnaces in a clear light. He could explain even the escapement of the pump, that thick, long breathing that went on without ceasing, and which seemed to be the monster's congested respiration.

The workman, expanding his back at the tipping-cradle, had not even lifted his eyes on Étienne, and the latter was about to pick up his little bundle, which had fallen to the earth, when a spasm of coughing announced the carman's return. Slowly he emerged from the darkness, followed by the yellow horse drawing six more laden trams.

"Are there factories at Montsou?" asked the young man.

The old man expectorated, then replied in the wind:

"Oh, it isn't factories that are lacking. Should have seen it three or four years ago. Everything was roaring then. There were not men enough; there never were such wages. And now they are tightening their bellies again. Nothing but misery in the country; every one is being sent away; workshops closing one after the other. It is not the emperor's fault, perhaps; but why should he go and fight in America? without counting that the beasts are dying from cholera, like the people."

Then, in short sentences and with broken breath, the two continued to complain. Étienne narrated his vain wanderings of the past week: must one, then, die of hunger? Soon the roads would be full of beggars.

"Yes," said the old man, "this will turn out badly, for God does not allow so many Christians to be thrown on the street."

"We don't have meat every day."

"But if one had bread!"

"True, if one only had bread."

Their voices were lost, gusts of wind carrying away the words in a melancholy howl.

"Here!" began the carman again very loudly, turning towards the south. "Montsou is over there."

And stretching out his hand again he pointed out invisible spots in the darkness as he named them. Below, at Montsou, the Fauvelle sugar works were still going, but the Hoton sugar works had just been dismissing hands; there were only the Dutilleul flour mill and the Bleuze rope walk for mine-cables which kept up. Then, with a large gesture he indicated the north half of the horizon: the Sonneville workshops had not received two-thirds of their usual orders; only two of the three blast furnaces of the Marchiennes Forges were alight; finally, at the Gagebois glass works a strike was threatening, for there was talk of a reduction of wages.

"I know, I know," replied the young man at each indication. "I have been there."

Questions for discussion:

Historians have returned to the original writings of Marx and Engels, setting aside what was done in their names in the twentieth century, to understand the nature of early capitalism.

The Marxists took a different view of the role of labour. In the famous passage from *The Communist Manifesto*, Marx and Engels give their version of World History. In 1859 Marx expanded these thoughts in a smaller document, *A Contribution to the Critique of Political Economy*. How does the Marxist view differ from the forces of history as described by Adam Smith, David Ricardo and John Stuart Mill?

What ideas from the English Radicals can be detected in the work of Marx and Engels?

The novel *Germinal* is a gritty social realist account of a strike in France in the 1870s. How does the author, Émile Zola, prepare us for this instance of class conflict?

Going further:

D.K. Fieldhouse, *The Colonial Empires: A Comparative Study from the Eighteenth Century*, Weidenfeld and Nicholson, London, 1966

Louis Hartz, *The Peopling of New Societies*, Harcourt, Brace & World, New York, 1964

Lewis Mumford, *The City in History: Its Origins, Its Transformations, and Its Prospects*, Harcourt, Brace and World, New York, 1961

Sheldon Pollock, 'The death of Sanskrit', *Comparative Studies in Society and History*, vol. 43, 2001, pp. 392-426

Frank Thistlethwaite, 'Migration from Europe overseas in the nineteenth and twentieth centuries', XIe Congr. International des Sciences Historiques, *Rapport*, 5, 1960, pp. 32-60

John Tully, *The Devil's Milk: A Social History of Rubber*, Monthly Review Press, New York, 2011

Marshall Young, Oxford Business School, as quoted by Jo Owen in *First*, Second Quarter, 2007, pp. 16-17

Unit 20

The Great War and Bolshevism

Important lessons in nationality were taught at the onset of the Great War to European schoolboys. The French child was taught to recite this poem:

> Child, upon these maps do heed/ This black stain to be effaced/ Omitting it, you would proceed/ Yet better it in red to trace
>
> Later, whatever may come to pass/ Promise there to go you must/ To fetch the children of Alsace/ Reaching out their arms to us/ May in our fondest France Hope's green saplings to branch/
>
> And in you, dear child, flower/ Grow, grow, France awaits its hour

The English boy learnt to recite the following:

> To rid the map of every trace
> Of Germany and of the Hun
> We must exterminate that race
> We must not leave a single one
> Heed not their children's cries
> Best slay all now, the women, too
> Or else someday again they'll rise
> Which if they're dead, they cannot do

While the German schoolboy was taught to say:

> We have one and only enemy
> Who digs the grave of Germany

> Its heart replete with hatred, gall and envy
> We have one and only enemy
> The villain raises its murderous hand
> Its name, you know, is England

The First War World fed off these national identities.

These three poems make up the opening scene of three schoolboys in the movie, *Joyeux Noël*, (2005), a powerful evocation of the feelings in 1914. Part of the difficulty in understanding the carnage of the Great War is that we need to recognise that the Europeans could not imagine what was about to happen. There had been a century of peace since 1815, a focus on building empires, and large migrations of workers (especially the Atlantic Crossing). The British Empire set the pattern: an old kingdom became a new empire in this period.

The Great War can be well understood as a clash of empires. The largest empires were the chief combatants: Germany and the Ottoman Empire on one side; Britain and France on the other. Those with smaller empires were slower to become engaged in this conflict (Italy in 1915; America in 1917). Russia withdrew from the conflict in 1917 owing to its Revolution. Australia and other colonies of the combatant nations were drawn into the horrors of the Great War. Except for three jurisdictions (Australia; South Africa; Ireland, then part of Britain), every one of the 23 combatant nations used conscription to dragoon its men into fighting for empire. Men did not willingly serve in the horrors of this war. This was the British Industrial Revolution coming to a violent climax, with modern industry at the service of war.

Nineteenth-century America and the Closing of the Frontier, 1890

America sees itself in messianic terms. In President George W. Bush's first Inaugural Address, on 20 January 2001, *Psalms* 18.10 is quoted: '... After the Declaration of Independence was signed, Virginia statesman John Page wrote to Thomas Jefferson: "We know the race is not to the swift nor the battle to the strong. Do you not think an angel rides in the whirlwind and directs this storm?'" What aspects of its history explain America's messianic tendency?

Americans saw themselves as inhabiting a place of possibility, because the New World was free from the taints and mistakes of the Old. Americans had a sense of having fought a successful revolution against an Old World monarchy. They believed in classlessness, and in democracy – though all white men did not get the vote till 1828. The US historian William Appleman Williams famously remarked that Americans were so beloved of their own Revolution that they could not imagine any other way of achieving self-determination. The Monroe Doctrine (1823) was a brash assertion of the young republic, declaring that no other nation could interfere in its immediate neighbourhood. It was also still an agricultural society – with voting fixed for November, after the harvest had been brought in, and President taking office, at noon on 20 January, to allow him to get to Washington DC.

The young Republic's first major challenge came in 1861. The American Civil War, running from 1861 to 1865, cost 600,000 American lives – more casualties than all other wars in which Americans have fought since 1776. It was not a moral war about the existence of black slavery in the young democratic Republic. It was a war between two parts of the nation that were moving in different economic directions. If the South had not attempted to secede from the Union, it is doubtful that slavery would have been abolished in 1865.[54] As it was, the compromises made to the defeated Southerners after the War meant that for some observers the true end of the War was not 1865, but 1965, with the passage of the Civil Rights Act. The position of the ex-slaves did not materially improve during that intervening century.

The two huge Civil War armies were voluntary, suggesting the degree to which men from both sides held firmly to their sense that their side

---

54 Adam I.P. Smith, *The American Civil War*, Palgrave Macmillan, Basingstoke, Hampshire, 2007.

Harvard's Memorial to the 136 Union dead, ignoring the 71 graduates who died in the Confederate causes [Harvard University]

was right in this conflict, and that political (or economic) differences mattered. The public and the soldiers were closely connected, in the South because the war was fought on local soil, and in the North because the newspapers reported battles within hours of them being fought. This glare of publicity, and some of the technology used (railways, telegraphs, machine guns) made it a modern war, but it was never lifted above the simple masculine notions of military heroism that would end on the Western Front in 1916. At Harvard there is a memorial board outside

Winslow Homer, *Bell-Time*, depicts the grim life of New England mill workers, 1868 [Robert Pascoe]

the Sanderson Theatre listing all its men who died in the Union cause – visitors can be heard to remark cynically it is 'a monument to Southern marksmanship'. Both sides still to this day hail their heroes and see the War as a series of set-piece battles.

From about the 1840s the United States had been dividing economically into two parts. The free states of the North were expanding rapidly in population, with land-sales out West and people moving into Iowa (which became a state in 1846), Wisconsin (1848) and, following the gold rushes, California (1850). The Californian gold rushes in some ways were symbolic of the new power of the North. More importantly, these Northern states were increasingly becoming a market economy, with greater flows of labour and capital.

However, the South was still more powerful economically. Mississippi, doomed by the Civil War to generations of poverty, was the wealthiest state in the Union at the outset of the War.[55] Across the South, the price

---

55 Smith, *The American Civil War*, p. 17.

of slaves was rising, as was the value of the South's products (tobacco, coffee, sugar, cotton). The South was closely interwoven with the Atlantic economy, but in other respects was surprisingly feudal. It was feudal in its parcellised sovereignty – the young American republic's distrust of centralised government had meant that every state retained considerable local power. Each of the 15 slave-holding states was also quite variegated internally, with an uneven distribution of slave-owning properties. Unlike the slave economies further south in the Caribbean and Latin America, the American South was never dominated demographically by its slaves, and its ratio of female to male slaves meant that its slave population was growing dramatically in the decades before 1861. The Caribbean slave economies were male-dominated. And, as in feudal Europe, there was a concentration of slaves in few hands. Only three per cent of families were plantation owners, each with more than 20 slaves, and owned half of America's slave population.[56] These slaves were not paid a wage for their services, but instead were bound by generations of loyal service to their white owners. The relationship that developed between slaves and their owners was quintessentially 'feudal'. In the eleven states that combined to form the breakaway Confederacy, there were 5.5 million whites and 3.5 million (mostly slave) blacks.

As America became a two-economy republic, the rules governing the slaves in the South became tougher. For example, George Washington's method of reconciling his democratic instincts with his ownership of slaves – that they be manumitted on his widow's death – was declared illegal in the South. The calls for Abolition in the North simply hardened the resolve of Southern slaveholders that they would not compromise their slave-based economy. The War, when it came, was as bloody as it was inevitable.

President Lincoln was sufficiently animated by this carnage to deliver his well-known Gettysburg Address, with the immortal lines:

---

56 Smith, *The American Civil War*, p. 16.

Four score and seven years ago our fathers brought forth on this continent a new nation, conceived in liberty, and dedicated to the proposition that all men are created equal. Now we are engaged in a great civil war, testing whether that nation, or any nation so conceived and so dedicated, can long endure. We are met on a great battlefield of that war. We have come to dedicate a portion of that field, as a final resting place for those who here gave their lives that that nation might live. It is altogether fitting and proper that we should do this. But, in a larger sense, we can not dedicate, we can not consecrate, we can not hallow this ground. The brave men, living and dead, who struggled here, have consecrated it, far above our poor power to add or detract. The world will little note, nor long remember what we say here, but it can never forget what they did here. It is for us the living, rather, to be dedicated here to the unfinished work which they who fought here have thus far so nobly advanced. It is rather for us to be here dedicated to the great task remaining before us – that from these honored dead we take increased devotion to that cause for which they gave the last full measure of devotion – that we here highly resolve that these dead shall not have died in vain – that this nation, under God, shall have a new birth of freedom – and that government of the people, by the people, for the people, shall not perish from the earth.

The Gettysburg Address draws from the ancient Greek practice of oratory [Unit 4] and emboldened future US presidents, such as Barack Obama [Unit 24] to strive to meet this highest standard of public speaking.[57]

The effects of the Civil War were powerfully depicted in Winslow

---

57 Dennis Glover, *The Art of Great Speeches*, Cambridge University Press, Cambridge UK, 2011.

Fifth Avenue, Easter 1900: American cities were growing and teeming with immigrants

Homer, *The Brush Harrow*, 1865. Two boys are left to do a man's work, and lonely birds circle in the sky. With the devastation caused by this war, America turned to European immigration to find labour for its factories and farms. It expanded westwards, creating a moving frontier of people, their carts, and their stock. The American Revolution was finally concluded in 1890, with the closing of this frontier. Frederick Jackson Turner, based in Wisconsin, in 1893 argued that the frontier experience had transformed all (White) Americans (explaining their rugged individualism, their democratic instinct, and the military training they had received from the Indian Wars). The Turner thesis helps explain many aspects of American history: the weakness of the American Left, the decimation of the Indians, the nation's gun culture, the power of the Hollywood Western, and the American 'fragment'.[58] In sporting terms, the new national game of baseball was a powerful emblem of this westward expansion. With baseball the English game of cricket grew an outfield, an expanse beyond the urban diamond. America saw itself as a nation that could hit the ball into the outer.[59] Turner also recognised the significance of the European migration. America was undoubtedly built by the 'Atlantic Crossing'.[60]

Industrial innovation then had its effect on America in the years after the War. There had been an earlier tradition of the Yankee inventor, the practical Puritan who could make anything work. This figure was wittily portrayed by Mark Twain in his whimsical novel, *A Connecticut Yankee in the Court of King Arthur*. America welcomed technicians, especially immigrants from Great Britain, such as the Welsh and the Cornish, who could work the mining technology of Colorado or build ships in New York. American industry became renowned for its successful cross-overs, such as 3M, a stationery firm that had originally developed sandpaper.[61] Nineteenth-century America grew, however, with unequal access to capital. Blacks, Italians and Jews found it harder to borrow money than Whites. A final factor was the role of universities in this period of American history, as the German research university proved crucial to American industrial capitalism, having been adopted and developed in many states of the nation.

---

58 Louis Hartz, *The Peopling of New Societies*, Harcourt, Brace & World, New York, 1964.
59 Allen Guttmann, *From Ritual to Record: The Nature of Modern Sports*, Columbia University Press, New York, 1979.
60 Frank Thistlethwaite, 'Migration from Europe overseas in the nineteenth and twentieth centuries, XIe Congr. International des Sciences Historiques, *Rapport*, 5, 1960, pp. 32-60.
61 Jim Collins and Jerry I. Porras, *Built to Last: Successful Habits of Visionary Companies*, HarperCollins, New York, 1994.

By the end of the nineteenth century, America was a growing urban industrial power, with a strong industrial bourgeoisie. This was the so-called Age of the Robber Barons. Much of the red-blooded capitalism of this era was dramatised by investigative writers, known as the 'muckrakers'. These included Lincoln Steffens, Jacob Riis, and Upton Sinclair, whose expose of the Chicago meat industry, *The Jungle* (1906), was based on his undercover employment there.[62]

Freud, 1900

While America was still young and growing, Europe was more dominant at the beginning of the new century. Fin-de-siècle Vienna was an important meeting ground for ideas that would profoundly shape the twentieth century. Sigmund Freud's *The Interpretation of Dreams* (which appeared in 1900) was a product of this culture. Freud exposed the naiveté of much nineteenth-century thinking. He revealed that there were inner processes at work within people that demanded explanation. He defined the unconscious, repression, infantile sexuality, and the tripartite division of the mind into the ego (the self), superego (the conscience), the id (desire).

Freud borrowed the idea of the 'talking cure' from a colleague – he found that if he let people talk in free association about their lives, childhood traumas, long repressed, came to the surface. These traumas were often of a sexual nature, Oedipal for men and Elektra for women, involving one's parents. Hypnosis and dream analysis were developed by the Freudians as strategies to elucidate these personal insights. Although man had been elevated by Darwin, Freud showed people are driven by very basic desires.

German-speaking cities were the intellectual centres of the day. Vienna was significant amongst these. It contained a honeycomb of coffee-houses, with marble-topped tables where intellectuals could spend

---

62 One of Sinclair's later novels, *Oil!* (1927) was loosely adapted into the film, *There Will Be Blood* (Paul Thomas Anderson, dir. 2007).

their days, writing on headed paper, with newspapers and encyclopedias at their elbow, places to talk and discuss the ideas in circulation at the time. Vienna became the home of 'the smart Jew', no longer reviled as 'crafty'. They were accused by anti-Semites of inventing Modernism.

Vienna became renowned for its art and design, and literature. Gustav Klimt's famous *The Kiss* (1907-08) wraps Viennese sexuality in Byzantine gold. The film *Eyes Wide Shut* (Stanley Kubrick, 1999) is based on a novella set in Vienna around this time, *Dream Story* (1926), by the Austrian writer Arthur Schnitzler.

Modernism, 1910

Modernism had its roots in the late nineteenth century but is conventionally defined as beginning in about 1910. Virginia Woolf dated its origins to December 1910. It crossed all fields, including music, architecture, and fiction. It became associated with Paris, the Bloomsbury Group in London, and New York.

Modernism can be defined as the application of Freudian ideas in cultural expression, including the rejection of the 'final authorities' – God, government, science, and Reason. The roll-call of Modernists is impressive in its size and range: Bertolt Brecht, Joseph Conrad, Henri Duchamp, T. S. Eliot, William Faulkner, Walter Gropius, James Joyce, Wassily Kandinsky, D. H. Lawrence, Le Corbusier, Henri Matisse, Pablo Picasso, Luigi Pirandello, Ezra Pound, Marcel Proust, Rainer Maria Rilke, Gertrude Stein, Igor Stravinsky, Giuseppe Ungaretti, Mies van der Rohe, William Carlos Williams, Virginia Woolf, and William Butler Yeats.

The poem 'XII' by William Carlos Williams is often used as the epitome of Modernism:

> so much depends
> upon
> a red wheel
> barrow

> glazed with rain
> water
>
> beside the white
> chickens.

Williams made his living as a general practitioner, which is important to understanding this poem, but many of the Modernists represented a new kind of artist. Many artists chose to lead Bohemian lives, and their artworks emphasised revolutionary change in preference to evolutionary progress. Examples include Stravinsky, The *Rite of Spring* (1913), Duchamp, *Nude Descending a Staircase, No. 2*, and Picasso, *Les Demoiselles d'Avignon*. Stravinsky's ballet music confronted traditional taste just as profoundly as Picasso's prostitutes glared at the onlooker, while Duchamp's woman looked as mechanical as the stairs she descended. These artists were declaring that the received wisdom of space and time could no be longer be trusted, and scientific research uncovered the Special Theory of Relativity (Albert Einstein) and the sub-atomic particles (Niels Bohr), parallel discoveries to those of the Modernists. Modernism began on a positive note, but the events that unfolded in 1914 would change all that.

The rise of Germany, 1871-1914

Germany was re-established as a unitary state in 1871. This was the Hohenzollern dynasty, otherwise known as the Second Reich, if the First Reich was the Holy Roman Empire, 800–1806. The new German state flexed its muscles, and the French defeat in the 1871 war not only led to the Paris Commune [Unit 18], but also the loss of Alsace-Lorraine to the new German state. (It is to this loss that the schoolboy's recitation refers, 'to fetch the children of Alsace'.) Otto von Bismarck ('the Iron Chancellor') kept the socialists under Eduard Bernstein in check, even though they were Europe's biggest Marxist party, by his 'carrot and stick' approach.

The Great War, 1914-1918

Up to 1914, much of Europe's energy had been focused on building global empires, and the main ideological conflict had been between capitalism and socialism. The two world wars, provoked by Europeans, produced a destruction of people and human settlements on an unprecedented scale. Partly as a consequence of these two world wars, human invention produced an astonishing range of new technologies (including aviation, tanks, motor vehicles, television, radar, atomic power), albeit at a huge human cost. There is no doubt that the Great War was caused by the Germans. (The Great War is the preferred term for this conflict, because it was not renamed the First World War until the coming of the Second World War.)

Leading up to 1914, the European powers had engaged in a series of diplomatic moves that led to formal treaties. These were not the cause of the Great War, but were merely part of the international mechanism that caused to happen. In its quest for imperial power, Germany had struck a Triple Alliance with Austria and Italy (while France and Russia also signed a treaty in 1884). This German imperial rivalry was to have disastrous consequences. Germany had supported the Boers against the British in the war of 1899–1902. The Germans also helped the Ottomans after their military disaster in the Balkans War of 1912. Germany now challenged Britain and France in the Middle East. Germany began building a navy to rival Britain's. In turn, by launching a new steam battleship, all big-gunned, the famous *HMS Dreadnought*, in 1906, the British provoked 'the Dreadnought crisis', as it was called.

However, Germany provoked the War. Germany tried to engineer a Treaty with the British favourable to itself. Germany never imagined Britain would ally itself with its traditional enemies, France and Russia. After all, there had been 400 years of hostility between the British and the French. But in 1904 they signed the Entente Cordiale, partly to resolve their problems with the Scramble for Africa. France was to take Morocco, Britain Egypt, and so on.

This then was a war that could not be imagined. It was sparked by the 1914 assassination of Ferdinand, Archduke of Austria-Hungary, by a Serbian in Sarajevo. There was a degree of national hatred among the Europeans that is difficult to understand today. It was an imperial war even in the manner of its conduct, a fact felt keenly by Australians. Putting one's colonial soldiers on the front line became each empire's main gambit. The French used Senegalese, British deployed their 'White Gurkhas' (the ANZACs).

In the slogan of the day, 'War is a bayonet with a worker at each end', and this was especially true of the Great War. The application of heavy industry to human warfare caused a horrific loss of life and injury. Men followed their officers blindly into battle up and down the Western Front. Neither side could prevail, but the addition of the Americans on the Allied side in 1917 certainly helped. The Australians performed well, from 1916, following their experience at Gallipoli in 1915. The mental pain of war was called 'shell shock' (and is now better known as PTSD, Post-Trauma Stress Disorder).

National honour was strengthened by this war, as each side counted its casualties after 1918. The dead could be summoned by post-war politicians seeking to explain this war, but the wounded were ignored, as they could answer back.[63]

The Russian Revolution, 1905-1921

This Great War is a necessary context for understanding the first successful revolution carried out in the name of Karl Marx. Contrary to his expectations it took place in a society that was more feudal than capitalist.

Traditional Russia comprised 100 million peasants. Russia had serfs until 1861. It was ruled by a nobility and a tiny middle class. The Czar held absolute power – he had no parliament to answer, not even a cabinet, but retained a strong bureaucracy and secret police. It was old-fashioned Eastern Absolutism [Unit 13].

---

63 Marina Larsson, *Shattered Anzacs: Living with the Scars of War*, UNSW Press, Sydney, 2009.

The Russian Revolution has to be understood as comprising four stages. The first, centred on St Petersburg (Petrograd) in 1905 was really a trial run. Then, in February 1917 came the abdication of the Czar. Thirdly, from 24 October to 26 October 1917, was the nub of the revolution, as Lenin's Bolsheviks seized the Winter Palace in St Petersburg, the event usually called the November 1917 Revolution. (Russia was still using the pre-Gregorian or Julian calendar.) Finally, in the Civil War, 1917-1921, the counter-revolutionary White Army was defeated by the Red Army under the command of Leon Trotsky.

The 1905 revolt was instigated by the incompetence of the government as shown in its defeat during the Russo-Japanese War (1904). Troops fired on peaceful protestors; strikes, naval mutinies and peasant risings followed. The revolt was crushed, but some change was clearly necessary, and a Duma (parliament) was formed. When Russia joined the Great War, the peasantry was ill-equipped and bore the brunt of war. Aside from the casualties, food rations were cut and once again the government seemed incapable of organising its military forces.

Bolshevik propaganda included the alleged affair between the Tsarina and Rasputin

The Bolshevik propaganda was effective. In one poster, a naked Tsarina Alexandra was shown in the arms of the priest Rasputin. The Bolsheviks, although numbering only 35, 000 people out of 130 million Russians, took over the revolution when the Czar quit in 1917. From then the momentum of change was with this left-wing arm of the revolution, and Lenin was swept to power on the promise of land and food, with an immediate withdrawal from the war.

The 'Americanisation' movement after the Great War, 1919-1924

The social effect of the War was felt in all the combatant nations. Fears of political unrest in America led to the Palmer raids of 1919, an attempt to round up all dissidents, many of whom seemed to be foreigners. To stem the flood of unwanted immigrants, the US Congress passed the 1924 Quota Laws, setting restrictions on the numbers of immigrants from each source country based on the 1890 Census. So groups who had arrived in bigger numbers after 1890, such as the Italians, were systematically excluded. So, although the 'huddled masses' who had built America were acknowledged, some national groups proved more welcome than others. The arrest on murder charges of the Italian-American anarchists Sacco and Vanzetti, and their long campaign for justice, ending in their execution, became a warning to dissidents that extreme political views would not be tolerated.

In this context Americans were reluctant to get entangled in the affairs of the Old World. Despite the leading role played by President Woodrow Wilson at Versailles, and America's part in founding the League of Nations, the US Congress refused to join the new League, and it was doomed from the start. From 1920 America retreated into its own affairs, until jolted from this isolationism with the Japanese bombing of Pearl Harbor in 1941. This period of so-called 'Americanisation' saw much of the conservative basis of contemporary America laid down.

It also saw the beginning of the rise of the United States, the main theme in world history of the second half of the twentieth century.

Primary source: Narratives of the Great War

Bill Bland, 'Letter from a former English University Lecturer', 1916

[extracted from Lyn McDonald, *1914–1918: Voices and Images of the Great War*, Pollinger, 1988]

18 February 1916 [France]

Darling, I can't bear you to be unhappy about me. Don't be grey and old, my darling. Think of the *cause*, the cause. It is England, England, England, always and all the time. The individual counts as nothing, the common cause everything. Have faith, my dear. If only you will have faith in the ultimate victory of the good, the true, and the beautiful, you will not be unhappy even is I never return to you. Dear, if one's number is up, one will go under. I am here, and I shall either survive or not survive. In the meantime, I have never been truly happier.

P.S. Hardship be damned! It's all one long blaze of glory.

[Captain Bill Bland served in the 22nd Battalion, Manchester Regiment, 7th Manchester Pais; this letter is in the Imperial War Museum. What was his fate? Did he return safely?]

Robert Graves, *Goodbye to All That*, 1929

[repr. Penguin, Harmondsworth UK, 1960]

I used to congratulate myself on having quite blindly chosen the Royal Welch Fusiliers, of all regiments in the army. 'Good God!' I used to think. 'Suppose then when the war broke out I had been living in Cheshire, and had applied for a commission in the Cheshire Regiment.' How ashamed I should have been to find in the history of that regiment – the old Twenty-second Foot, just senior in line to the Royal Welch, the Twenty-third – that it had been deprived of its old title 'The Royal Cheshires' as a punishment for losing a battle. (This was a quite unhistorical libel, but we all believed it.) Or how lucky not to have joined the Bedfords, who were making a name for themselves in this war, but were still called 'The

Peacemakers'; for they had only four battle-honours on their colours, none more recent than the year 1711, and we misquoted their regimental motto as: 'Thou shalt not kill!' [It was actually the famous French phrase *Honi Soit Qui Mal Y Pense*, 'Shamed Be He Who Thinks Evil Of It'.] Even the Black Watch had a stain on its record; and everyone knew about it. If a Tommy of another regiment went into a public bar where men of the Black Watch were drinking, and felt brave enough to start a fight, he would ask the barmaid not for 'pig's ear', which is rhyming slang for beer, but for a pint of 'broken square'. Then belts would be unbuckled. [In the Sudan in 1885, the Black Watch had adopted a square formation, but the Madhi's forces had broken it.]....

The troop-train consisted of forty-seven coaches, and took twenty-four hours to arrive at Béthune, the railhead, via Saint Omer. We detrained at about 9 p.m., hungry, cold, and dirty. Expecting a short journey, we had allowed our baggage to be locked in a van; and then played nap throughout the journey to keep our minds off the discomfort. I lost sixty francs, which was over two pounds at the existing rate of exchange. On the platform at Béthune, a little man in filthy khaki, wearing the Welsh cap-badge, came up with a friendly touch of the cap most unlike a salute. He had orders to guide us to the battalion, at present in the Cambrin trenches, about ten kilometers away. Collecting the draft of forty men we had with us, we followed him through the unlit suburbs of the town – all intensely excited by the noise and flashes of the guns in the distance. None of the draft had been out before, except the sergeant in charge. They began singing. Instead of the usual music-hall songs they sang Welsh hymns, each man taking a part. The Welsh always sang when pretending not to be scared; it kept them steady. And they never sang out of tune.

We marched towards the flashes, and could soon see the flare-lights curving across the distant trenches. The noise of the guns grew louder and louder.

[The book is actually strongly anti-war – this becomes more obvious further in.]

Kande Kamara, *Memories of a West African in France*

[Oral Testimony recorded 22–24 September 1976, from Joe Harris Lunn, 'Kande Kamara speaks: An oral history of the West African experience in France, 1914–1918', in Melvin E. Page, *Africa and the First World War*, Macmillan, London, 1987, pp. 44–48]

... One of my younger brothers... was shot in the thigh... and he cried out... "Brother, they've shot me." But I didn't look at him – I didn't help him – because during wartime, even if your friend is shot dead, you would continue facing the enemy to save your own life. Because [officers] were watching you, and if you were afraid to shoot the enemy... your own people would shoot you down... I didn't say anything; I kept quiet. I wasn't looking at him, but tears were running down my face.

Wilfred Owen, 'Dulce et Decorum Est'

[from Siegfried Sassoon, ed., *Poems*, Chatto and Windus, London, 1920]

> Bent double, like old beggars under sacks,
> Knock-kneed, coughing like hags, we cursed through sludge,
> Till on the haunting flares we turned our backs
> And towards our distant rest began to trudge.
> Men marched asleep. Many had lost their boots
> But limped on, blood-shod. All went lame; all blind;
> Drunk with fatigue; deaf even to the hoots
> Of tired, outstripped Five-Nines that dropped behind.
>
> Gas! GAS! Quick, boys! – An ecstasy of fumbling,
> Fitting the clumsy helmets just in time;
> But someone still was yelling out and stumbling,
> And flound'ring like a man in fire or lime . . .
> Dim, through the misty panes and thick green light,
> As under a green sea, I saw him drowning.
> In all my dreams, before my helpless sight,
> He plunges at me, guttering, choking, drowning.

> If in some smothering dreams you too could pace
> Behind the wagon that we flung him in,
> And watch the white eyes writhing in his face,
> His hanging face, like a devil's sick of sin;
> If you could hear, at every jolt, the blood
> Come gargling from the froth-corrupted lungs,
> Obscene as cancer, bitter as the cud
> Of vile, incurable sores on innocent tongues,
> My friend, you would not tell with such high zest
> To children ardent for some desperate glory,
> The old Lie: Dulce et Decorum est
> Pro patria mori.

[Owen enlisted in the Britsh Army in 1915; he died of wounds on 4 November 1918. Five-Nines are German artillery shells; what are some other technical terms in this poem?]

Erich Maria Remarque, *All Quiet on the Western Front*

[trans. A. W. Wheen, Fawcett Books, New York, 1929, pp. 1–18]

Kantorek had been our schoolmaster, a stern little man in a grey tailcoat, with a face like a shrew mouse. He was about the same size as Corporal Himmelstoss, the "terror of Klosterberg". It is very queer that the unhappiness of the world is so often brought on by small men. They are so much more energetic and uncompromising than the big fellows. I have always taken good care to keep out of sections with small company commanders. They are mostly confounded little martinets.

During drill-time Kantorek gave us long lectures until the whole of our class went, under his shepherding, to the District Commandant and volunteered. I can see him now, as he used to glare at us through his spectacles and say in a moving voice: "Won't you join up, Comrades?"

… Yes, that's the way they think, these hundred thousand Kantoreks! Iron Youth! Youth! We are none of us more than twenty years old. But youth? Youth! That is long ago. We are old folk.

A German author looks back at the Great War:
Erich Maria Remarque [germanoriginality.com]

E.P.F. Lynch, *Somme Mud: The War Experiences of an Infantryman in France, 1916–1919*

[ed. Will Davies, Random House Australia, Milsons Point NSW, 2006]

[Trench warfare was horrific, as the Australian Edward Lynch explains in this extract, part of the chapter detailing the attack on Messines following the underground explosions:]

Morning dawns and we find that during the night, a communication sap has been dug right up to the N.Z. line of trenches through that heavy shelling. Men have fiercely worked under that barrage all night and these men are the Maoris of New Zealand. You Maoris'll do us! [Australians do not usually realise Maori is the plural of Maori.]

It's daylight now. Eleven of us are in an old Fritz trench going through our packs, searching for food for we're starving, but they yield nothing so we crawl about searching for equipment left behind by wounded men. An officer comes up and tells us that the battalion, helped by two companies of the 40th Battalion, is again to hop-over and retake Owl Trench and Owl Support. He wants some of us to find a supply of enemy bombs as our grenades and running short.

Longun and I get a couple of bags each and wander around the Fritz trench to find some bombs. We crawl down his old broken dugouts, strike matches and gingerly step over torn dead Fritz everywhere.

'Come on, out of this. We'll find enough up on top. This rattin' is no good to me,' Longun complains, so we get up in the open again, just as an enemy barrage comes down hard and solid. We can't get back to our mates and have a rotten ten minutes crouched in a little trench till the barrage is over.

We go back, hand over our bombs and then hurry along to see if any food has been left for us. Just as we round a bend of the trench, we find one of the men we left, his two legs absolutely shattered. Desperate from fear, he lies on his side frantically clawing away at the trench wall to get cover. The sight of this poor unstrung, dying fellow is terrible. We marvel that any man so mangled can live, even for a minute.

Round the bend we hurry, afraid to speak, afraid of what we expect to find. Three men are dead where we left them sitting as went off for bombs. Another man lies tossed across the side of the trench. There's no sign of Dark or the other three men we left, but smashed rifles, town and frayed equipment and little spots of blood that tell us a shell landed fair amongst the party. We go on to the next bay where the men there tell us that Dark escaped lightest with only a leg wound and the other three were taken out also. We ask why the man with shot-off legs wasn't taken out too and we're told that the stretcher-bearers gave him no hope. Back we go to get a stretcher for him, but the bearers knew best. The poor wretch is dead.

'We advance in five minutes,' is passed along, and Longun and I rush around to find a rifle each and equipment as ours are all smashed up from the shell burst.

It's 8.30 a.m. as we hop-over again to retake the positions we lost last night. Our guns are keeping a heavy barrage on the enemy trench. We move on, passing our dead who fell yesterday. We are nearing Owl Trench now and see a few of our wounded who have been out all night. The poor wretches roll over and feebly wave to us, hoping to be saved.

On we go through rifle and machine-gun fire. Owl Trench is just ahead. Our barrage lifts from it and we see the men of our first wave throwing their bombs into it and then jumping in with the bayonets going. Enemy prisoners climb out and begin to make their way back.

With a rush we are passing them and trying to make them understand to take our wounded back as they go.

Owl Trench is under us. We cross it and race on towards where our sells are bombarding Owl Support. Closer and closer to the bursting shells we crawl. The barrage lifts and with a mad charge we're into the trench yelling. I see Fritz climbing out with hands held high. Others kneel in the trench and hold their arms up or cover their eyes in fear. The position is ours.

'Men wanted on the left!' is roared by someone and I rush along to where a bomb fight is going on. The din is terrific. Our shouts mingle with the calls of Fritz. Egg bombs and stick bombs fly at us. Men are falling everywhere, but still our men are throwing their Mills grenades. I rush up and throw the two bombs I have left. Someone yells at me from on top of the trench and I jump up there and lie beside young Jacko and fire at the Fritz bombs are coming from. The Fritz give way and our men are steadily advancing along the trench. We can't see any more enemy heads to fire at so we jump down, pull the spades out from under out equipment and get to work throwing earth up on our parapet.

A sergeant rushes by. 'Pass all bombs to the left.' And a few are passed along. An officer comes along inspecting the position and encouraging to dig on. Word comes to load all rifles to the full and we pause our digging and get our rifle magazines full. A young officer staggers along the trench, his head swathed in blood-stained bandages. His face is white and nervous-looking. As he passes by, led along by a stretcher-bearer, he keeps on repeating, 'We can still say the old 45th has never lost a position, boys.'

We continue working on. It's now well into the afternoon. An enemy bombardment opens upon us. We expect it to stop any moment and to have Fritz counter-attack but the bombardment keeps on. Every now and again a shell gets the trench as stretcher-bearers race up and down. We expect Fritz to come over and men's heads bob up above the trench, take a hurried glance and pop down again. Still no sign of Fritz counter-attack and still the shells fall upon us.

It's almost dark now. The shelling stops abruptly and a massed formation of Fritz is coming for us, bayonets streaking silver in the fading light. 'Come on, into them!' And we line the parapet and empty our rifles at them. They are mowed down, but more take their places. For a few minutes we fire and the counter-attack scatters as the men break and run. Into the fleeing backs we fire until they are out of sight. Our rifles are hot. We're flushed and excited. Bang! Crash! And down we get under the trench wall as the barrage is on to us again.

For over three hours we get shelled then all is quiet. The quietness seems strange, unnatural. Our bearers are getting the wounded out. Those of us who are still left line the trench watching, listening and waiting for the next counter-attack. Jacko and I, nervous, unstrung, and hungry, sit against the trench wall almost asleep, worn out and despondent.

Towards morning some tea tasting of petrol is passed around and we drink all we can get and bags of dates also; the first food to reach our post since we came in from Kortypyp early yesterday morning. Longun, Jacko and I eat dates until we are almost sick. No shortage of them, as a supply sufficient for the whole battalion came up and the far greater part of the old 45th is now lying dead or on its way to hospital.

It's just breaking day and the three of us get in some sniping at lost Fritz poking about down a gully. We reckon we got fourteen of them between us. The last of our stretcher parties come in. They have been out behind us all night searching for wounded.

Morning drags on. Shells are falling spasmodically on our trench. One lands fair above us and we dive sideways. I feel a red-hot pain in my left wrist as a piece of shell gets me. My watch falls and I grab my wrist, which is bleeding freely. The pain is severe and the whole arm is numb, but I know the wound isn't deep. Jacko rescues my watch and I slip it into my pocket. We examine the wound. The shell fragment has cut the leather band of the watch strap and made a long, deep flesh wound. Logun bandages it and tells me to make out whilst it's a bit quiet, but I can't do that as many a man in the trench has wounds ten times as bad and is carrying on with the job.

Another hour goes by. Longun and Jacko are away somewhere digging. My arm is sore and very swollen already so I have been left on 'look out' duty.

'Nulla!' I hear Longun frantically call. He walks up to me in a dazed sort of way. 'Come here.' His voice breaks. He's out of his calmness for the first time since I've known him. Without a word he turns and slouches away, head bent between sagging shoulders. I follow and see him stop along the trench and hear a forced cheerfulness from him as he softly says, 'How's it now, old chap? Here's Nulla.' And there lying against the back of the trench is poor little Jacko dying.

Big, terrified eyes flickering above a strangely blue-tinged frightened face. A man is supporting him against the trench. His right thigh is a great, black, blood-edged hole of mangled flesh from which protrude pieces of reddish bone. His thin little girlish lips are twitching. I can't speak. I want to cheer him up, to make him believe he'll be all right, but I can't speak. Jacko seems to be receding into the trench wall. Two frail little boyish hands paw towards me. I grab them and Longun's hands close over ours and I feel Longun's hands trembling above mine as I hold Jacko's two.

'Your fellows been... been good... to me. Ole man... ole...' And he shudders, his brave little shoulders droop. 'Tell Daddy I found it, Mummy. Ole man, ole man, ole... ' And we grab him as he falls and lower him down, dead.

[Look up Lynch's subsequent military career for some insights into this narrative.]

Siegfreid Sassoon, 'The Redeemer', *The Old Huntsman*

>   DARKNESS: the rain sluiced down; the mire was deep;
>   It was past twelve on a mid-winter night,
>   When peaceful folk in beds lay snug asleep;
>   There, with much work to do before the light,
>   We lugged our clay-sucked boots as best we might
>   Along the trench; sometimes a bullet sang,
>   And droning shells burst with a hollow bang;
>   We were soaked, chilled and wretched, every one;
>   Darkness; the distant wink of a huge gun.
>   I turned in the black ditch, loathing the storm;
>   A rocket fizzed and burned with blanching flare,
>   And lit the face of what had been a form
>   Floundering in mirk. He stood before me there;
>   I say that He was Christ; stiff in the glare,
>   And leaning forward from His burdening task,
>   Both arms supporting it; His eyes on mine
>   Stared from the woeful head that seemed a mask
>   Of mortal pain in Hell's unholy shine.
>   No thorny crown, only a woollen cap
>   He wore--an English soldier, white and strong,
>   Who loved his time like any simple chap,
>   Good days of work and sport and homely song;
>   Now he has learned that nights are very long,
>   And dawn a watching of the windowed sky.
>   But to the end, unjudging, he'll endure

Horror and pain, not uncontent to die
That Lancaster on Lune may stand secure.
He faced me, reeling in his weariness,
Shouldering his load of planks, so hard to bear.
I say that He was Christ, who wrought to bless
All groping things with freedom bright as air,
And with His mercy washed and made them fair.
Then the flame sank, and all grew black as pitch,
While we began to struggle along the ditch;
And someone flung his burden in the muck,
Mumbling: 'O Christ Almighty, now I'm stuck!'

Poems of Giuseppe Ungaretti (1888–1970)

[Ungaretti was born in Egypt, where his father died working on the Suez Canal and his widowed mother set up a shop on the edge of the desert. Despite a flirtation with Fascism after the War, he became a passionate pacificist later in life.]

Veglia
Cima Quattro il 23 dicembre 1915

Un'intera nottata
buttato vicino
a un compagno
massacrato
con la sua bocca
digrignasta
volta al plenilunio
con la congestione
delle sue mani
penetrata

The horror of the Great War: Italian soldiers killed by the Austrians at Cividale del Friuli, 1917

nel mio silenzio
ho scritto
lettere piene d'amore
Non sono mai stato
tanto
attaccato alla vita

[The Watch: Spending an entire night/ thrown alongside/ a masscared comrade/ with his mouth/ sneering/ toward the full moon,/ with the congestion/ of his hands/ penetrating/ my silence/ I have been writing/ letters/ full of love. Never have I been/ so/ attached to life.]

Horror and pain, not uncontent to die
That Lancaster on Lune may stand secure.
He faced me, reeling in his weariness,
Shouldering his load of planks, so hard to bear.
I say that He was Christ, who wrought to bless
All groping things with freedom bright as air,
And with His mercy washed and made them fair.
Then the flame sank, and all grew black as pitch,
While we began to struggle along the ditch;
And someone flung his burden in the muck,
Mumbling: 'O Christ Almighty, now I'm stuck!'

Poems of Giuseppe Ungaretti (1888–1970)

[Ungaretti was born in Egypt, where his father died working on the Suez Canal and his widowed mother set up a shop on the edge of the desert. Despite a flirtation with Fascism after the War, he became a passionate pacificist later in life.]

Veglia
Cima Quattro il 23 dicembre 1915

Un'intera nottata
buttato vicino
a un compagno
massacrato
con la sua bocca
digrignasta
volta al plenilunio
con la congestione
delle sue mani
penetrata

The horror of the Great War: Italian soldiers killed by the Austrians at Cividale del Friuli, 1917

nel mio silenzio
ho scritto
lettere piene d'amore
Non sono mai stato
tanto
attaccato alla vita

[The Watch: Spending an entire night/ thrown alongside/ a masscared comrade/ with his mouth/ sneering/ toward the full moon,/ with the congestion/ of his hands/ penetrating/ my silence/ I have been writing/ letters/ full of love. Never have I been/ so/ attached to life.]

Soldati

Bosco di Courton luglio 1918

Si sta come

d'autunno

sugli alberi

le foglie.

[Soldiers: Just as/ in autumn/ on the trees/ they are the leaves.]

Giuseppe Ungaretti in his Italian infantry uniform
at the time he began writing his war poems

Questions for discussion:

The documents in Units 20-24 introduce us to texts as cultural documents. How can we apply literary techniques to the interpretation of primary source documents?

In these Great War narratives, compare the implicit attitudes to crucial issues in wartime in this range of texts. What can we infer from these narratives about the varying attitudes to war, and the Great War in particular, in the cultures and nations represented by these veterans? It is not enough to say simply that trench warfare was grim and forbidding, as soldiers reacted differently to it, or at least wrote about it differently.

Examples of some of the issues we might discuss:

How did regimental military pride work in some national contexts? (Refer to Graves)

What were some of the reasons for men signing up to fight? (Remarque, Bland, Kamara, Owen)

How did the rank-and-file relate to the officer class? (Remarque, Lynch)

What was the attitude to mutiny and desertions? (Remarque)

What distinctions were made between black and white soldiers? (Kamara, Lynch)

How did soldiers deal with their fear? (Graves, Lynch)

What was the scale of death? (Ungaretti, Lynch)

How did the soldiers deal with the sight of mutilated bodies in the trenches? (Graves, Ungaretti, Sassoon, Lynch)

How did the Great War controvert much of the thinking about heroism and war during the nineteenth century? How was national pride understood by each of these authors? Why are the literary responses to the War so vivid? What genre of literary expression helped survivors make sense of the War?

Going further:

James Collins and Jerry I. Porras, *Built to Last: Successful Habits of Visionary Companies*, HarperCollins, New York, 1994

Dennis Glover, *The Art of Great Speeches*, Cambridge University Press, Cambridge UK, 2011

Allen Guttmann, *From Ritual to Record: The Nature of Modern Sports*, Columbia University Press, New York, 1979

Louis Hartz, *The Peopling of New Societies*, Harcourt, Brace & World, New York, 1964

Marina Larsson, *Shattered Anzacs: Living with the Scars of War*, UNSW Press, Sydney, 2009

Adam I.P. Smith, *The American Civil War*, Palgrave Macmillan, Basingstoke, Hampshire, 2007

Frank Thistlethwaite, 'Migration from Europe overseas in the nineteenth and twentieth centuries, XIe Congr. International des Sciences Historiques, *Rapport*, 5, 1960, pp. 32-60

Giuseppe Ungaretti, *Il porto sepolto* ('The Buried Port'), 1916 and 1923

Andrew Wheatcroft, *The World Atlas of Revolutions*, Simon & Schuster, New York, 1983

Units 21-24: The Rise of the United States

The rise of the United States was a gradual process, starting at Versailles in 1919, and concluding with the end of the Cold War in 1991. America's ascent to global supremacy took place in a period when the Europeans and the Japanese were divided by Fascism, the Second World War, and then by Postcolonialism. From 1945 to 1962 America and its allies enjoyed a Long Boom. But the Sixties saw the undermining of Western hegemony, and around 1975 it seemed that American power had come to an end. America found an economic solution in Neo-liberalism and a political escape via the New World Order. With the demise of the Soviet Union, America reigned alone. Would that dominant place in world affairs be challenged by China, or even India? That remains a key question for the twenty-first century.

Unit 21

Fascism, World War 2, Postcolonialism

With the Great War was produced the so-called 'lost generation'. The trauma of the war caused a general despair among Europeans and Americans alike. The Great War did for the general population what Modernism had done for the intellectuals; it stripped away all facades of power, glory and authority. Half the population moved to the Left, with communist parties coming into existence across the world; the other half moved to the Right, favouring the repression of Bolshevism.

A key figure in this 'lost generation' was the writer Ernest Hemingway (1899-1961). Hemingway tottered on crutches in Paris, where he settled with the first of his four wives and joined the café society, writing *The Sun Also Rises* (1926). In the Great War Hemingway had served as an

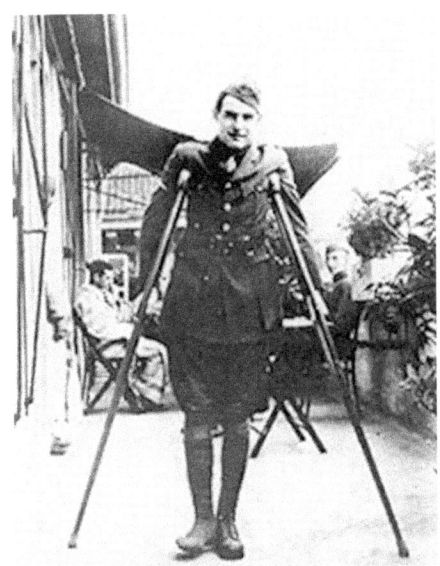

Ernest Hemingway in Paris

ambulance driver, and was wounded in 1918, as recounted in *A Farewell to Arms* (1929), written in his admirably sparse style that evoked the numbing futility of this war. The novel ends with the death of Lieutenant Frederic Henry's beloved Catherine:

> I went into the room and stayed with Catherine until she died. She was unconscious all the time, and it did not take her very long to die.
>
> Outside the room, in the hall, I spoke to the doctor, "is there anything I can do to-night?"
>
> "No. There is nothing to do. Can I take you to your hotel?"
>
> "No, thank you. I am going to stay here a while.' '
>
> "I know there is nothing to say. I cannot tell you -- "
>
> "No," I said. "There's nothing to say."

Interwar America, as depicted in Grant DeVolson Wood, *American Gothic*, 1930
[Friends of American Art Collection, Art Institute of Chicago]

"Good-night," he said. "I cannot take you to your hotel?"

"No, thank you."

"It was the only thing to do," he said. "The operation proved -- "

"I do not want to talk about it," I said.

"I would like to take you to your hotel."

"No, thank you."

He went down the hall. I went to the door of the room.

"You can't come in now," one of the nurses said.

"Yes I can," I said.

"You can't come in yet."

"You get out," I said. "The other one too."

But after I had got them out and shut the door and turned off the light it wasn't any good. It was like saying good-by to a statue. After a while I went out and left the hospital and walked back to the hotel in the rain.

This final page is regarded by some as the epitome of good writing, as it so perfectly captures the grief of a man.

Meanwhile America retreated into isolationism. In his masterwork, *American Gothic* (1930), Grant DeVolson Wood captured the mood of this period. The stern father-figure holds out his fork as if to ward off strangers; behind them is their house, whose interior cannot be seen through the curtains. Wood's subjects are a dentist and his sister who represent the conservative caution of Americans in this period.

F. Scott Fitzgerald's *The Great Gatsby* uses a powerful allegory to make a similar point. Gatsby had been born on the frontier to humble parents in 1890, just as the frontier was closing [Unit 20]. By 1922 he had returned from the Great War, during which America had sought to support the Allied cause. The conservative Europeans saw him as a gauche upstart, and he was brought down by their guile. This novel mirrors the anxieties

Italy deals with its 'mutilated victory':
A Great War memorial in Tuscany [Robert Pascoe]

Americans of the 'lost generation' felt about their society, scorned as second-rate by the Europeans. Only the eye of God, represented by the optician's billboard, knew the truth.

In Australia, many veterans moved to the Right in politics. 'Further Right than Tommy White' became a catchphrase to describe Tommy White. White became a POW of the Ottomans, and returned to Australia to write his best-seller, *Guests of the Unspeakable*, which justified his right-wing politics. White served as a Minister in two conservative governments, and almost became Prime Minister.

Europe suffered a failure in democracy. Europe was now to face a century of decline, with two world wars and the Great Depression.[64] The crisis began with the Paris Peace Conference of 1919 (Treaty of Versailles). The Allies (France, Britain, British Empire, Japan, Italy, first Russia, later USA) declared themselves as victors over Germany, Austria-Hungary, Bulgaria and the Ottoman Empire. The Austro-Hungarian Empire collapsed, leading to the creation of Czechoslovakia, Austria, Hungary and the Kingdom of Serbs, Croats and Slovenes.

The Paris Peace Conference had important outcomes. The fear of Bolshevism led to the new states of Estonia, Latvia and Lithuania being detached from the newly Communist Russia. (Russia was not invited to Paris). Poland, Finland and Irish Free State were formed as new states. Romania grew in size. Germany was allowed to keep most of its territory, due to a fear of Bolshevism spreading (but was punished in other ways). Many minorities were not able to achieve nationhood (such as the Macedonians, Armenians, Basques, and Catalans). The world's political systems became more sophisticated in an attempt to respond to these demands. There were new international institutions created (notably the League of Nations), women were granted the franchise in many jurisdictions, and mass political parties became the norm. In the history of ideas the 1914–1945 era saw remarkable new ideas and theories, such as the Frankfurt School, Bauhaus, and the Garden City movement. The process of decolonisation was set in train, so the irony was that a pair of world wars brought about by rival imperial powers contributed to the end of those very empires.

As for Marxism, the success of the Bolsheviks in the Russian Revolution had proved that societies which were more feudal were ripe grounds for state-directed collectivism. But in those societies which had more advanced democratic capitalist institutions, such as Germany and

---

64 Juan L. Linz, and Alfred Stepan, *The Breakdown of Democratic Regimes*, Johns Hopkins University Press, Baltimore MD, 1978; Charles S. Maier, *Recasting Bourgeois Europe*, Princeton University Press, Princeton NJ, 1975; Karl J. Newman, *European Democracy between the Wars*, tr. Kenneth Morgan, George Allen & Unwin, London, 1970.

Britain, Marxism became allied with the union movement and radical social movements to become 'social democracy' or 'Labourism'. In this form it moved further and further away from the kind of Communism which developed in Soviet Russia. Marxism, once divided in this way, lost political ground in both contexts. In Russia, the Stalinists concentrated more and power in the apparatus of government, while in the capitalist jurisdictions the Labour Parties began to define themselves as opposed to both Communism and political conservatism.

In two European societies that did not fit the communist or capitalist model neatly – Italy and Germany – a new model of political movement emerged. This was Fascism, invented in Italy and then transformed in Germany into National Socialism.

The rise of Fascism in Italy was the work of Benito Mussolini. Mussolini, it is important to recall, was originally a socialist. Like other famous Italian leaders to the present day, he was also a journalist with excellent propaganda skills and a capacity to organise. Like Germany, Italy had been humiliated by the Great War. Although on the winning side of the conflict, it was a 'mutilated victory', with little to show for the win. The Italian Government was in disarray and a revolutionary moment existed. The Red riots throughout the War continued after 1918, leading to pitched battles in the streets, with Bologna and Milan being the main points of conflict. Mussolini took the Fascist message into the hills of central Italy. His new Fascist Party won no seats in the Parliament in 1919, but 35 in 1921. He was the first Italian leader to identify a genuinely national class on which to build a political movement. The social classes of the North included the bourgeoisie, the petit-bourgeoisie, and the proletariat. The classes of the South were the aristocracy, the wealthier peasants, and the poorer peasants. By speaking to the interests of the northern petit-bourgeoisie and the 'grandi contadini', he was able to forge a new national social class where previously none had existed. This alliance of northern and southern interests gave him a firm political basis.

The elite turned to Mussolini for help in defeating the Communists;

he staged the March on Rome in 1922 to take over as prime minister, at the invitation of the king. This was the last time he made the mistake of wearing a top hat and tails in public life.

The defeat of the Italian Left followed soon after. In the streets, Blackshirts continued to battle with Left-leaning Italians, especially in Tuscany and Emilia-Romagna. By these means of physical violence Mussolini was able to assume power by 1926. The anti-fascists were sent to island prison camps; the most famous prisoner was Antonio Gramsci, a celebrated Marxist. A command economy developed under Mussolini. Mussolini did not fundamentally change Italy; rather, he gave it a sense of regularity and order. For example, he required all motorists to drive on the right, and he built the world's first motorways, the 'autostrate'.[65] With his domestic reform stalled by the mid-1930s, Mussolini turned to foreign adventurism. In 1935–36 the Italians invaded Ethiopia, and in 1939 Albania, as part of Mussolini's dream to own 'mare nostrum', 'our sea', the Mediterranean.

Within this defeat of the Left, there was a clear lesson. Marxism clearly failed to prevail on the streets of the post-war Italian cities. However, Gramsci gave Marxism a new understanding of how the ruling class actually ruled, an understanding that has been important in subsequent neo-Marxist analyses. Gramsci's adaption of Marxism turned its economic base on its head. Antonio Gramsci's *Prison Notebooks* were not fully translated into English until 1971, and they came as a shock, as they affirmed much of what the New Left was then thinking. He argued that the modern ruling class uses 'egemonia' (hegemony) as well as 'dominio' (command). This argument called for a modification of the old base-determines-superstructure model. Marxism had to take account of the ways in which the ruling class wins consent for its rule. Mussolini's sophisticated use of radio and other mass media helped explain his rule.

---

65 Before Mussolini the 'contadini' drove on the left side of the road, the 'cittadini' on the right. The first 'autostrata' was built between Milan and Varese in 1924–26 by Piero Puricelli.

Intellectuals, said Gramsci, must become 'organic' to the working class if they want a revolution.

Soon after the success of Fascism in Italy, Wall Street collapsed. The Great Depression of the early 1930s was a turning point of the twentieth century. It began in 1926, with a fall in commodity prices, sending ripple effects around the world. World trade sank to 35 per cent of its 1929 levels. In the capitalist economies there were no safeguards to prevent unemployment, which reached its peak in 1932. In the command economies this was not a problem. Some historians now argue that the Second World War had a basic economic cause – industrial Germany needed the raw materials produced by Eastern Europe.

But to understand the ascent of Hitler and National Socialism we need to go back to 1919. Germany was the loser in the Great War. It suffered harsh peace terms at Versailles, in keeping with the ideas of the time. It lost all its colonies across the world (the very empire it had gone to war to develop), and also considerable territory at home. Its western border was demilitarised and it was forced to reduce the size of its armed forces. Germany also faced crippling 'reparations' (financial

50 million Marks, worthless money in Weimar Germany [Marita Grafe-tshur]

compensation) to the Allies for the material cost of the war. The result of these penalties was runaway inflation by 1923. German money became almost worthless. Not surprisingly, the new German State (the Weimar Republic) could not function properly. The German polity was beset by splintered parties, which constantly recombined as governments rose and fell. The Nazis (on the extreme Right) and the Communists (extreme Left) both had their own private armies.

The Nazi takeover began with them winning only three per cent of the vote in 1928, but 37 by 1932. In his campaigning, Hitler denounced the Treaty of Versailles, the Jews, the Communists, and the existing government for their incompetence. The German Right began to think Hitler could be of use to them. President Paul von Hindenburg appointed him Chancellor in 1933, and a coalition government comprising nine conservatives and three Nazis was formed. Within a few months the parliamentary building (the Reichstag) had been burnt down (justifying the rounding up of Communists), freedom of opinion was abolished, and legal protections against wrongful arrest were removed. Another election, this time staged, was held, and in July 1933 all other political parties were dissolved. The Third Reich was proclaimed. Many of Hitler's opponents and more socialistic followers were purged when he destroyed his paramilitary 'Sturmabteilung' (SA) in mid-1934. On 2 August 1934 Hindenburg died and Hitler was proclaimed Führer (leader, guide).

Nazi ideology was central to the Third Reich. Hitler was the source of all authority. It was he as Führer who interpreted the national will. Hitler aimed to reconstruct German society – to wipe out class and religious divisions and to replace them with a heightened national consciousness. As a 'master race', Germans were entitled to more land. Hitler used propaganda, processions and rallies to great effect, following the lead of the mass political tactics pioneered by Mussolini. As early as March 1935 (more than a decade before America), the Germans were making regular television broadcasts into public halls and the homes of elite

Nazis.[66] In 1935 the Jews were deprived of German citizenship, and on 9-10 November 1938 a night of State-sanctioned violence, 'Crystal night' ('kristallnacht') was directed at Jewish businesses and synagogues. The 'Final Solution', with at least six million Jews slaughtered in camps, began in 1942.

Hitler's relationship with the Jews was infamous. It is not even clear where Hitler's anti-semitism came from. In *Mein Kampf* he said he was offended by the sight of Orthodox Jews when he moved to Vienna at the age of 14 in 1903. No doubt Viennese Jews challenged everyday assumptions of German superiority. One theory has Hitler's experience of gas warfare on the Western Front as inspiring the gas chambers. It is possible that it was not until 1941 that he thought of the 'Final Solution' – after all, Jews were valuable in the German military even under the Third Reich, and many had served with distinction in the Great War.

The Holocaust reverberates in people's lives to this very day. The Melbourne artist and Holocaust survivor, Felix Tuszynski, like many others, still has nightmares of this experience.

The lead-up to the Second World War really began in 1936, when Hitler moved troops into the demilitarised Rhineland, to test the Allied will. Emboldened by this, in 1938 Hitler moved German forces into Austria, which then became part of the Reich. As Austria was German-speaking, this 'Anschluss' was reluctantly accepted by Britain and France. Later that same year the Germans put the squeeze on Czechoslovakia, with its German minority in Sudetenland. This crisis was resolved by Britain and France giving way (the 'appeasement') at Munich. In early 1939 Hitler broke this agreement, and occupied most of Czechoslovakia. Then Hitler signed a non-aggression pact with Russia – which meant he could invade Poland, and he did so. This event triggered the Second World War.

---

66 Michael Kloft, dir., *Television under the Swastika*, DVD, 52 min., colour & b/w, 1999.

The Spanish Civil War

Meanwhile, in Spain, a third right-wing dictator, Franco, came to power. The Spanish Civil War proved to be the only twentieth-century conflict in which all the major groups met. Spain had stayed out of the Great War, but became embroiled in Morocco, where its army lost 12,000 soldiers to Rif bedouin. In Madrid the army seized power under General Prima de Rivera (1923–1930). A republic was then formed, but it failed to deal with the nation's problems, including the Basque and Catalan separatists, and the anti-clerical anarchists and socialists. General Francisco Franco began the uprising in Spanish Morocco. Seville fell on the first day, but in Granada the Republicans resisted. As many as 25,000 people died in the area around the Alhambra. The war officially lasted three years, with foreign interventions on both sides (1936–1939). Later more famous for *1984* and *Animal Farm*, George Orwell (the pen-name of Eric Arthur Blair) wrote his *Homage to Catalonia* (1938) based on these experiences. The Germans were decisive in Franco winning the war, hoping he would side with them. But Franco wisely decided to keep out of the Second World War, and his regime survived until 1982 (he had died in 1975). This kind of survival could have been Mussolini's fate too, had Italy also remained neutral.

The Second World War

In many ways the Second World War grew logically out of the Great War. Versailles was an imperfect settlement. The antagonists were divided along economic lines at first: command economies versus capitalist economies, at least until Hitler invaded Russia. Many of their differences could not be settled using diplomatic or economic means.

There is no doubt that Hitler was an accomplished military commander.[67] Hitler had a major fault as a military leader, in that he was bored with logistics and the problems of bringing up supplies. He also understood the use of army and air force power far better than he

---

67 Rupert Matthews, *Hitler, Military Commander*, Arcturus, London, 2003.

understood the navy. His genius was in coordinated attacks involving sudden concentrations of firepower, including his use of paratroopers. September 1939 was his biggest triumph, with his invasion of Poland. In 1940 Hitler overran Denmark, Norway, and then France. In September 1940, Hitler lost the Battle of Britain (the air war against the British).

Operation Barbarossa was launched on 22 June 1941, and this became the most important date in the twentieth century, as the Anglo-American alliance could not have defeated Hitler's Germany without the Soviet Union.[68] In this conflict, 'Everything depended on two men... On 22 June 1941 Hitler wanted a war with Russia, no matter what... At the same time Stalin did not want a war with Germany, he did not want to fight Hitler...'[69]

Why did Germany and the Soviet Union agree on the Treaty of 1939? Stalin and Hitler were not hostile to each other, but can we really reduce historical explanation to the operations of powerful men? We can concede there is always a politics, even in a dictatorship, such as Hitler's relationship with his generals, and his early successes improved his position with them. The German military had a proud tradition that went back to the Prussians, and Hitler, as an outsider, earned their grudging respect.

This can be seen in Hitler's key directives, during 1940 and 1941, as the military commander. On 31 July 1940 he ordered that preparation for war with the Soviet Union commence. On 18 December 1940 Hitler ordered detailed plans, and then on 21 June 1941 the 'Dortmund' command was issued. Operation Barbarossa was part of Hitler's strategic thinking in early 1941. Hitler presented himself to the world as a bulwark against Communism. He wanted the Treaty to deter the British from going to war against him. He told his generals the eventual war against the Soviet Union was to be 'a war of annihilation', different from other

---

68 John Lukacs, *June 1941: Hitler and Stalin*, Yale University Press, New Haven CT, 2006, p. 2.
69 Lukacs, *June 1941*, p. 4.

wars, not merely a grab of territory. Unfortunately, the war in the Balkans delayed Barbarossa by five weeks; Hitler decided against a Middle East incursion. Hitler's obsession with the Eastern Front and letting the British survive can be explained by seeing Eastern and Southern Europe as part of the new German order, one that would compete with Britain and America. Germany would create an Empire equivalent to the British, but one based in Eastern Europe – and possibly stretching to Africa and the Middle East. He was not interested in a unified Europe – rather, a Greater Germany. He assumed Germany could manage an Empire just as the British had done – but without the same experience. Hitler failed to understand that empires require an accommodation with the natives. Because German imperialism was based on extreme nationalism, that was never understood. Nazis had a pathological love of violence – this violence was exercised against any resistance.

Hitler's military tactics were as sophisticated as his strategic thinking. Hitler was a master of the 'blitzkrieg', the coordinated incursion of army and air force power into a single area, successful in 1938, 1939, and 1940. The British could not be defeated by German naval forces led by Hitler, making the focus on the Eastern Front more logical in 1941. However, Barbarossa violated Hitler's doctrine of a single attack – here there were three – which he justified as denying the Russians space in which to regroup. But this meant that the Germans were forced to cut supplies to their troops and hope for a quick win.

Hitler put a lot of effort into thinking about Eastern Europe as a theatre of war in 1941. He interviewed Great War veterans about the Pripet marshes, and determined that in the summer they could be used, at least by his infantry, thus denying them to Russian partisan forces.

Meanwhile Stalin was also engaged in strategic thinking. He wanted to keep out of another European war and allow the capitalist nations to weaken themselves. So he resisted suggestions from Churchill that the Soviet Union join an alliance against Hitler. Stalin understood that Marx was wrong to assume nations would disappear. Stalin decided to build up

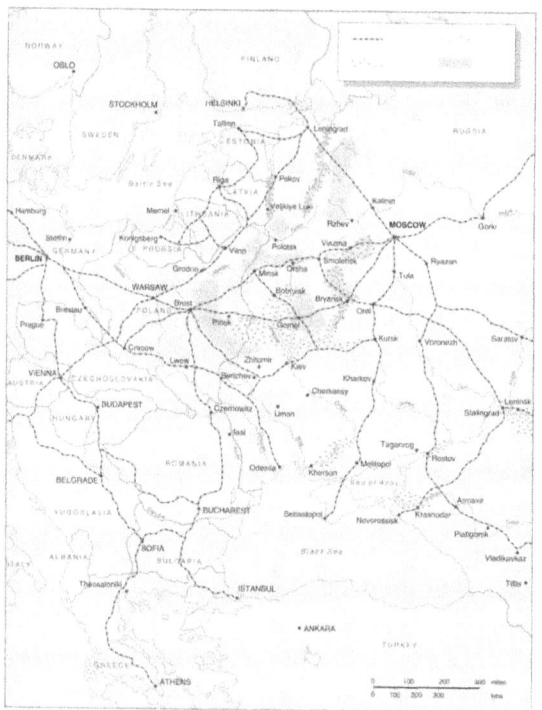

Hitler's Eastern Front in 1941, with the Pripet Marshes in the centre of what would become Operation Barbarossa

a powerful communist State as a countervailing force to what he foresaw would be belligerent nations opposed to the Soviet Union. Stalin ignored the information warning him of an imminent German invasion.

The German people admired the statecraft in Hitler's decision to invade the Soviet Union. Stalin was personally shattered and went into hiding for days, offering his resignation.

So the battle began. Hitler put 17 Panzer divisions in the field, deployed against the very successful Soviet T-34 tanks. As usual, he was careless about supply lines. These Panzers were intended to race into the Soviet Union and outflank the enemy troops from the rear.

Hitler took a direct interest in Germany's military strategies

The worst result of the German invasion, however, was the mass murder of Jewish people.[70] It is also significant that German military brutality toward the Russian people convinced them that Stalin's regime was less ruthless than Hitler's would be.[71]

Later in 1941 the US entered the War and helped defeat the German submarines in the Atlantic. In October 1942, The British won at El Alamein (with Australian help) and by May 1943 the German and Italian troops in North Africa were defeated. In 1943 the Anglo-American invasion of Italy led to the fall of Mussolini, and the creation of a

---

70 Lukacs, *June 1941*, p. 133-34.
71 Geoffrey Megargee, *Barbarossa 1941: Hitler's War of Annihilation*, Tempus, Stroud UK, 2007 [2006].

modern, unified Italy. They landed on the southern coast of Sicily, at Gela.[72] Popular tradition has it that the American troops were assisted in their rapid conquest of the island by the American mafia.[73]

In January 1943 the Russians won at Stalingrad, on the Volga, south of Moscow. In June 1944 the Anglo-American forces made their landings at Normandy. On 20 July 1944 the von Stauffenberg Plot failed.[74] During December 1944, an attempted German break-out at Ardennes was blocked. On 30 April 1945 Hitler committed suicide in his Berlin bunker. The European war was over.

The Pacific War

The Second World War occupied a second theatre, that of the Pacific. Here the morality of war, always abysmal, sank to new depths. The Japanese occupation of Nanking had been brutal, and this event set the tone for this theatre of the war. The Japanese conquest of East Asia was stunning in both its speed and its brutality. The Japanese soldiers had the benefit of 'comfort women', a euphemism for Korean women used as prostitutes, servicing an impossible number of Japanese men each day. Japanese soldiers were later given permission to cannibalise Australian troops in New Guinea.

In truth, the Japanese lacked the capacity to invade Australia, but prime minister John Curtin talked of their aggression as a prelude to an invasion of Australia. The Japanese briefly considered an invasion of the Soviet Union from the East, but Australia was beyond their military reach. Anti-Communism in the United States made it difficult for President Roosevelt to support the Soviet Union, but the war with Japan was a different prospect altogether.

Turning back the Japanese was a high priority for the Allies. Australian

---

72 This was the beach Leonardo Sciascia chose for his humorous story of Sicilian boat people in the 1950s, 'Il lungo viaggio'.
73 Peter Robb, *Midnight in Sicily*, Duffy & Snellgrove, Sydney, 1996, pp. 52-56.
74 This event is well described in the movie, *Valkyrie*, (Bryan Singer, dir. 2008).

troops were withdrawn from the Middle East by Curtin, against Churchill's wishes, and re-deployed in New Guinea. The Americans pushed northwards to Japan, with Australian troops left to mop up the nearby islands. The Pacific War continued into the later months of 1945 after the European War was won. The Pacific War saw several important military innovations, such as the perfection of the amphibious assault by American troops, and the use of the ultimate weapon at Hiroshima and Nagasaki.

The Pacific War ended later in 1945, with the American use of atomic and hydrogen bombs on Nagasaki and Hiroshima. This is still highly controversial, to this day the only use of nuclear weapons in human history. It was perhaps justified by the American leadership as a warning to the USSR in advance of the Cold War that seemed inevitable.

The Second World War raises important historical and ethical questions.[75] Was appeasement the right policy for Great Britain and other Western powers to follow in the 1930s? Could the Vatican have been more effective in opposing the policies of the Nazi State? Was the German population a willing supporter of the Nazi regime? Was the fall of France in 1940 inevitable? Was Churchill really the great war leader that the British imagine? Were German forces in the East inevitably going to fail? Was Joseph Stalin a great war leader? Can the segregationist policies of the US armed forces during the Second World War be justified on the grounds that integration would have impeded the war effort? Was the Allied bombing of enemy cities such as Dresden, Hamburg, and Tokyo necessary? Was the atomic bombing of Hiroshima and Nagasaki justified? And, did the British and the French understand that the Second World War was the beginning of the end for their respective empires?

There were some important lessons to be drawn from the Second World War. One was the loss of confidence in the European empires, including notions of British superiority. The United States entered the war in 1941 innocent of what might happen. The US Jeep was seen as

---

75 Denis Showalter, *History in Dispute*, St James Press, Detroit, vols 4 and 5, 2000.

the New World alternative to the Panzer. In 1939 the US had only the eighth largest army in the world: now, after 1945, it was the 'superpower' facing the USSR in the Cold War.

The Second World War intensified the pessimism of the intellectuals. In October 1945 Jean-Paul Sartre returned to his native city and gave an important speech on existentialism, entitled 'Paris in Year Zero'. He famously argued that 'man was condemned to be free'. He turned Rousseau's dictum on its head. We were free, if only we knew it. Yet most people, he said, live in 'bad faith', and freedom could only be found by leading the authentic life. His message struck a chord. A generation of intellectuals around Sartre remained fiercely anti-American and, until May 1968, defended the Soviet Union, arguing that Stalinism was at least honest in its use of atrocious violence. American troops stationed in post-war France were surprised by the hostility of a population they had done so much to liberate.

The Frankfurt School

In the meantime, the carnage of the twentieth century inspired German intellectuals to ask how we might marry Freud's insights with those of Marx? This is the essence of the Frankfurt School. The Frankfurt School for Social Research was affiliated with the University of Frankfurt and was private funded. When Max Horkheimer took the directorship in 1930 he argued that their research mandate was to develop a critical theory of society rather than a descriptive sociology – to use the latest findings of all social sciences, with an emancipatory intent. Their key research question was, 'Why didn't the German working class follow the Marxist lead?' By yoking Freud to Marx, the Frankfurt School showed that regimes such as Nazism controlled not only the economic base of society but, more fundamentally, people's internal lives. Now the State had taken over the instrumental rationality of the economic. Since the beginning of the Enlightenment, Reason had become too dominant – the calculable was all that was valued. Capitalism had colonised the cultural industry.

A key member of the Frankfurt School was Walter Benjamin (pronounced Valter Ben-yamin). Benjamin described the effect of the Great War in these words: 'Men returned... grown silent – not richer, but poorer in communicable experience... A generation that had gone to school on a horse-drawn streetcar now stood under the open sky in a countryside in which nothing remained unchanged but the clouds,

Frantz Fanon

and beneath these clouds, in a field of force of destructive torrents and explosions, was the tiny, fragile human body.'

The Frankfurt School was to prove a force in post-war America, since its leaders were admitted as refugee intellectuals. The experience of Frankfurt School émigrés in America underlined their attitudes to totalitarian society. Herbert Marcuse came to see American society as worse than Nazi Germany. Here he developed his notion of 'repressive tolerance' – for example, sexual permissiveness within a society that has a large porno industry. The Frankfurt School became a link with the New Left that emerged in post-1962 America. Marcuse became the darling of the American New Left.

Postcolonialism

The end of empire released new social theories on the colonial experience. Frantz Fanon, a French-Caribbean intellectual, wrote *Black Skin, White Masks* (1952) as a doctoral thesis at Lyon, followed by *The Wretched of the Earth* (1961). Postcolonialism had an optimism not evident in other forms of Marxism. The Palestinian-American Edward Said rejected the 'Orientalism' (1978) through which the Middle East had been understood. The Indian Gayatri Chakravorty Spivak developed the concept of the 'subaltern' position. Harvard's Homi K. Bhabha praised hybridity as a modern identity. As a product of imperial failure and implosion, postcolonialism proved in many ways to be a more positive project than neo-Marxism.

Primary sources:

Anne Frank, *The Diary of a Young Girl*, and Charlotte Delbo, *Auschwitz and After*

Anne Frank, *The Diary of a Young Girl*

[tr. B.M. Mooyard-Doubleday. Some of these extracts and commentaries are adapted from the website www.annefrank.org, accessed 8 January 2009]

Sunday, 14 June, 1942

On Friday, June 12th, I woke up at six o'clock and no wonder; it was my birthday. But of course I was not allowed to get up at that hour, so I had to control my curiosity until a quarter to seven. Then I could bear it no longer, and went to the dining room, where I received a warm welcome from Moortje (the cat).

Anne Frank (second from left) playing with friends in Amsterdam [www.annefrank.org]

Soon after seven I went to Mummy and Daddy and then to the sitting room to undo my presents. The first to greet me was *you*, possibly the nicest of all [this diary]. Then on the table there were a bunch of roses, a plant, and some peonies, and more arrived during the day.

I got masses of things from Mummy and Daddy, and was thoroughly spoiled by various friends. Among other things I was given *Camera Obscura*, a party game, lots of sweets, chocolates, a puzzle, a brooch, *Tales and Legends of the Netherlands* by Joseph Cohen, *Daisy's Mountain Holiday* (a terrific book), and some money. Now I can buy *The Myths of Greece and Rome*–grand!

Then Lies called for me and we went to school. During recess I treated everyone to sweet biscuits, and then we had to go back to our lessons.

Now I must stop. Bye-bye, we're going to be great pals!

Saturday, 20 June, 1942

I haven't written for a few days, because I wanted first of all to think about my diary. It's an odd idea for someone like me to keep a diary; not only because I have never done so before, but because it seems to me

Anne Frank received this diary as a gift for her 13th birthday [www.annefrank.org]

Loose sheets making up Anne Frank's revised diary [www.annefrank.org]

that neither I – nor for that matter anyone else – will be interested in the unbosomings of a thirteen-year-old schoolgirl. Still, what does that matter? I want to write, but more than that, I want to bring out all kinds of things that lie buried deep in my heart.

...I don't want to set down a series of bald facts in a diary like most people do, but I want this diary itself to be my friend, and I shall call my friend Kitty...

My father [Otto] was thirty-six when he married my mother [Edith], who was then twenty-five. My sister Margot was born in 1926 in Frankfort-on-Main, I followed on June 12, 1929, and, as we are Jewish, we emigrated to Holland in 1933...

The rest of our family, however, felt the full impact of Hitler's anti-Jewish laws, so life was filled with anxiety. In 1938 after the pogroms, my two uncles (my mother's brothers) escaped to the U.S.A. My old grandmother came to us, she was then seventy-three. After May 1940 good times rapidly fled: first the war, then the capitulation, followed by the arrival of the Germans, which is when the sufferings of us Jews really began. Anti-Jewish decrees followed each other in quick succession. Jews must wear a yellow star, Jews must hand in their bicycles, Jews are banned from trams and are forbidden to drive. Jews are only allowed to do their shopping between three and five o'clock and then only in shops which bear the placard 'Jewish shop'. Jews must be indoors by eight o'clock and cannot even sit in their own gardens after that hour. Jews are forbidden to visit theatres, cinemas, and other places of entertainment. Jews may not take part in public sports. Swimming baths, tennis courts, hockey fields, and other sports grounds are all prohibited to them. Jews may not visit Christians. Jews must go to Jewish schools, and many more restrictions of a similar kind.

So we could not do this and were forbidden to do that. But life went on in spite of it all. Jopie used to say to me, 'You're scared to do anything, because it may be forbidden.' Our freedom was strictly limited. Yet things were still bearable....

Sunday morning, 5 July, 1942

Dear Kitty,

Our examination results were announced in the Jewish Theatre last Friday. I couldn't have hoped for better... When we walked across our little square together a few days ago, Daddy began to talk of us going into hiding...

...Yours, Anne

Wednesday, 8 July, 1942

Dear Kitty,

Years seem to have passed between Sunday and now. So much has happened, it is just as if the whole world had turned upside down. But I am still alive, Kitty, and that is the main thing, Daddy says.

Yes, I'm still alive, indeed, but don't ask where or how. You wouldn't understand a word, so I will begin by telling you what happened on Sunday afternoon.

At three o'clock (Harry had just gone, but was coming back later) someone rang the front doorbell. I was lying lazily reading a book on the veranda in the sunshine, so I didn't hear it. A bit later, Margot appeared at

Anne Frank, May 1942 [www.annefrank.org]

the kitchen door looking very excited. 'The S.S. have sent a call-up notice for Daddy', she whispered...

I was more frightened than ever and began to cry...

... Into hiding–where would we go, in a town or the country, in a house or a cottage, when, how, where...?

These were questions I was not allowed to ask, but I couldn't get them out of my mind. Margot and I began to pack some of our most vital belongings into a school satchel. The first thing I put in was this diary, then hair curlers, handkerchiefs, schoolbooks, a comb, old letters; I put in the craziest things with the idea that we were going into hiding. But I'm not sorry, memories mean more to me than dresses.

...I fell asleep immediately and didn't wake up until Mummy called me at five-thirty the next morning. Luckily it was not so hot as Sunday; warm rain fell steadily all day. We put on heaps of clothes as if we were going to the North Pole, the sole reason being to take clothes with us.

No Jew in our situation would have dreamed of going out with a suitcase full of clothing...

...Moortje, my little cat, was the only creature to whom I said farewell....

...Continued tomorrow.

Yours, Anne

Thursday, 9 July, 1942

Dear Kitty,

So we walked in the pouring rain, Daddy, Mummy, and I, each with a school satchel and shopping bag filled to the brim with all kinds of things thrown together anyhow.

We got sympathetic looks from people on their way to work. You could see by their faces how sorry they were they couldn't offer us a lift; the gaudy yellow star spoke for itself....

...The hiding place itself would be in the building where daddy has his office...

I will describe the building: there is a large warehouse on the ground floor which is used as a store.... A wooden staircase leads form the downstairs passage o the next floor... The right-hand door leads to our 'Secret Annexe'. No one would ever guess that there would be so many rooms hidden behind that plain grey door. There's a little step in front of the door and then you are inside.

There is a steep staircase immediately opposite the entrance. On the left a tiny passage brings you into a room which was to become the Frank family's bed-sitting-room, next door a smaller room, study and bedroom for the two young ladies of the family. On the right a little room without windows containing the washbasin and a small W.C. compartment, with another door leading to Margot's and my room. If you go up the next flight of stairs and open the door, you are simply amazed that there could be such a big light room in such an old house by the canal....

...Yours, Anne

Saturday, 11 July, 1942

Dear Kitty,

Daddy, Mummy, and Margot can't get used to the sound of the Westertoren clock yet, which tells us the time every quarter of an hour. I can. I loved it from the start, and especially in the night it's like a faithful friend. I expect you will be interested to hear what it feels like to 'disappear'; well, all I can say is that I don't know myself yet...

...Yours, Anne

Sunday, 27 September, 1942

Dear Kitty,

Just had a big bust-up with Mummy for the umpteenth time; we simply don't get on together these days and Margot and I don't hit it off any too well either...

Mrs Van Dann had another tantrum. She is terribly moody. She keeps hiding more of her private belongings. Mummy ought to answer each Van Daan 'disappearance' with a Frank 'disappearance'. How some people do adore bringing up other people's children in addition to their own...

...Yours, Anne

Monday, 28 September, 1942

... Anyhow, I've learned one thing now. You only really get to know people when you've had a jolly good row with them. Then and only then can you judge their true characters!

Yours, Anne

Friday, 9 October, 1942

Dear Kitty

I've only got dismal and depressing news for you today. Our many Jewish friends are being taken away by the dozen. These people are treated by the Gestapo without a shred of decency, being loaded into cattle trucks and sent to Westerbork, the big Jewish camp in Drente. Westerbork sounds terrible: only one washing cubicle for a hundred people and not nearly enough lavatories. There is no separate accommodation. Men, women, and children all sleep together. One hears of frightful immorality because of this; and a lot of the women, and even girls, who stay there any length of time are expecting babies.

It is impossible to escape; most of the people in the camp are branded as inmates by their shaven heads and many also by their Jewish appearance.

If it is as bad as this in Holland whatever will it be like in the distant and barbarous regions they are sent to? We assume that most of them are murdered. The English radio speaks of their being gassed.

Perhaps that is the quickest way to die…

… Nice people, the Germans! To think that I was once one of them too! No, Hitler took away our nationality long ago. In fact, Germans and Jews are the greatest enemies in the world.

Yours, Anne

Thursday, 29 October, 1942

Dear Kitty

…Following Daddy's good example, Mother has pressed her prayer book into my hand. For decency's sake I read some of the prayers in German; they are certainly beautiful but they don't convey much to me. Why does she force me to be pious, just to oblige her?

Wednesday, 13 January, 1943

Dear Kitty,

Everything has upset me again this morning, so I wasn't able to finish a single thing properly.

It is terrible outside. Day and night more of those poor miserable people are being dragged off, with nothing but a rucksack and a little money. On the way they are deprived even of these possessions. Families are torn apart, the men, women, and children all being separated. Children coming home from school find that their parents have disappeared. Women return from shopping to find their homes shut up and their families gone...

And, as for us, we are fortunate. Yes, we are luckier than millions of people. It is quiet and safe here, and we are, so to speak, living on capital...

Yours, Anne

Tuesday, 10 August, 1943

Dear Kitty

...When I jump out of bed in the morning, ... I go to the window, take down the blackout, sniff at the crack of the window until I feel a bit of fresh air, and I'm awake.... Do you know what Mummy calls this sort of thing? 'The art of living'–that's an odd expression...

Yours, Anne

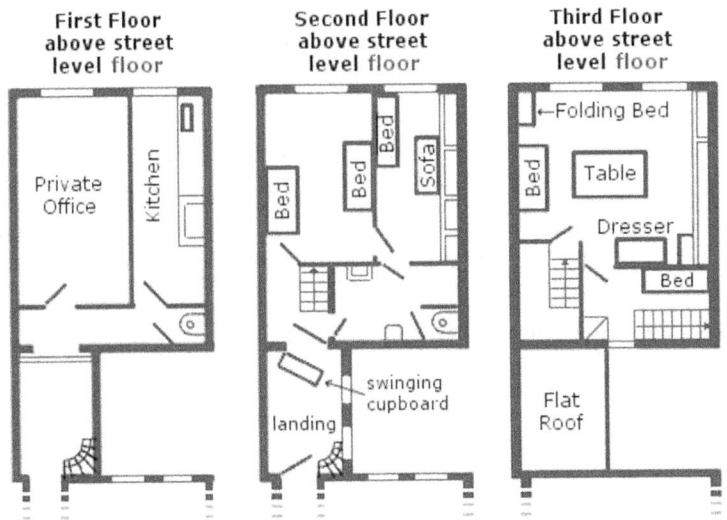

Floor plan of the office building with the Secret Annex where the Frank family hid
[http://www.geocities.com/afdiary/gifs/annexe_floorplan.gif]

Sunday, 27 February, 1944

Dearest Kitty

From early in the morning till late at night, I really do hardly anything else but think of Peter. I sleep with his image before my eyes, dream about him and he is still looking at me when I awake....

But how and when will we finally reach each other? I don't know quite how long my common sense will keep this longing under control.

Yours, Anne

Monday, 20 March, 1944

Dear Kitty,

...a little shadow has fallen on my happiness. I've thought for a long time that Margot liked Peter quite a lot too. How much she loves him I don't know, but I think it's wretched. It must cause her terrible pain each time I'm with Peter, and the funny part of it is that she hardly shows it....

[Margot then wrote Anne a letter about this situation, which Anne shared with her diary, as well as her reply and Margot's rejoinder.]

[On 28 March 1944, the people in hiding heard a special Dutch news report broadcast from London, on *Radio Oranje* (Radio Orange). Dutch Cabinet Minister Gerrit Bolkestein announced that diaries and other important documents would be gathered when the war ended, as a record of what happened to the Dutch people during the Second World War, to be preserved for future generations. The people immediately thought of Anne's diary.]

Tuesday, 4 April, 1944

Dear Kitty

For a long time I haven't had any idea of what I was working for any more; the end of the war is so terribly far away, so unreal, like a fairy tale...

I must work [at study], so as not to be a fool, to get on, to become a journalist, because that's what I want! I know that I can write, a couple of my stories are good, my descriptions of the 'Secret Annexe' are humorous, there's a lot in my diary that speaks, but–whether I have real talent remains to be seen....

I want to get on; I can't imagine that I would to have lead the same sort of life as Mummy and Mrs Van Daan and all the women who do their work and are then forgotten....

[Anne Frank began the serious work on her book around 20 May 1944. She revised the major portion of her original diary in the short time left until the arrest of the people in hiding on 4 August 1944. Working on loose sheets of coloured paper, she frequently made simple corrections in the text. Sometimes she deleted entire passages because she thought these were too personal. She still addressed all the letters in her diary to Kitty, her imaginary friend. The last diary entry that Anne had a chance to rewrite on these loose sheets was dated 29 March 1944.]

[On Friday, 4 August 1944, a day like any other day, an *SS*-officer and three Dutch policemen entered the building and demanded to be escorted to the Secret Annex. The people in hiding were betrayed. They were taken to Westerbork and then to Auschwitz. There the men were separated from the women. Edith, Margot and Anne ended up in the women's camp Auschwitz-Birkenau. There, Bloeme Evers-Emden occasionally spoke to Edith and her daughters, whom she knew from the Jewish high school in Amsterdam. After the war she said about this encounter: 'I talked to them occasionally. They were always together, the three of them, mother and daughters. What you could have possibly interpreted from "The Secret Annex", that there was disharmony between them, was erased by existential necessity. They were always together the three of them and they definitely received a lot of support from each other.' In Auschwitz-Birkenau, Edith became friends with Rosa de Winter. Rosa survived Auschwitz and on the journey home met Otto Frank. She told him that his wife had died. In 1945 Rosa described her remembrances of the camp: 'Constant selections... Edith, someone

I know well, is also with me, she's had to give up her two daughters, 15 and 18 years old. We comfort each other and have become friends, we are preparing ourselves for the worst... Edith and I are always together...'
In her memoirs, Rosa de Winter describes Edith's death: 'Edith falls ill, has a high fever. I want her to go to the Ambulance (hospital). But there is a great fear of being gassed because every week Dr Mengele goes to these barracks for the sick to pick out those women who in his eyes are too emaciated to remain alive. Despite everything, I take Edith there. Her fever is higher than 104°F and she is immediately admitted to the Revier (barracks for the sick)'. This was at the end of November 1944. Shortly afterwards Rosa herself becomes so ill that she also ends up in a Revier. At the beginning of January 1945 the temperature is minus 40°F, and Rosa is still in the barrack. 'One morning new patients arrive. Suddenly, I recognise Edith, she comes from another sick barrack ward. She is but a mere shadow of herself. A few days later she died, totally worn out.' Margot and Anne also died; Otto survived and published his daughter's memoirs, but in an edited form.]

Charlotte Delbo, *Auschwitz and After*

[tr. Rosette C. Lamont, Yale University Press, New Haven CT, 1995]

None of Us Will Return

Today, I am not sure that what I wrote is true.
I am certain it is truthful.

Arrivals, Departures

People arrive. They look through the crowd of those who are waiting, those who await them. They kiss them and say the trip exhausted them.

People leave. They say good-bye to those who are not leaving and hug the children.

There is a street for people who arrive and a street for people who leave.

There is a café called "Arrivals" and a café called "Departures".

There are people who arrive and people who leave.

But there is a station where those who arrive are those who are leaving, a station where those who arrive have never arrived, where those who have left never came back.

It is the largest station in the world.

…They did not know there is no arriving in this station.

They expect the worst – they do not expect the unthinkable.

And when the guards shout to line up five by five, the men on one side, women and children on the other, in a language they do not understand, the truncheon blows convey the message so they line up by fives ready for anything.

…there are married couples who stepped out of the synagogue the bride all in white wrapped in her veil wrinkled from having slept in the floor of the cattle car.

Charlotte Delbo in her best-known pose [http://en.wikipedia.org/wiki/Charlotte_Delbo]

The bridegroom in black wearing a top hat his gloves soiled.

Parents and guests, women holding pearl-embroidered handbags.

All of them regretting they could not have stopped home to change into something less dainty.

The rabbi holds himself straight, heading the line, he has always been a model for the rest.

There are boarding-school girls wearing identical pleated skirts, their hats trailing blue ribbons. They pull up their knee socks carefully as they clamber down, and walk neatly five by five, holding hands, unaware, as though on a regular Thursday school outing. After all, what can they do to boarding-school girls shepherded by their teacher? She tells them, 'Be good, children!' They don't have the slightest desire not to be good.

... A band will be dressed in the girls' pleated skirts. The camp commandant wishes Viennese waltzes to be played every Sunday morning.

A blockhova will cut homey curtains from the holy vestments worn by the rabbi to celebrate the Sabbath no matter what, in whatever place.

A kapo will masquerade by donning the bridegroom's morning coat and top hat, with their girlfriend wrapped in the bride's veil. They'll play 'wedding' all night while the prisoners, dead tired, lie in their bunks. Kapos can have fun since they're not exhausted at the end of the day.

Charlotte Delbo at Auschwitz [http://www.cheminsdememoire.gouv.fr/image/Biographies/DelboAuschwitz.jpg]

Questions for discussion:

The Holocaust matters for many reasons – but possibly most of all because it is the first significant occasion during which memory becomes a negative rather than positive human attribute – we call this the 'memory of trauma', and it is an invention of the twentieth century. For the first time in world history, memory was not a safe haven, but rather a place of chillingly distressful remembrances. And what had been a soldier's disease, affecting at least 5 per cent of veterans, became the ailment of civilians.

Once humankind had experienced the Holocaust, and it had become a widespread memory (after the 1980s), the victims of other traumas since the Second World War found it possible to find the language to talk about the genocides of Indigenous peoples, the Armenian genocide, Stalin's Terror, Pol Pot, Bosnia and Kosovo, and Rwanda.

Delbo's work remains keenly read for her accounts of other people's traumas as well, notably in *Days and Memory* (*La mémoire et les jours*, 1985). Delbo's account of trauma leads us to the proposition that the deceased victims of trauma remain 'undead' – part of her task is to speak on their behalf, and at times her role as an author is subverted by these undead who speak directly to us as readers without her agency. The phrase 'None of Us Will Return' can now be understood. No inmate will be able to go back to life as it was before the camp. Many of them, Delbo included, came to understand they had a moral duty *not* to forget, on behalf of their fellow prisoners who died.

Those who were executed at Auschwitz are technically 'undead', because they were given none of the respect due the dead. The act of 'remembering' must be performed by these 'undead', that is, the people who lost their lives in the trauma. It is a larger story than the Holocaust. For example, the ghostly figures who appear in films like *The Cabinet of Dr Caligari* and other German Expressionist masterpieces of the Weimar period tell us of the trauma of the Great War. Contemporary Hollywood is fixated by those who see dead people, such as the child in *The Sixth Sense*, or Buffy the Vampire Slayer.

Going further:

Paul Fussell, *Wartime: Understanding and Behavior in the Second World War*, Oxford University Press, New York, 1998

Robert Graves, *Goodbye to All That*, Penguin Books, Harmondsworth UK, 1960 [1929]

John Keegan, *The Battle for History: Re-Fighting World War Two*, Pimlico, London, 1997 [1995]

John Keegan, *A History of Warfare*, Pimlico, London, 1994 [1993]

Juan L. Linz and Alfred Stepan, *The Breakdown of Democratic Regimes*, Johns Hopkins University Press, Baltimore MD, 1978

John Lukacs, *June 1941: Hitler and Stalin*, Yale University Press, New Haven CT, 2006

Charles S. Maier, *Recasting Bourgeois Europe*, Princeton University Press, Princeton NJ, 1975

Rupert Matthews, *Hitler, Military Commander*, Arcturus, London, 2003

Nazi concentration camps, as mapped by Jen Rosenberg, 1988
[history1900s.about.com/.../holocaust/blmap.htm]

Evan Mawdsley, *World War II: A New History*, Cambridge University Press, Cambridge UK, 2009

Mark Mazower, *Hitler's Empire: Nazi Rule in Occupied Europe*, Allen Lane, London, 2008

Geoffrey Megargee, *Barbarossa 1941: Hitler's War of Annihilation*, Tempus, Stroud UK, 2007 [2006]

John Mosier, *Cross of Iron: The Rise and Fall of the German War Machine, 1918-1945*, Henry Holt & Co., NY, 2006

Karl J. Newman, *European Democracy between the Wars*, tr. Kenneth Morgan, George Allen & Unwin, London, 1970

Bryan Perrett, *The Taste of Battle: Front Line Action, 1914–1991*, Cassell, London, 2000

Peter Robb, *Midnight in Sicily*, Duffy & Snellgrove, Sydney, 1996

Denis Showalter, *History in Dispute*, St James Press, Detroit, vols 4 and 5, 2000

Peter Watson, *A Terrible Beauty*, Weidenfeld & Nicolson, London, 2000

Unit 22

The Long Boom

> Harry Truman, Doris Day, Red China, Johnnie Ray,
> South Pacific, Walter Winchell, Joe DiMaggio,
> Joe McCarthy, Richard Nixon, Studebaker, television
> North Korea, South Korea, Marilyn Monroe,
> Rosenbergs, H-bomb, Sugar Ray, Panmunjom
> Brando, "The King and I" and "The Catcher in the Rye"
> Eisenhower, vaccine, England's got a new queen,
> Marciano, Liberace, Santayana goodbye

We didn't start the fire
It was always burning
Since the world's been turning
We didn't start the fire
No we didn't light it
But we tried to fight it

> Joseph Stalin, Malenkov, Nasser and Prokofiev
> Rockefeller, Campanella, Communist Bloc,
> Roy Cohn, Juan Peron, Toscanini, Dacron,
> Dien Bien Phu falls, "Rock Around the Clock"
> Einstein, James Dean, Brooklyn's got a winning team,
> Davy Crockett, Peter Pan, Elvis Presley, Disneyland,
> Bardot, Budapest, Alabama, Krushchev,
> Princess Grace, "Peyton Place", trouble in the Suez

'We Didn't Start The Fire' is Billy Joel's apologia for American imperialism during the period from the late 1940s. The song is a naïve account of American history and its involvement in world affairs. Billy Joel explains: 'I had turned 40. It was 1989 and I said, "Okay, what's happened in my life?" I wrote down the year 1949. Okay, Harry Truman was president. Popular singer of the day, Doris Day. China went Communist. Another popular singer, Johnnie Ray. Big Broadway show, *South Pacific*. Journalist, Walter Winchell. Athlete, Joe DiMaggio. Then I went on to 1950 [...]. It's one of the worst melodies I've ever written. I kind of like the lyric though…'

Naïve or not, the song perfectly captures the sense of smug confidence felt by many Americans after 1945. How can we understand the abundant self-confidence of America in this period?

Overall, in general, how can we explain America's rise to world dominion, a feature of world history after 1945? The 1950s is often described as a Long Boom. One suggestion is that capitalism, especially in America, succeeded in delivering sufficient wealth to people that any thoughts of revolutionary overthrow were discarded. The American economy, having been bolstered by the war effort, continued to grow. This is part of the answer, but it does not explain why America in particular should have assumed so powerful a role in world history.

The Long Boom of the 1950s saw the enunciation of a 'pax americana' which would protect the world from the military and economic agonies of the first half of the twentieth century. Even as a young republic the United States had sought a place in world affairs. The Monroe Doctrine (1823) had asserted a regional role for itself in its immediate neighbourhood, following the attempt by the British to re-open hostilities with the War of 1812. The idea of 'American peace' was constructed after the Civil War and suggested a society that had learned to put economic development ahead of war between its states, unlike Europe. The US remained isolationist until 1917, and again, following Versailles, until 1941. This particular history suggested to its intellectuals that American was 'exceptional': it seemed that this was a society like no other, thanks to its Revolution and the opportunities it gave to people from the Old World. In this context the 'containment' of Communism after 1945 was seen as critical to maintaining this peace. This was a double-edged idea of 'peace', therefore, as it rested on the assembly of a fearsome arsenal of weaponry.

The Cold War (1945-1991)

This arsenal was kept in storage during the decades known as the Cold War. The Cold War took its name from the fact that, unlike the two previous world wars of the twentieth century, it never quite got to the point of all-out war between the key belligerent states, America and the Soviet Union, and their main allies. Instead their wars were local conflicts, fought through proxies. The causes of the Cold War were straightforward. Europe lay exhausted by the two World Wars and the Great Depression. The USA and USSR emerged from the Second World War as its victors, divided by opposing ideologies. Germany was divided into West and East, each a satellite of the Americans and the Soviets. Europe was divided by an 'Iron Curtain', a piece of hyperbole borrowed by the British leader, Winston Churchill, for a speech he gave in Missouri in 1946. In 1961 Berlin became divided by the Berlin Wall, a powerful symbol of this division, as the East Germans sought to prevent communication between the two halves of the city. (The pulling down of this Wall in 1989 marked the beginning of the end of the Cold War.) With its lack of real fighting, the Cold War required a high level of espionage.[76]

In its conduct of the Cold War, the American State became more powerful, developing its capacity for both coercive and hegemonic power. During the late 1940s, under President Truman, much of the machinery for fighting the Cold War was built. The National Security Act of 1947 rationalised the American defence establishment, formed a separate US Air Force, and created the CIA (Central Intelligence Agency). The

---

76 Phillip Deery and Mario del Pero, *Spiare e tradire: Dietro le quinte della Guerra Fredda*, Feltrinelli, Milan, 2011.

Marshall Plan supported European States in their post-war rebuilding. The Truman Doctrine (1947) promised aid to both Greece and Turkey to prevent the expansion of Soviet influence in the eastern Mediterranean. The North Atlantic Treaty Organisation (NATO) was formed in 1949 to unite the military forces of North America and Western Europe. In 1950 Truman committed Allied troops to the Korean War, following Chinese expansion in the aftermath of its 1949 revolution.

Against the grain, Truman won the 1948 election, but in 1952 the Republicans finally took office, under Dwight ('Ike') Eisenhower. McCarthyism was now the dominant political mood, and suffused all aspects of American life. In 1956 Eisenhower was re-elected, and there was a sense of business as usual in America. But in 1957 the Sputnik crisis alerted Americans to the contest in which they were embroiled: against all odds, the Russians launched a space vessel before the Americans. The 1960 election was a contest between Richard Nixon and a Catholic candidate, John F. Kennedy, who somehow succeeded in winning office. He was the first successful Catholic candidate and an unashamed liberal. Kennedy steered the nation through the Cuban Missile Crisis of October 1962, when the Soviet Union attempted to place nuclear weapons on the nearby island. Kennedy negotiated their removal with adroit diplomacy.

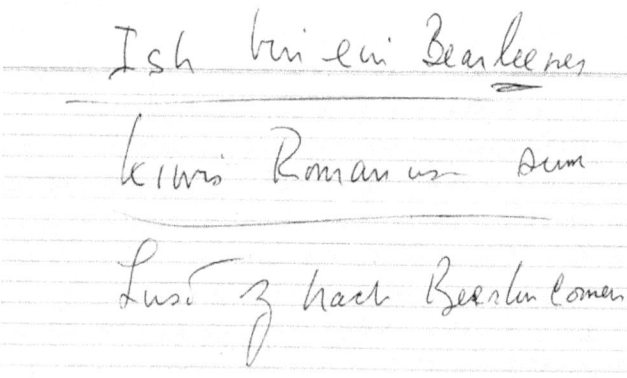

John F. Kennedy delivering his speech in Berlin on 26 June 1963 (next page), with the help of phonological notes to render German and Latin in his pronounced Boston accent

The following June he gave his famous speech, 'Ich bin ein Berliner' ('I am a Berliner') as a protest against the building of the Berlin Wall. He uses the phrase twice, right at the end and near the start: 'Two thousand years ago, the proudest boast was "Civis romanus sum". Today, in the world of freedom, the proudest boast is "Ich bin ein Berliner!"... All free men, wherever they may live, are citizens of Berlin, and therefore, as a free man, I take pride in the words "Ich bin ein Berliner!"'[77]

---

[77] It is an urban myth that the Germans chuckled at Kennedy's reference to himself as 'a jam doughnut' (a Berliner), as it is obvious from the faces in the crowd in the youtube.com version that his meaning was clear.

The Cold War dominated the discourse of 1950s America. For example, the engineers who built the US superhighways used the need to defend America with mobile tanks as the rationale for constructing the system. Academic freedom was severely constrained.[78] It is difficult from this distance to appreciate the level of anxiety produced by the Cold War, forcing people to take sides in what was seen as an all-out conflict between the US and the USSR.

The two faces of the modern State

The American State became extremely sophisticated in its imperial reach. Empire was now not just a matter of ruling territory (as it had been for the French and the British in their respective colonial empires). American dominance lay in being able to impose its will without the expense of conquest and colonial government. America emerged from the Second World War with military bases throughout world and world-wide financial investments. Like other States, the American State arrogates to itself a monopoly use of violence (its coercive function), and the American State is also a repository of knowledges (its hegemonic function). We need to deal with these two kinds of rule quite separately.

The coercive function is the more obvious. The American use of coercion was demonstrated in 1945 with the use of nuclear bombs at Hiroshima and Nagasaki. But during the late 1940s, the 1950s, and the 1960s, this power was exerted around the globe. Once the Soviets also had nuclear weapons, the policy of Mutual Assured Destruction (MAD) ensured that neither side would deploy its intercontinental missiles. The economic power of post-war America was consolidated via the building of international organisations and treaties. At its base, this coercive function depended upon legal knowledge and international treaties, such as, in this period, the General Agreement on Tariffs and Trade, GATT, 1947; NATO, 1949; ANZUS, 1952; SEATO, 1954; the Baghdad

---

[78] André Schriffin, ed., *The Cold War & The University: Toward an Intellectual History of the Postwar Years*, The New Press, New York, 1997.

Pact, 1955; the International Atomic Energy Treaty, 1957; and the Arms Control and Disarmament Agency, 1961. In military terms, the most significant technological advance by 1962 was the use of helicopters and mobile ground forces in Vietnam. The limitations of this technology only became obvious in retrospect. Economic power was based on the Marshall Plan and other international arrangements, as the Americans were determined to learn the lessons of Versailles. (Indeed, the War Guilt clause of Versailles was replaced by the highly selective Nuremberg trials, and the Japanese war criminals were mostly excused.)

But it is impossible to explain America's superpower success without considering its hegemonic role in the world of ideas. While coercive power is essentially military and economic, hegemonic power deals with knowledge, persuasion, culture and the rather less material aspects of State operations. Indeed, one of the key arguments for regarding America as the greatest power in human history is precisely this combination of the coercive and the hegemonic. Previous empires (Rome, the Aztecs, Absolutist Europe) had relied on coercive strategies, or in other cases (Confucian China, medieval Islam, the modern French Empire) mostly on hegemonic strategies. But the US domination of world affairs after 1945 was finely balanced between these twin aspects of governmental rule.

In carrying out its functions of hegemonic rule the State draws on different kinds of understanding, relying on a broader range of social sciences, especially the disciplines of economics and sociology.[79] Relevant examples in this period included the Grand Theory of sociologist Talcott Parsons, offered as an alternative to Marxist social theory; the work in modernisation theory of the economist W.W. Rostow, who proposed a universal model of economic development; and the critique of 'amoral familism' by the political scientist, Edward Banfield, who eulogised small-town America as an alternative to the style of social life he identified in the underdeveloped world.

---

79 T.S. Simey, *Social Science and Social Purpose*, Constable, London, 1968, offers a cross-national perspective on this development, looking at the UK, the US and Germany.

Thus the State moved through distinctive disciplinary layers, across the twentieth century, as it sought to increase its hegemonic capacity. Its basic departments of State – such as the military departments, customs and immigration – rely mostly on the legal disciplines. The immigrants arriving at Ellis Island, in New York harbour, for instance, were processed according to the legal understandings of the time, such as the Quota Laws of the early 1920s. A second set of departments, such as Treasury, foreign affairs, and trade, were built on economic understandings, particularly from Roosevelt's New Deal onwards. Finally, and more recently, there are those departments which rely on sociological insights, such as environmental protection and homeland security. (These are more recent developments, from the 1970s onwards.[80])

Thus the American State derives its hegemonic power in its stock of knowledges about the world. Its legal knowledge, collected in the White House, the State Department, and the Central Intelligence Agency comprises knowledges about territory, populations, languages, diplomacy, all matters of value to America in its global policing. Economic knowledge, collected in Treasury, the banking and other industry regulators, the Internal Revenue Service is essentially knowledges about prices and incomes, rules of trade, and so on. Sociological knowledge, collected in think tanks and private consultancies is knowledges about foreign governments, political divisions, and public opinion. Already quite sophisticated in the 1950s, this range of knowledges would become quite impressive in the early twenty-first century, with the American State able to absorb vast quantities of 'big data' from its 'Five Eyes' program (spying agencies in the US, the UK, Canada, Australia and New Zealand).

Harlem, Hollywood and Harvard

American knowledge and culture is constantly produced, processed and reproduced. How this is all held together can be conveniently summed

---

[80] A good reference for this deployment of sociological knowledge is Mark H. Moore, *Creating Public Value: Strategic Management in Government*, Harvard University Press, Cambridge MA, 1995.

Robert Johnson

up by the 'Harlem-Hollywood-Harvard' formula. Harlem represents the folk culture of America, Hollywood its mass or popular culture, and Harvard its art or scholarly culture.

All new ideas or social movements begin in the neighbourhood. America is unusual in that it generates its own ideas and is resistant to foreign ideas. New ideas emerge in their raw form, such as in immigrant Italian culture. Places like Boston's North End, New York's Little Italy, and Paterson NJ are sources of fresh insights, melding imported and local traditions into Italo-American hybrid culture. Similarly, Afro-American folk culture is very strong, with developments in US popular music beginning with Robert Johnson in the 1930s. Indeed, R&B derives from the workaday music performed by Black slaves on the old plantations, and influenced the modern songwriting of Led Zeppelin, Eric Clapton, the Rolling Stones and many other bands. Songs made famous by the Rolling Stones such as 'Love in Vain' and 'Stop Breakin' Down Blues' are Afro-American in origin. Tap Dancing was originally African Juba dancing. The examples can be readily multiplied.

This cultural innovation from the street ('Harlem') becomes massified, and then disseminated by 'Hollywood'. So Italo-American products, ideas, and images include the Stop and Shop food chain; Mario Puzo's novel, *The Godfather*, and the film series to which it gave rise; and Bruce Springsteen's gritty music from New Jersey. 'Every important idea in Western culture appeared in American film, 1935-1945', says a character in a risqué novel of the Sixties.[81] Hollywood grew in esteem in the Long Boom. It won the confidence of American moviegoers in their millions. Dozens of new films appeared each year. Some flopped. Some became box-office successes. What they had in common was an attempt to translate the big stories of the Western tradition to the silver screen. This element of hegemony had its positive side also. Any social or political cause that was depicted on screen, such as Black equality, received significant legitimation if it was portrayed in a Hollywood movie. It was also in Hollywood that many of the debates of the era, such the vexed issue of Communism and McCarthyism, were played out. Rival film-makers on either side of the ideological divide put across their views via their movies.

Finally, there is art culture, abbreviated as 'Harvard'. With the Italian heritage, to pursue that theme, Italian Renaissance art was studied by college students on study abroad, such as at the Harvard campus, Villa I Tatti, in Florence. In the US Italo-American writers of note included Gregory Corso, Don DeLillo, Lawrence Ferlinghetti, and Camille Paglia. In art culture, the new cultural work is examined, tested and reproduced by American universities.

In this complex cultural framework, what explains the failure of the

---

81 Gore Vidal, *Myra Breckinridge*, Little, Brown, Boston, 1968.

American Left? [82] Why has the US been so effective in dealing with its dissidents? Herbert Marcuse theorised that America was as hegemonic in its exercise of power as the regimes with which the Frankfurt School was originally interested. One part of the puzzle is that Blacks, Italians, and Jews were historically excluded from Ivy League universities – instead, they found their voice via Hollywood. (This absence of a wide cross-section of American youth from 'Harvard' also explains why the Ivy League schools do not star in college football!) But it is also important to recognise that US culture is now powerfully self-reflexive, so that issues of colour and class are negotiated through its major cultural institutions – Harvard and Hollywood.

The Beats and pop art

There was a moment during the Long Boom when the conservatism of the era was questioned by a small artistic elite, a group of White writers and poets known as the Beat Generation. These included poets such as Allen Ginsberg, Gregory Corso, and Lawrence Ferlinghetti, and writers such as Jack Kerouac, *On The Road*, 1957. Their roots were Italo-American, French-Canadian and Jewish-American. The Beat was centred on San Francisco, but in the Sixties some of their ideas entered popular music and was influential around the Western world, in the work of singers such as Bob Dylan, Woody Guthrie, and Joan Baez.

Beat poetry was whimsical and at the same time political in a small-p sense. A good example is Lawrence Ferlinghetti's 'Underwear':

> I didn't get much sleep last
> night
> thinking about underwear
> Have you ever stopped to
> consider
> underwear in the abstract

---

[82] A basic reference on this vexed issue is Christopher Lasch, *The Agony of the American Left*, Knopf, New York, 1969.

Lawrence Ferlinghetti outside his City Lights Bookshop, San Francisco

When you really dig into it
some shocking problems are
raised
Underwear is something we
all have to deal with
Everyone wears
some kind of underwear
Even Indians wear
underwear
Even Cubans
wear underwear
The Pope wears underwear

Human Destiny in Human Hands

The Governor of Louisiana wears
underwear
I saw him on TV
He must have had tight underwear
He squirmed a lot
Underwear can really get you in a bind
You have seen the underwear ads for
men and women
so alike but so different
Women's underwear holds things up
Men's underwear holds things down
Underwear is one thing
men and women do have in common
Underwear is all we have between us
You have seen the three-color pictures
with crotches encircled
to show the areas of extra strength
with three-way stretch
promising full freedom of action
Don't be deceived
It's all based on the two-party system
which doesn't allow much freedom of
choice
the way things are set up
America in its Underwear
struggles thru the night
Underwear controls everything in the
end
Take foundation garments for instance
They are really fascist forms
of underground government

Richard Hamilton, *Just what is it that makes today's homes so different, so appealing?*, 1956 [Kunsthalle Tübingen]

> making people believe
> something but the truth
> telling you what you can or can't do
> Did you ever try to get around a girdle
> Perhaps Non-Violent Action

Pop art (associated with Andy Warhol and Roy Lichenstein) arose simultaneously in the US and in Britain. Like Beat, pop art was critical of the good life of the Long Boom. The foundational work was Richard Hamilton's *Just What Is It That Makes Today's Homes So Different, So Appealing?* (1956). It was perhaps from Beat that The Beatles took their name in August 1959. These movements in the US and Britain were harbingers of what was to follow in the Sixties.

The world outside America, 1945-62

What was it like to live in this period of absolute American hegemony? And what was happening outside America during the Long Boom? Decolonisation proceeded apace in Asia, Africa, and Latin America, leading to independence for China, India, and many other postcolonial nations. Meanwhile, Europe was recovering from the world wars --- the Rome Olympics in 1960 is traditionally dated as the point where the Italian economy had recovered. Each of these economies developed according to local understandings of economic theory and practice, rather than according to the one American model.[83]

As in America, this was a period of political conservatism in much of Europe, Australia and elsewhere.

Britain and France were exposed by the Suez Crisis of 1956, which marked the end-point of their imperial histories. There were no rival states of any significance to America. China was suffering under Mao, while the Soviet Union struggled under its heavy defence budget throughout these years and facing the truth about Stalin.

In many parts of the world the 1950s was characterised by extreme poverty and weak governments. It was not clear what would happen next, and there were fears of a Third World War.

The Kennedy Government as Camelot (1960-63)

Under Kennedy America saw itself as a new Camelot, a reference to that legendary British kingdom ruled by King Arthur and his Knights of the Round Table. Kennedy himself was Arthurian in his magical charm and power. America was at the height of its powers, seemingly invincible. All that ended with Kennedy's killing. Although he was the fourth President to be assassinated, this one seemed to be more of a turning point than

---

[83] A good textbook on this is David Kennett, *A New View of Comparative Economics*, Thomson, South-Western, Mason OH, 2004.

the previous ones (Lincoln, 1865; Garfield, 1881; McKinley, 1901).[84] His assassination in Dallas, Texas, on 22 November 1963, brought Camelot to a shattering end. The proliferation of conspiracy theories that emerged to explain this shock caused the US Government, years later, to produce all the known documents on the case.[85] The date became enshrined in American public memory, like the attack on Pearl Harbor before it (7 December 1941) and the attack on the Twin Towers subsequently (11 September 2001).

Would this American dominance of world affairs be challenged with the death of such a charismatic leader? That was the question of 1963, and the subsequent dozen or so years, now known as the Sixties, would bring a surprising answer.

---

84 There is a persistent legend that William Harrison entered the presidency in 1840 with the curse of Tecumseh over his head, which explains why every president elected in the twentieth year (1840, 1860, 1880 etc.) has died in office, until Kennedy.
85 US National Archives, 'The President John F. Kennedy Assassination Records Collection' http://www.archives.gov/research/jfk/ [accessed 12 July 2013].

Primary source:

Nine stories retold by Hollywood, 1945-1962

Here are nine movies made in Hollywood during the Long Boom, from 1945 to 1962. They are listed in the order in which they appeared. Review their plots and, if necessary, check them on youtube.com.

The context in which these movies were produced is important to understand. From 1948 Americans could purchase a television set for their homes. The TV became as much part of the American Dream as a car in every garage and a chicken in every pot. Hollywood responded with a burst of creativity and new technologies. Widescreen movies were introduced, beginning with *Shane*; there was some 3-D; and drive-in cinemas proved popular. By the end of the decade almost all movies were shot in colour, since TV remained black-and-white. In all, the size of cinema audiences in the US halved in this period. And yet the new movie stars of 1950s Hollywood cemented the rise of the celebrity in American society. The Academy Awards became more glamorous, and lent an air of critical legitimacy to the business of movie-making. Hollywood continued to export American ideals abroad. If domestic audiences were shrinking, Hollywood was now the dominant movie factory in worldwide terms.[86] Hollywood had begun as a national cinema, but now became international and a symbol of American life.

The nine movies, in chronological order:

A Tree Grows in Brooklyn, 1945. A classic tale of immigrant America. It was director Elia Kazan's first movie, with actor James Dunn as the alcoholic father of an Irish-American family living in Brooklyn in 1912, and Dorothy McGuire as his long-suffering wife. She cleans their apartment building and collects rags to make a living. The children think she is not

---

86 Residents of a new suburb in faraway Perth, Western Australia, when given a free choice to name their locality, had no hesitation but to agree on 'Hollywood'!

A Tree Grows in Brooklyn

a good mother because she needs to work long hours to provide for the family, but their perception of her is based on what turn out to be outmoded ideas about the role of a mother in a New York tenement in the early twentieth century.

It's a Wonderful Life, 1946. Directed by Frank Capra, this movie was filmed on a 'movie ranch', a property in southern California set up to shoot movies, especially Westerns. It was a three-block set, with dozens of buildings and with animals allowed to roam free to give it the appearance of a real town. Clarence Odbody (Henry Travers) is George Bailey's guardian angel, sent down from Heaven when George (played by James Stewart) is feeling suicidal. Clarence has a kinder opinion of George than he does himself. He shows him how the town would have been if he had not undertaken his charitable works there. Clarence is given his wings as an angel because he succeeds in turning George's life around, prompting the comment from George's daughter alongside the Christmas tree: 'Look, Daddy. Teacher says, "Every time a bell rings

It's a Wonderful Life

an angel gets his wings.'" This scene of a Christmas tree bell ringing is reprised in *National Lampoon's Christmas Vacation* (Jeremiah S. Chechik, dir., 1989). *It's a Wonderful Life* explores the limits of human agency in a world where divine forces still operate.

Shane (George Stevens, dir. 1953). Some say this is the best Western ever made, or at least equal to *The Searchers* (John Ford, dir. 1956). 'A Stranger Rides Into Town…': this is so often the premise of the Western genre, and here it is a gunslinger who calls himself 'Shane', played by Alan Ladd. Shane takes the side of a homesteader and his wife (Marian Starrett, played by Jean Arthur in her last movie role) in their war with a cattle baron. It is possible that Shane and Marian had a relationship in the past. The Starretts' little boy, young Joey (Brandon deWilde) treats Shane as a hero. Shane advocates the use of guns to settle disputes, but also concedes the days of the Wild West are drawing to an end. Jack Palance

Shane

The Defiant Ones

plays the black-hatted bad man of the movie, a killer named Jack Wilson, hired by the cattle baron. In the final saloon scene, Shane kills Wilson in a gunfight. He is slightly wounded but reassures Joey that he will be alright as he rides off into the sunset, perhaps to die quietly on his own. *Shane* was the first movie to use a widescreen. It also uses a wire to yank the actors backwards when they are shot from in front. *Shane* has sound effects that make its gunshots realistic.

The Defiant Ones, 1958, directed by Stanley Kramer in black-and-white. Two convicts – one black (Noah Cullen, played by Sidney Poitier), one white (Joker Jackson, acted by Tony Curtis) – escape from the authorities after a truck accident, but are shackled together. To survive they must learn to cooperate. They find they have far more in common than the colour of their skin had suggested. When a scheming woman, Billy's mother (Cara Williams), tries to break them up, they help each other stay together, even though it leads to their recapture. The film ends with them as happy prisoners.

The Nun's Story (Fred Zinnemann, dir. 1959). Audrey Hepburn stars as a young Belgian woman who wants to become a nun in order to work in the Congo. Having entered the order as Sister Luke, she is assigned instead to a Belgian mental home, but eventually does end up in the Congo. She is clear about what she wants to do with her life, but fate keeps intervening. In the Congo she becomes a nurse at a white hospital, working for the atheistic genius Dr Fortunati (played by the Australian actor Peter Finch), with whom there is some sexual tension. She contracts TB, but he is able to invent a local cure for her. However, she is required to return to Belgium and gives up her vocation when the Nazis invade Belgium.

On The Beach, 1959. Set in Melbourne, Australia, this is a Stanley Kramer film about the end of the world following a nuclear war. One submarine survives because it was under water during the holocaust. The commander of the *USS Sawfish* (Gregory Peck), imagining he is now widowed, falls in love with an alcoholic woman in Melbourne (Ava

The Nun's Story

On The Beach

The Apartment

Gardner). A publicist used the line, 'If you are going to make a film about the end of the world, then Melbourne is the place to make it.' Such was the novelty of Hollywood moviemaking in Australia's second city that the film crews had to contend with hundreds of well-wishers around every set. The end of humanity seems inevitable, and they must all deal with that reality. Man's folly has led to this catastrophe, and the world is almost totally submerged.

The Apartment (Billy Wilder, dir. 1960). An ambitious young man, Buddy Boy (Jack Lemmon), lends his apartment for his male workmates to use for illicit affairs. One of the women caught up in this progression of liaisons is Fran (Shirley MacLaine). Buddy Boy becomes something of a mentor to her and in their time together they learn to play Gin Rummy, so the film ends with the immortal line, 'Shut Up and Deal!'

Psycho, 1960. Directed by Alfred Hitchcock, this has become one of the most famous films of all times. The plot is simple enough. A young

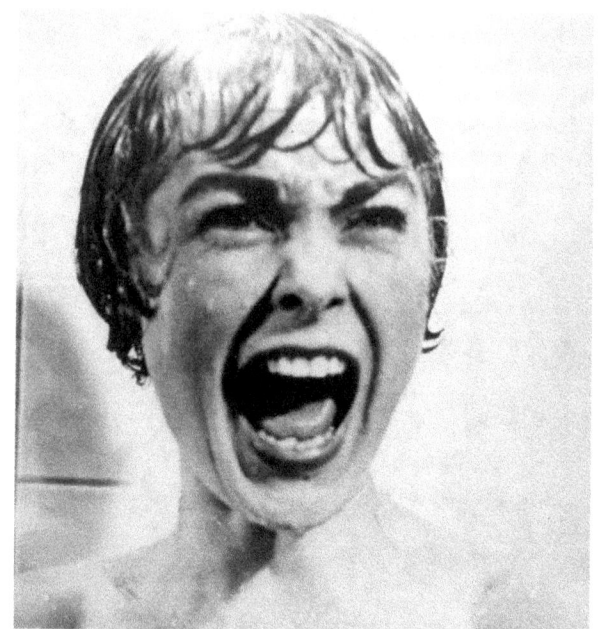

Psycho

The Man Who Shot Liberty Valance

woman, Marion Crane (Janet Leigh) has embezzled her employer and ends up booking into a quiet motel whose owner-manager is the strange Norman Bates (played by Anthony Perkins). The film features the infamous shower scene that has become something of a movie cliché. There is a murderer loose in the Bates Motel, but his or her identity is not all obvious.

The Man Who Shot Liberty Valance, 1962. John Ford directed this black-and-white movie. Liberty Valance (Lee Marvin) terrorises a town on the American frontier until he is shot and killed. A rancher, Tom Doniphon (John Wayne) has pulled the trigger, but credit goes to a local lawyer, Ransom "Ranse" Stoddard (James Stewart) who goes on to a successful career in politics as a result. Doniphon was in love with Hallie (Vera Miles), but she fell in love with Stoddard, eventually marrying him, and Doniphon conceded her to him. Years later, with Doniphon's death, when a journalist discovered the truth, he tore up his notes and proclaimed: 'This is the West, sir. When the legend becomes fact, print the legend.'

Questions for discussion:

Review the nine stories of the West that can be traced back to the time of the ancient Greeks [Unit 4]. Which of these nine stories does each of these movies retell? What makes you say that?

How does each story get revised in this process of retelling? To what overall effect?

What is the role of Hollywood in American life in the 1945-1962 period?

Going further:

Archive.org contains many moving images and sound recordings relevant to modern US history, such as: Cuban Missile Crisis −76 items; Lawrence Ferlinghetti −20 items; Jack Kerouac −977 items [accessed 12 July 2013] This archive is growing steadily.

Phillip Deery and Mario del Pero, *Spiare e tradire: Dietro le quinte della Guerra Fredda*, Feltrinelli, Milan, 2011

David Kennett, *A New View of Comparative Economics*, Thomson, South-Western, Mason OH, 2004

Christopher Lasch, *The Agony of the American Left*, Knopf, New York, 1969

Mark H. Moore, *Creating Public Value: Strategic Management in Government*, Harvard University Press, Cambridge MA, 1995

André Schriffin, ed., *The Cold War & The University: Toward an Intellectual History of the Postwar Years*, The New Press, New York, 1997

T.S. Simey, *Social Science and Social Purpose*, Constable, London, 1968

US National Archives, 'The President John F. Kennedy Assassination Records Collection' http://www.archives.gov/research/jfk/ [accessed 12 July 2013]

Gore Vidal, *Myra Breckinridge*, Little, Brown, Boston, 1968

Unit 23

The Sixties and the undermining of Western hegemony

Bruce Springsteen's classic 'Born in the USA' became a retrospective anthem of the 1960s protest against American involvement in Vietnam, with its evocative lyrics:

> I got in a little hometown jam
> And so they put a rifle in my hands
> Sent me off to Vietnam
> To go and kill the yellow man

Bruce Springsteen, born in 1949, was a teenager during these years, but saw enough in working-class New Jersey to understand the world in which he was growing up. His surname indicates a Dutch-Irish father, while his maternal grandparents were Neapolitans named Zerilli who landed at Ellis Island around the year 1900. Springsteen's music was inspired by the seaside towns of New Jersey where the band of which he was 'the Boss' played.

The period often described as the Long Boom saw the development of both coercive and hegemonic functions, and the rise of America as a genuine superpower. This dominance came to a major crisis with the OPEC oil crisis of 1973, the resignation in 1974 of President Nixon, and the defeat of the American forces in Vietnam in 1975. These were tangible crises in the context of a much deeper malaise, 'the Sixties', which began in about 1962 or 1963 (the moment of Kennedy's assassination).

The Sixties as a pivotal decade in World History

The decade opened with the 1962 Port Huron Statement. The best educated, white, middle-class Americans did not accept their inheritance; they wanted a different America from the one their parents had bequeathed them. They created the SDS (Students for a Democratic Society), which had branches all over the world, including Melbourne. SDS was led by activists such as Tom Hayden, Alan Haber, Todd Gitlin, Paul Booth, and Jim Monsonis.

In Rome the Second Vatican Council convened in 1962 and continued meeting until it concluded its business in 1965, promising a new kind of Catholicism. When America's first Catholic President was assassinated on 22 November 1963, he was replaced by vice-president 'LBJ' (Lyndon Baines Johnson), who went on win the subsequent presidential election in 1964 and escalated the Vietnam War.

In 1968 Richard ('Tricky Dicky') Nixon won election as President for the Republicans. He faced increasing student and popular protest against the War. Episodes such as the Kent State killings in 1970 showed how divisive the War had become. In 1969 the journalist Seymour Hersh broke the story of the My Lai massacre 18 months earlier, while in 1971 the so-called 'Pentagon Papers' exposed the broader US involvement in Indochina. Nonetheless in 1972 Nixon was re-elected in a landslide after visiting China and the USSR in pursuit of 'détente'.

Then came three events in quick succession which demonstrated the fragility of America as a superpower. The US democratic system was challenged by the revelation of the Watergate scandal (1972–74) and the resignation of Nixon. In October 1973 another War between Israel and its Arab neighbours led to the OPEC oil crisis. And in April 1975 US forces evacuated Saigon and admitted their defeat in the Vietnam War.

The Sixties, defined by historians as the years from about 1962 to 1975, had proved to be one of the most decisive single decades in World History.

The Second Vatican Council

Signs of change were evident in the world's largest religion from about 1958, with the election of a progressive, Pope John XXIII, to the papacy. The Church was then archly conservative. It had done little to oppose

Fascism and Nazism; it played an anti-Communist role in most nations during the Cold War; and it did little to involve its adherents ('the laity') in its decision-making. John XXIII wanted to change all that, so he embarked on a radical reform of a very traditional church. He summoned all the church leaders to Rome for a general meeting, a Council. In each of the four years from 1962 to 1965 the world's bishops converged on Rome for the twenty-first Council of the Church, humanity's longest-running parliament.

The Second Vatican Council made sweeping changes to the conduct of its rituals, most of which survived the inevitable counter-revolution. Henceforth, the Mass would be conducted in the vernacular, instead of Latin. Instead of performing the Eucharist with his back to them, the priest would now turn to face the worshippers. The laity would have a larger role in the Church, with a wider range of people (including women) reading Scripture and otherwise assisting the priest in the rituals of the Church. Jews were no longer to be described as 'perfidious', responsible for the death of Jesus.

The Catholic Church now declared itself to be a pilgrim church, on a journey to win peace and salvation, instead of a fixed monolithic entity that blocked change.[87] As the momentum of change increased during the Sixties, many young men joined the priesthood to help bring about what they saw as desirable change in the world.

The New Left

A similar sense of enthusiasm was evident in the Students for a Democratic Society, which grew in numbers very quickly and built campus chapters from its headquarters in New York. Their rallying cry was a denunciation of anti-communism, and they saw McCarthyism ebb as their demands for free speech grew stronger. A key defining event in this free-speech movement was the Berkeley Student Revolt, 1964–65, which pitted them

---

[87] Robert Pascoe, *The Feasts & Seasons of John F. Kelly*, Allen & Unwin, Crows Nest NSW, 2006.

The music of The Beatles, shown here on their Abbey Road record cover, was once associated with political protest

against the Governor of California, future President Ronald Reagan. This was a youth revolution, with a suspicion of people who were more than 30 years old. Interwoven with this campus agitation was the so-called 'hippie revolution' a social movement preaching political activism, drug use and sexual promiscuity. Its motto was 'Tune in, turn on, drop out!' This new leftism, known as the New Left, was distinguished from the Old Left in its insistence that social revolution should begin from individual values and lifestyle – sexual preference, colour, and other individual traits worth fighting for. A better society could be constructed not so much through the older insistence on a reform of the means of production, but rather through an individual commitment to leading lives without war, poverty, injustice and the other ills of affluent societies like America. Popular music became associated with political protest, in both Rhythm and Blues (derived from Afro-American Delta music) and folk music (Joan Baez, Bob Dylan) in both America and Britain (The Beatles, the Rolling Stones).[88]

The New Left originated in America but its ideas spread abroad, carried by the global influence America possessed worldwide. A good example was the 'mai '68' uprising in Paris. Students were once again the cause of this popular protest, with students at the Sorbonne supporting those at Nanterre in their demand for better education. Within a week, schools, universities, factories, and public servants went out on a wildcat strike, involving 11 million people (roughly two/thirds of the French workforce). The Government of Charles De Gaulle was taken completely by surprise: he fled to a French military base in Baden-Baden, Germany, and then promised fresh elections. The rebels were divided among themselves, with a conflicting set of demands, and the Gaullists increased their majority in the parliament.

In 1969 the SDS dissolved and its more revolutionary members formed the Weathermen, a group that was prepared to use violence against the US Government in retaliation for its conduct of military operations in Vietnam and elsewhere.

'The Years of the Bullet' in Europe

The Red Brigades and other European and Japanese militant groups were inspired by the more militant American New Left groups, such as the Weathermen. Italian historians call the 1970s 'the Years of the Bullet' ('Anni di piombo'). Italy was wealthier after the boom of 1960, but most of this new wealth was trapped in the hands of the post-war elites. The Christian Democrats (DC), a party formed by Alcide De Gasperi in 1943, controlled Italy though its adroit connections to local elites (allegedly including the mafia in Sicily). Secret right-wing paramilitary groups also emerged. In all, 2000 Italians were killed for political reasons between 1969 and 1981. The low point was the kidnapping and murder

---

[88] Ian MacDonald, *Revolution in the Head: The Beatles' Records and the Sixties*, third edition, Vintage, London, 2005.

Aldo Moro as prisoner of the Red Brigades

of Aldo Moro, the Prime Minister and a progressive member of the DC, in 1978.[89]

The Cultural Revolution in China

A curious social experiment that was a parody of what had been happening in the West, the Cultural Revolution was the second disaster to befall the Chinese people, following the death of millions during a famine in the years 1958 to 1962. The Cultural Revolution was launched by Mao in 1966 and lasted until his death in 1976. Young zealots, the Red Guards, were dispatched to scourge the country of supposed bourgeois

---

89 Peter Robb, *Midnight in Sicily*, Duffy & Snellgrove, Sydney, 1996.

elements, leading to the persecution of teachers and other professional people. 'Intellectuals' (graduates) were sent to the countryside to undertake peasant work.

Curiously, a comparable persecution was unleashed in Indonesia in October 1965 by General Suharto, leading to the killing of one million Communists, mostly teachers and other intellectuals. In Cambodia a decade later a similar purge was ordered by Pol Pot, the leader of the government, leading to the death of up to three million people.

The true extent of these and other atrocities is still being researched by historians.

The Women's Movement

An important corollary of the American New Left was rise of 'second-wave' feminism. The first wave was the suffragette movement, around the turn of the nineteenth century, which saw women win the right to vote in many countries. Now the feminist demand was more widely based. Betty Friedan's *The Feminine Mystique* (1963) dealt with 'the problem with no name': the impossibility of living up to the image of the good suburban housewife and mother as depicted by Hollywood. Second-wave feminists like Germaine Greer understood the New Left leaders were males, as chauvinist as their predecessors. Using arguments that echoed the Enlightenment-era arguments of Wollstonecraft, this generation of feminists wanted to subvert patriarchy in general terms. Women, until now a conservative force in Anglophone societies, from the 1960s helped radicalise many areas of life, including academic scholarship.

Black Power

The Port Huron Statement identified the continuing inequality of Blacks in America as an issue. The New Left was a White movement, but the upheaval of the Sixties created an opportunity for Afro-American protest as well. James Baldwin's 1963 classic, *The Fire Next Time* burst out onto a more innocent readership. Its beautiful, long sentences that went on for ever drew readers into the logic of his argument. A centrepiece of the book is the scene where we meet Elijah Muhammad in a Chicago mansion, surrounded by acolytes who assure him in chorus that every remark he makes is correct, 'Yes, that's right'. Elijah's Nation of Islam taught that Allah was a Black god who contended with the Christian White deity, and that next time there would not be another flood, but a holocaust, the 'fire' in the book's title. The Holocaust looms large in Baldwin's reasoning. If the Germans could do that to the Jews, what was to stop the American Whites subjecting the Black Americans to the gas chambers? Should Blacks acquiesce to the White way of life in America? 'Do I really *want* to be integrated into a burning house?', asks Baldwin rhetorically.[90]

The civil rights movement in America began as a local issue, led by Martin Luther King and other pacifists, who were moderates. But it soon escalated, leading to violent riots throughout US cities in the mid-1960s. One of these activists, Stokely Carmichael, in 1966 became the head of the Student Non-Violent Coordinating Committee (SNCC, pronounced 'Snick'), and declared: "This is the twenty-seventh time I have been arrested and I ain't going to jail no more! The only way we gonna stop them white men from whuppin' us is to take over. What we gonna start sayin' now is Black Power!'. Carmichael moved on to join the Black Panthers, a militant form of Black Power that demanded smashing Western ideas of hegemony.

Ethnic revival in America

In 1938 a Norwegian-American historian, Marcus Lee Hansen (1892-1938) predicted that the grandchildren of immigrants to America would want to remember what it was about their identity that the sons wanted to forget in their rush to become accepted as Americans. Hansen's Law proved to be true in the late 1960s. With the rise of feminism and Black

---

90 James Baldwin, *The Fire Next Time*, Dial Press, New York, 1963, p. 81.

activists, leaders of the immigrant minorities in America followed suit, demanding equality with what they perceived to be the dominant Anglo-American minority. The Irish, the Italians and other European minorities in America looked to have been assimilated, but in the late Sixties began to question their cultural origins and identity. Each objected to the way their parents and grandparents had been assimilated into an American 'melting pot'. The underlying assumption in assimilation theory was that as immigrant groups became more materially successful they would surrender their ancestral folkways and become more patriotic Americans. However, many of the early leading champions of ethnic diversity were Jewish-American scholars, such as Harvard's Oscar Handlin, who rediscovered their ethnicity as they became wealthier. These Americans looked to Israel as a touchstone of their Jewish identity. Irish-Americans favoured the incorporation of Northern Ireland into the Republic, while Italo-Americans also formed their own lobby, the National Italian American Foundation (NIAF).

'The Greening of America'

By the late 1960s it seemed that everything about American life that had seemed to be settled at the beginning of the 1960s was now up for grabs. *The Greening of America* was an extremely popular book of 1970 that attempted to summarise these various manifestations of dissent. Its author, Charles A. Reich, was a Yale law professor (who later outed himself as a gay). Among others, he taught both Hillary Rodham and her boyfriend Bill Clinton. Reich argued that America began with Consciousness I (agrarian society), followed by Consciousness II (organisation man), but now had reached Consciousness III (the counterculture). It appeared as if America had revolutionised itself from within.

In the early 1970s a number of events threatened American domination in the world.

The Yom Kippur War of October 1973

In October 1973, still smarting over their earlier defeats in 1948 and 1967, Egypt and Syria launched a surprise attack on Israel during its holiest public holiday. Israel, although warned by the Jordanian king Hussein, had no advance warning, having grown complacent since the 1967 Six-Day War. Neither America nor the USSR welcomed the war, though both re-supplied their allies. It led to the first direct Arab-Israeli talks since 1948 and the Camp David Accords. However, the OPEC nations (Organization of Petroleum Exporting Counties), led by Saudi Arabia, imposed an oil embargo on the US in retaliation for its role in the Yom Kippur War, leading to America's 1973 energy crisis. American superiority in global economic matters was seriously questioned for the first time since 1945.

Watergate, Nixon's resignation, the fall of Saigon

Meanwhile, opposition to the Vietnam War, especially in the US, made the New Left a mainstream cause. The Watergate scandal of 1974 resulted from a break-in of that hotel in 1972 by five men later found by the FBI to be funded by the Committee to Re-Elect the President. Hubris had meant that Nixon had arranged for all his White House conversations to be recorded. When these were handed over to judicial authorities by order of the courts, he was found to be personally involved in the Watergate scandal. Nixon resigned in 1974 before he could be impeached by the Congress; his vice-president, Gerald Ford, took over and pardoned him. By April 1975 the US forces had quit Saigon, and the Americans conceded their first military defeat in the Cold War.

American hegemony had reached its lowest ebb. In 1975 it was not evident that US hegemony in world affairs would continue.

The historiography of World History

Largely because of the rise of the New Left, History as a discipline had undergone enormous changes by 1975. Historiography, the study of historians and historical writings, had become an important sub-discipline. What follows is a list of some of the prominent historians who contributed to World History, listed chronologically. At time of their writing these were secondary sources – some now might considered 'primary', reflecting their time and place. In general they follow the pattern of deo-centric and anthro-centric explanations, with some interesting exceptions.

Herodotus (c.484–c.425 BCE), the 'Father of History', wrote in his *The Histories* (c.445 BCE) about the war between the Greeks and the Persians. He was criticised because he liked a good story – we can see the oral sources very evidently in his narrative. Herodotus was broadly accurate about Egyptian history – he was stronger in his treatment of the Egyptians because they were a different culture. His contemporary was Thucydides (c.460-c.395 BCE), an historian of the Peloponnesian Wars, who was far more technical and drier. He was a military man who rejected the deo-centric approach.

Augustine of Hippo (354-430), in *The City of God* (413-426) understood History as the struggle between good (the City of God) and evil (the City of Earth). Hebrew stories stressed a divine purpose in History. Greco-Roman histories emphasised origins and founding stories – they were more secular. Christian history combined both. Augustine renounced lust late in life for political reasons. On the Muslim side, Ibn Khaldun (1332–1406) wrote the *Muqaddima* (1375–1378). He argued that deserts produce a strong sense of social solidarity among Bedouin. They create a conquering dynasty and move to the city. But over time the dynastic leaders become estranged from their kinsmen and a new Bedouin group, fresh from the desert, takes over. Later he added an economic dimension – the second dynastic leaders' expenses grow too fast and are beyond the means of the peasantry to afford.

Post-Enlightenment history struggled to find anthro-centric explanations. In his *Phenomenology of Spirit* (1807) G.W.F. Hegel (1770-1831) saw a progressive development of Reason through his dialectical approach. Every thesis produces its own antithesis that leads to a new synthesis. Hegel adopted the Reformation view that man is striving to meet God's will ('Spirit'). But he also accepted the Enlightenment insistence on secular rationalism. Despite humanity's discordant efforts, there is a purpose to history. God's will is met by rational legal systems and enlightened citizens. History comprises four great eras: Oriental, Greek, Roman, German.

One of Hegel's students, Karl Marx (1818–83), in works such as *The Eighteenth Brumaire of Louis Bonaparte* (1869) advanced a materialist conception of history. Human labour is at the centre of how we should understand societies: 'humans make their own history but not in conditions of their own choosing'. In this formulation he turned Hegel on his head. Forces of production are determinate of human history, beginning with primitive communism, and followed by the ancient, slave, feudal, Asiatic, capitalist and socialist modes of production. Crucial to historical materialism are a society's level of economic development; changes in the mode of production; the resulting class divisions; and class struggle.

H.G. Wells (1866–1946) was a famous socialist and science-fiction writer, who wrote an *Outline of History* (1920). One of his last works, *World Brain* (1936) anticipates the Internet.

Oswald Spengler (1880–1936), in *The Decline of the West* (1926–28), rejected the linear view of history, including the traditional division into ancient, medieval and modern. He identified eight so-called 'high cultures': the Egyptian, the Chinese, the Babylonian, the Indian, the Mayan, the Magian (Semitic and Islamic), the Greco-Roman, and the Faustian (modern West). Each was a separate organism lasting a thousand years – their demise was inevitable, plant-like. Spengler reflected the pessimism of post-Great War Germany.

Christopher Dawson (1889–1970), the author of *Religion and World History* (1975) was a Catholic historian. The first Catholic to be offered a professorship in the Harvard School of Divinity (1958), he drew on Augustine to show that European history was a struggle between Christian principles and the reality of life. European missionaries were important as the agents of colonialism. Europeans should return to the medieval idea of individual conscience and rational argument.

Arnold J. Toynbee (1889-1975), the author of *A Study of History* (12 volumes, 1934-1961) deplored nationalist historiography and reacted against Spengler. He identified 31 civilisations in all, beginning with Sumerian, Akkadian and Hittite, Egyptian, Aegean, Indus, Orthodox Christian, Western and Islamic. Toynbee considered writing and religion to be the key ingredients of civilisations. He believed there was a universal church and that civilisations were moving together. Later in life he began to accept technological explanations.

In *Man Makes Himself* (1936) Vere Gordon Childe (1892-1957) synthesised the available archaeological evidence from a materialist perspective. He wanted to understand artefacts as they were actually used. Childe is the only Australian in this list – he failed to get a tutorship at the University of Queensland in 1922 because he was a socialist, so in 1927 became the Abercromby Professor of Archaeology at Edinburgh. He invented the concepts of 'Neolithic Revolution' and 'Urban Revolution'.

Fernand Braudel (1902-85) wrote *A History of Civilizations* (1994). He contended that History should be divided into *la longue durée* (the geographic and climatic factors), *la moyenne durée* (socio-economic) and *la courte durée* (the political and diplomatic). In this he relegated Marxist accounts to the periphery of explanations of human history. The *Annaliste* school proved popular in America and Australia, but not in Britain. When applied to France his method produced an essentialist view of its culture.

The Spanish Seaborne Empire (1966) was one of the maritime histories written by J. H. Parry (1914-82), the Gardiner Professor of Ocean History and Affairs at Harvard. He taught a popular subject on the history of maritime transport, nicknamed 'Boats' by the students, in which he popularised the view that so much of World History was oceanic.

William H. McNeill (1917-), author of the iconic *The Rise of the West* (1963) is a Canadian. He was inspired by Toynbee and Spengler, but did not see civilisations as discrete. His critics call him ethnocentric and Whiggish. He sees change as induced by contact and conflict between cultures: the key agents of diffusion and interaction are epidemic diseases, parasitism, military and industrial technologies, and human migrants.

The incomplete writings of Marshall G. S. Hodgson (1922–68) were collected by his students in the book *Rethinking World History* (1993). With McNeill and L. S. Stavrianos he comprised the 'Chicago School'. He was an Islamicist who concentrated on the Afro-Eurasian Historical Zone (the *Oikoumene*). He invented the concept of 'ecumenes', periods of intense interregional trade and contact.

Jean-François Lyotard (1924–98) in *The Postmodern Condition*

Michel Foucault

(1979/1984) offered a challenge to 'grand narrative' – there is so much discontinuity in the contemporary world that World History becomes an impossible task because it must rely heavily on grand narratives of all kinds.

In *The Order of Things* (1966), Michel Foucault (1926-84) applied his theory of knowledge to World History. The 'discourse' typical of each *episteme* is more important than the ideas of great thinkers because it shapes the way in which people examine, describe and control the world and themselves. For example, Renaissance thinking was magical, connecting words and meanings, followed by a rational Classical age that saw everything demonstrably representable.

Janet L. Abu-Lughod (1928-) in *Before European Hegemony: The World System, AD 1250-1350* (1989), argues that the origins of modern Europe lie not in the sixteenth century, but in the thirteenth century, when the relationship with the Islamic world was better developed in the aftermath of the Crusades.

Benedict Anderson (1936-) is best-known for *Imagined Communities* (1983). As a British historian of southeast Asia, he is interested in development of nationalism in the late eighteenth Century as a new kind of community where face-to-face interaction was replaced by print culture, especially the newspaper.

His younger brother, Perry Anderson (1938-) attempts in *Passages from Antiquity to Feudalism* (1974) to apply Marxist theory to world history in the Classical period, followed by *Lineages of the Absolutist State* (1974). He is a widely read scholar with great erudition.

Felipe Fernández-Armesto (1950-) in *The World: A History* offers an exciting attempt to re-orient World History away from a Eurocentric base. The biographer of Christopher Columbus, he invented the notion of the Columbian Exchange, and then attempts to see world history in global terms.

Francis Fukuyama (1952-) wrote an influential book, *The End of History and the Last Man* (1992) in which he argued that democracy is the

Perry Anderson

ideal state. No further progress will be made or will be necessary after the collapse of the Soviet Union in 1989. However, the war in Iraq caused him to re-think his position during 2006.

This survey of world historians shows that historians tend toward one of four 'world hypotheses' in organising their narratives. These are 'Contextualist', moving from general observations to particular examples, 'Mechanist', searching for laws that explain human societies operating like clockwork, 'Organicist', using botanical metaphors and this seeing History as a circular argument, and 'Formist', seeing History as a series of discrete people, periods and places that need to be evoked in their own terms.[91] Using these categories, the paragons of World History are Braudel (a Contextualist), Marx (a Mechanist), Spengler (the Organicist par excellence), and Herodotus (a classic Formist). These four categories are difficult to synthesise, as each represents a root metaphor.

---

91 Robert Pascoe, *The Manufacture of Australian History*, Oxford University Press, Melbourne, 1979 applies these categories to Australian History.

Primary source:

Students for a Democratic Society, The Port Huron Statement (1962)

[This is the text of original draft of the 1962 Port Huron Statement, as distributed by Alan Haber to the attendees at the SDS Northeast Regional Conference, April 23, 2006]

Introduction: Agenda for a Generation

Every generation inherits from the past a set of problems – personal and social – and a dominant set of insights and perspectives by which the problems are to be understood and, hopefully, managed. The critical feature of this generation's inheritance is that the problems are so serious as to actually threaten civilization, while the conventional perspectives are of dubious worth. Horrors are regarded as commonplace; we take universal strife in stride; we treat newness with a normalcy that suggests a deliberate flight from reality.

SDS founder, Tom Hayden, and Jane Fonda, with whom he was married from 1973 to 1989

How can the magnitude of modern problems be best expressed? Perhaps by means of paradox:

With nuclear energy whole cities could easily be powered, but instead we seem likely to unleash destruction greater than that incurred in all wars in human history;

With rockets we are emancipating man from terrestrial limitations, but from Mississippi jails still comes the prayer for emancipation of man on earth;

As man's own technology destroys old and creates new forms of social organization, man still tolerates meaningless work, idleness instead of creative leisure, and, educational systems that do not prepare him for life amidst change;

While expanding networks of communication, transportation, integrating economic systems, and the birth of intercontinental missiles make national boundaries utterly permeable and antiquated, men still fight and hate in provincial loyalty to nationalism;

While two-thirds of mankind suffers increasing undernourishment, our upper classes are changing from competition for scarce goods to reveling amidst abundance;

With world population expected to double in forty years, men still permit anarchy as the rule of international conduct and uncontrolled exploitation to govern the sapping of the earth's physical resources;

Mankind desperately needs visionary and revolutionary leadership to respond to its enormous and deeply-entrenched problems, but America rests in national stalemate, her goals ambiguous and tradition-bound when they should be new and far-reaching, her democracy apathetic and manipulated when it should be dynamic and participative.

These paradoxes convey tensions which demand the attention of every individual concerned with the future condition of man. The newness of them demands intellectual self-reliance from a younger generation that fears to be its own leadership. The complexity of them' requires a radical sense of appreciation, of facts and values, that few thinkers want to undertake. The dangers in them, that this is the first generation to know it might be the last in the long experiment at living, call not for detachment and retreat but for humility and initiative, not for hypnotic adoption of the politics of past and ranking orders, but for reflective working out of politics anew.

We are people of this generation, in our late teens and early or mid-twenties, bred in affluence, housed not in universities, looking uncomfortably to the world we inherit.

We are dismayed by the timidity of our elders and the privatism of our peers. The organizations we know, in which we are to be socialized as citizens, are unradical, in that they treat only of symptoms, not roots, or unpolitical, in that they are impelled more by outrage and static protest than measured analysis and assertive program, or simply hesitant, skirting the issues and blurring them with rhetoric, rather than admitting of problems both intellectual and political and nevertheless seeking a broad analysis of social issues.

We write, debate, and assert this manifesto, not as a declaration that we have the Final Cure, but to affirm that problems must be faced with an expression of knowledge and value, and in action.

In this affirmation we deny that problems can be faced by claiming they don't exist anymore, or that the government through expertise will solve what problems there are.

We do this as a basis for an organization, because as students we feel that only as we find some structured way of working together, sharing ideas, formulating program and engaging in action will the left become visible and responsible in America.

Our form is tentative – it will change as a response to growth, as we extend beyond our own age group – as we find ways to work with those whom the academic structure identifies as our teachers, as bridges can be extended to labor, the church, the liberal reform-and socialist political groups, as we form the necessary amalgamations with other liberal and radical centers on the campus and beyond. Our goal is to stimulate a left – new and, we think, young.

We seek to be public, responsible, and influential – not housed in garrets, lunatic, and ineffectual; to be visionary yet ever developing concrete programs – not empty or deluded in our goals and sterile in inaction; to be idealistic and hopeful – not deadened by failures or chained by a myopic view of human possibilities; to be both passionate and reflective – not timid and intellectually paralytic; to vivify American politics with controversy – not to emasculate our principles before the icons of unity and bipartisanship; to stimulate and give honor to the full movement of human imagination – not to induce sectarian rigidity or encourage stereotyped rhetoric ….

Towards American Democracy

Every effort to end the Cold War and expand the process of world industrialization is an effort hostile to people and institutions whose interests lie perpetuation of the East-West military threat and the postponement of change the "have not" nations of the world. Every such effort too, is bound to establish greater democracy in America. The goals of a domestic effort would be:

1. *America must abolish its political party stalemate.* A genuine, two party system, centered around issues and essential values, demanding allegiance to party principles, must supplant the current system of organized stalemate which is seriously inadequate to a world influx. It has long been argued that the very overlapping of American parties guarantees that issues will be considered responsibly, that progress will be gradual instead of intemperate, and that therefore America will remain stable instead of torn by class strife. On the contrary: the enormous party overlap itself confuses issues and makes responsible presentation of choice to the electorate impossible, that guarantees Congressional listlessness and the drift of power to military and economic bureaucracies, that directs attention away from more fundamental causes of social stability, such as a huge middle class, Keynesian economic techniques and Madison Avenue

advertising. The ideals of political democracy, then, and the imperative need for a flexible decision-making apparatus makes a real two-party system an immediate social necessity. What is desirable is sufficient party disagreement to dramatize major issues, yet sufficient party overlap to guarantee stable transitions from administration to administration.

Every time the President criticizes a recalcitrant Congress, we must ask that he no longer tolerate the Southern conservatives in the Democratic Party. Every time a liberal representative complains that "We can't expect everything at once" we must ask whether we received much of anything from Congress in the last generation. Every time he refers to "circumstances beyond control" we must ask why he fraternizes with racist scoundrels. Every time he speaks of the "unpleasantness of personal and party fighting," we should insist that pleasantry with Dixiecrats is inexcusable when the dark peoples of the world cry for American support.

2. *Mechanisms of voluntary association must be erected through which political information can be imparted and participation encouraged.* Political parties, even if realigned would not provide adequate outlets for popular involvement. Institutions should be created that engage people with issues and express a political preference, not as with the huge business lobbies which now exercise undemocratic power, but which carry political *influence* (appropriate to private, rather than-public, groupings) in the national decision making enterprise. Private in nature, these should be organized around single issues (medical care, transportation systems reform, etc.), concrete interest (labor and minority group organizations), multiple issues or general issues. These do not exist in quantity in America today. If they did exist, they would be a significant politicalizing and educative force, bringing people into touch with public life and affording them means of expression and action. Today giant lobby representatives of business interests are dominant, but not educative. The federal, government itself should counter the latter forces whose intent is often public deceit for private gain, but subsidizing the preparation and decentralized distribution of objective materials on all public issues facing government.

3. *Institutions and practices which stifle dissent should be abolished and the promotion of peaceful dissent should be actively promoted.* The first amendment freedom of speech, assembly, thought, religion and press should be seen as guarantors, not threats, to the national security. While society has the right to prevent active subversion of its laws and institutions, it has the duty as well to promote open discussion of all issues – otherwise it will be in fact promoting real subversion as the only means to implementing ideas. To eliminate the fears and apathy from national life it is necessary that the institutions bred by fear and apathy be rooted out: the House Un-American Activities Committee, the Senate Internal Security Committee, the loyalty oaths on federal loans, the Attorney General's list of subversive organizations, the Smith and McCarran acts. The process of eliminating these blighting institutions is the process of restoring democratic participation. Their existence is a sign of the decomposition and atrophy of the participation.

4. *Corporations must be made publicly responsible.* It is not possible to believe that true democracy can exist where a minority utterly controls enormous wealth and power. The influence of corporate elites on foreign policy is neither reliable nor democratic; a way must be found to subordinate private American foreign investment to a democratically-constructed foreign policy. The influence of the same giants on domestic life is intolerable as well; a way must be found to direct our economic resources to genuine human needs, not the private needs of corporations nor the rigged needs of a maneuvered citizenry.

Americans cannot trust the promise of the corporate bureaucracy to be "socially responsible". It must become structurally responsible to the people as well. Empirical study should determine the various ways in which this responsibility might be gained; strengthened congressional regulatory commissions; increased worker participation in management and other forms of multilateral decision-making; deliberate decentralization; actual transfer to public ownership, are a few major alternatives that must be considered.

5. *A truly "public sector" must be established and its nature debated and planned.* If war is to be avoided the "permanent war economy" must be as an *"interim* war economy." At some point, America must return to other mechanisms of economic growth besides public military spending. The most likely, a least desirable, return would be in the form of private enterprise. The undesirability lies in the fact of inherent capitalist instability, noticeable even with the bolstering effects of government intervention. In the most recent of post-war recessions, for example, private expenditures for plant and equipment dropped from $16 billion to $11.5 billion, while unemployment surged to nearly six million. By good fortune, investments in construction industries remained level, else an economic depression would have occurred. This will recur, and our growth in national per capita living standards will remain unsensational while the economy stagnates. The main *private* forces of economic expansion cannot guarantee a steady rate of grow, nor acceptable recovery from recession especially in demilitarizing world. Government participation in the economy is essential. Such participation will inevitably expand enormously, because stable growth of the economy, demands increasing investments yearly. Our present output of $450 billion might double in a generation, irreversibly involving government solutions. And in future recessions, the compensatory fiscal action by the government will be the only means of avoiding the twin disasters of greater unemployment and a slackening of the rate of growth. Furthermore, a close relationship with the, European Common Market will involve competition with numerous planned economies, and may aggravate American unemployment unless the economy here is expanding swiftly enough to create new jobs.

All these tendencies suggest that our future expansion rests upon our willingness to enlarge the "public sector" greatly. Unless we choose war as an economic solvent, future public spending *will be* of a non-military nature of a major intervention into civilian production by the government. The issues posed by this development are enormous:

a. How should public vs. private domain be determined? We suggest these criteria: 1) when a resource has been discovered or developed with public tax revenues, such as the space communications systems, it should remain a public resource, not be given away to private enterprise; 2) when monopolization seems inevitable, the public should maintain control of and industry, 3) when national objectives contradict seriously with business objectives as to the use of a resource, the former should prevail.

b. How should technological advances be introduced into a society? By a public process, based on publicly-determined needs. Technological innovations should not be postpones from social use by private corporations in order to protest investment in older equipment.

c. How shall the "public sector" be made public, and not the arena of a ruling bureaucracy of "public servants"? By steadfast opposition to bureaucratic coagulation, and to definitions of human needs according to problems easiest for computers to solve. Second, the bureaucratic pile-ups must be at least minimized by local, regional, and national economic *planning* -- responding to the interconnection of public problems' by comprehensive programs of solution. Third, and most important by experiments in *decentralization* based on the vision of man as master of his machines and his society. The personal capacity to cope with life has been reduced everywhere by the introduction of a technology that only minorities of man (barely) understand. How the process can be reversed – and we believe it can be – is one of the great sociological and economic asks before humane people today. Polytechnical schooling, with the individual adjusting to several work and life experiences, is one method. The transfer of certain mechanized task back into manual forms, allowing men to make whole, not partial, products, is not unimaginable. Our monster cities, based historically on the need for mass labor, might now be humanized, broken into smaller communities, powered by nuclear energy, arranged according to community decision. These are but a fraction of the opportunities of the new era: serious study and deliberate experimentation, rooted in a desire for human fraternity, may now result in blueprints of civic paradise.

6. *America should abolish squalor, terminate neglect, and establish an environment for people to live in with dignity and creativeness.*

   a. A program against *poverty* must be just as sweeping as the nature of poverty itself. It must not be just palliative,' but directed to the abolition of the structural circumstances of poverty. At a bare minimum it should include a *housing* act far larger than the one supported by the Kennedy Administration, but one that is geared more to low- and middle-income needs than to the windfall aspiration of small and large private entrepreneurs, one that is more sympathetic to the quality of communal life than to the efficiency of city-splitting highways. Second, *medical care* must become recognized as a lifetime human rights just as vital as food, shelter and clothing – the Federal government should guarantee health insurance as a basic social service, turning medical treatment into a social habit, not just an occasion crisis, fighting sickness among the aged not just by making medical care financially feasible but by reducing sickness among children and younger people. Third, existing institutions should be expanded so that the Welfare State cares for *everyone's* welfare according to need, *Social security* payments should be extended to everyone and should be proportionately greater for the poorest. A *minimum wage* of at least $1.50 should be extended to all workers (including the 16 million currently not covered at all).

   b. A full scale public initiative for *civil rights* should be undertaken despite the clamor among conservatives and liberals) about gradualism, property rights, and law and order. The executive and legislative branches of the Federal government should work by enforcement end, enactment against any form of exploitation of minority groups. No federal cooperation with racism is tolerable, from financing of schools, to the development of federally-supported industry, to the social gatherings of the Present. Laws hastening school desegregation, voting rights, and economic protection for Negroes are needed right now. And the moral force of the Executive Office should be exerted against the Dixiecrats specifically, and the national complacency about the race question generally. Especially in the North, where one-half of the country's Negro people now life, is not a problem to be solved in isolation from other problems. The fight against poverty, against slums, against the stalemated Congress, against McCarthyism, are all fights against the discrimination that is nearly endemic to all areas of American life.

c. The promise and problems of long-range *federal economic development* should be studied more constructively. It is an embarrassing paradox that the Tennessee Valley Authority is a wonder to foreign visitors by a "radical" and barely influential project to most Americans. The Kennedy decision to permit private facilities to transmit power from the $1 billion Colorado River Storage Project is a disastrous one, interposing privately owned transmitters between publicly-owned power generators and their publicly (and cooperatively) owned distributors. The contrary trend, to public ownership of power, should be generated in an experimental way.

d. The Area Redevelopment Act of 1961 is a first step in recognizing the underdeveloped areas of the United States. It has been rejected by Mississippi already, however, because of the improvement it bodes for the unskilled Negro worker. This program should be enlarged, given teeth, and pursued rigorously by Federal authorities.

e. *Mental health* institutions are in dire need; there were fewer mental hospital *beds* in relation to the numbers of mentally ill in 1959 than there were in 1948. Public hospitals, too, are seriously wanting; existing structures alone need an estimated $1 billion for rehabilitation. Tremendous staff and faculty needs exist as well, and there are not enough medical students enrolled today to meet the anticipated needs of the future.

f. Our prisons are too often the enforcers of misery. They must be either re-oriented to rehabilitative work through public supervision or be abolished for their dehumanizing social effects. Funds are needed, too, to make possible a decent prison environment.

g. *Education* is too vital a public problem to be completely entrusted to the province of the various states and local units. In fact, there is no good reason why America should not progress now toward internationalizing, rather than localizing, its educational system – children and young adults studying everywhere in the world, through a United Nations program, would go far to create mutual understanding. In the meantime the need for teachers and classrooms in America is fantastic. This is an area where "minimal" requirements hardly should be considered as a goal – there always are improvements to be made in the educational system, e.g., smaller classes and many more teachers for them, programs to subsidize the education of the poor but bright, etc.

h. America should eliminate *agricultural policies*, based on scarcity and pent-up surplus. In America and foreign countries there exist tremendous needs for more food and balanced diets. The Federal government should finance small farmers cooperatives, strengthen programs of rural electrification, and expand policies for the distribution of agricultural surpluses throughout the world (by Food-for-Peace and related UN programming).

i. Science should be employed to constructively transform the conditions of life throughout the United States and the world. Yet at the present time the Department of Health, Education and Welfare and the National Science Foundation together spend only $300 million annually for scientific purposes in contrast to the $6 billion spent by the Defense Department and the Atomic Energy, Commission. One-half of all research and development in America is directly devoted to military purposes. Two imbalances must be corrected – that of military over non-military investigation, and that of biological-natural-physical science over the sciences of human behavior. Our political system must then include planning for the human use of science: by anticipating the political consequences of scientific innovation, by directing the discovery and exploration of space, by adapting science to improved production of food, to international communications systems, to technical problems of disarmament, and so on. For the newly-developing nations, American science should focus on the study of cheap sources of power, housing and building materials, mass educational techniques, etc. Further, science and scholarship should be seen less as an apparatus of conflicting power blocs, but as a bridge toward supranational community: the International Geophysical Year is a model for continuous further cooperation between the science communities of all nations.

An Alternative to Helplessness

The goals we have set are not realizable next month, or even next elections, but that fact justified neither giving up altogether nor a determination to work only on immediate, direct, tangible problems. Both responses are a sign of helplessness, fearfulness of visions, refusal to hope: and tend to bring on the very conditions to be avoided. Fearing vision, we justify rhetoric or myopia. Fearing hope, we reinforce despair.

The first effort, then, should be to state a vision: what is the perimeter of human possibility in this epoch? This we have tried to do. The second effort, if we are to be politically responsible, is to evaluate the prospects for obtaining' at least a substantial part of that vision in our epoch: what are the social forces that exist, or that must exist' if we are to be at all successful? And what role have we ourselves to play as a social force?

1. In exploring the existing social forces, note must be taken of the Southern civil rights movement as the most heartening and exemplary struggle in this time of inactive democracy. It is heartening because of the justice it insists upon, exemplary because it indicates that there can be a passage out of apathy.

This movement, pushed into a brilliant new phase by the Montgomery bus boycott and the subsequent nonviolent action of the sit-ins and Freedom Rides has had three major results: first, a sense of self-determination has been instill in millions of oppressed Negroes; second, the movement has challenged a few thousand liberals to new social idealism; third, a series of important concessions have been obtained, such as token school desegregation increased Administration help, new laws, desegregation of some public facilities.

But fundamental social change – that would break the props from under Jim Crow – has not come. Negro employment opportunity, wage levels, housing conditions, educational privileges – these remain deplorable and relatively constant, each deprivation reinforcing the impact of the others. The Southern states, in the meantime, are strengthening the fortresses of the status quos and, are beginning to camouflage the fortresses by guile where open bigotry announced its defiance before. The white-controlled one-party system remains intact: indeed, conservative Republicans may have a greater interest in maintaining their coalition with Dixiecrats than in organizing a Republican Party in the South. Rural dominance remains a fact in nearly all the Southern states. Southern politicians maintain a continuing aversion to the welfare legislation that would aid their people. The reins of the Southern economy are held by conservative businessmen who view human rights as secondary to property rights. A violent anti-communism is rooting itself in the South, and threatening even moderate voices. Add the militarist tradition of the South and its irrational regional mystique and one must conclude that authoritarian and reactionary tendencies are a real obstacle to the small, voiceless, poor, and isolated democratic movements.

The civil rights struggle thus has come to an impasse. To this impasse, the movement responded this year by entering the sphere of politics, insisting on citizenship rights, specifically the right to note, the new voter registration stage of protest represents perhaps the first major attempt to exercise the conventional instruments of political democracy in the struggle for racial justice. The vote, if used strategically by the great mass of now-unregistered Negroes theoretically eligible to vote, will be a decisive factor in changing the quality of southern leadership from low demagoguery to decent statesmanship.

More important, the new emphasis on the vote heralds the use of *political means* to solve the problems of equality in America, and it signals the decline of the short-sighted view that "discrimination" can be isolated from related social problems. Since the moral clarity of the civil rights movement has not always been accompanied by precise political vision, and sometimes not even by a real political consciousness the new phase is revolutionary in its implications. The greatest of these implications seems to be the threat posed to the Dixiecrat domination of the political channels. An increased Negro vote drive in and of itself is not going to dislodge the racist power, but an accelerating movement through the courts, the ballot boxes and especially the jails is the most likely means of shattering the crust of political irresponsibility and restoring a semblance of democratic order, on local and state levels.

2. The broadest movement for *peace* in several years emerged in 1961-62. In its political orientation and goals it is much less identifiable than the movement for civil rights: it includes socialists, pacifists, liberals, scholars, militant activists, middle class women, same professionals, many students, a few unionists. Some have been emotionally single-issues: Ban the Bomb. Some have been academically obscurantist. Some have rejected The System (sometime both Systems). Some have attempted, too, to "work within" The System. Amidst these conflicting streams of emphasis however, certain basic qualities appear. The most important is that the "peace movement" has operated almost exclusively through peripheral institutions-almost never through mainstream institutions. Similarly, individuals interested in peace have nonpolitical social roles that cannot be turned to the support of peace activity. Concretely, liberal religious societies, anti-war groups voluntary associations, ad hoc committees haw been the political unit of the peace movement, and its human movers have been students, teachers, housewives, secretaries, lawyers, doctors, clergy. The units have not been located in spots of major social influence, the people have not been able to turn their resources fully to the issues that concern them. The results are political ineffectiveness and personal alienation.

The organizing ability of the peace movement thus is limited to the ability to state and polarize issues. It does not have an institution or the forum in which the conflicting interests can be debated. The debate goes on in corners; it has little connection with the continuing process of determining allocations of resources. This process is not necessarily centralized is however much the peace movement is estranged from it. National policy, though dominated to: a large degree by the "power elites" of the corporations and military, is still partially founded in consensus. It can be altered when there actually begins a shift in the allocation of resources and the listing of priorities by the people in the Institutions which hand social influence, e.g., the labor unions and the schools. As long, as the debates of the peace movement form only a protest, rather than an opposition viewpoint within the centers of serious decision-making. Then it is neither a movement of democratic relevance, nor is it likely to have any effectiveness except in educating more outsiders to the issue, It is vital, to be sure, that this educating go on (a heartening sign is the recent proliferation of books and journals dealing with peace and war problems), As a domestic concern for peace grows, coupled to the heavy pressures from newly-developing countries, the possibility for making politicians responsible to "peace constituencies" becomes greater.

But in the long interim before the national political climate is more open to deliberate, goal-directed debate about peace issues, the dedicated peace "movement" might well prepare a *local base*: by establishing civic committees On the techniques of converting from military to peacetime production, especially, To make war and peace relevant to the problems of everyday life, by relating it to the backyard (shelters), the baby (fallout), the job (military contracts) and making a turn toward peace seem desirable on these same terms – is a task the peace movement is just beginning, and can profitably continue.

3. Central to any analysis of the potential for change must be an appraisal of *organized labor*. It would be un-historical to disregard the immense influence of labor in making modern America a decent place in which to live. It would be confused to fail to note labors presence today as the most liberal of mainstream institutions. But it would be

irresponsible not to criticize labor for losing the idealism that once made it a driving movement. Those who expected a labor upsurge after the 1955 AFL-CIO merger can only be dismayed that one year later, in the Stevenson-Eisenhower campaign, the AFL-CIO Committee on Political Education was able to obtain solicited $1 contributions from only one of every 24 unionists, and prompt only 40 per cent of the rank-and-file to vote.

As a political force, labor generally has been unsuccessful in the post-war period of prosperity. It has seen the passage of the Taft-Hartley and Landrum-Griffin laws, and while beginning to receive slightly favorable National Labor Relations Board rulings, it has made little progress against right-to work laws. Furthermore, it has seen less than adequate action of domestic problems, especially unemployment.

This labor "recession" has been only partly due to anti-labor politicians and corporations. Blame should be laid, too, to labor itself for not mounting an adequate movement. Labor has seen itself as elitist, rather than mass-oriented, and as a pressure group rather than as an 18-million member body making political demands for all America. In the first instance, the labor bureaucracy is cynical toward, or afraid of, rank-and-file involvement in the work of the union. Resolutions passed at conventions are implemented only by high-level machinations, not by mass mobilization of the unionists. Without a significant base, labors pressure function is materially reduced since it becomes difficult to hold political figures accountable to a movement that cannot muster a vote from a majority of its members.

There are some indications, however, that labor might regain its missing idealism. First, there are signs within the movement: of worker discontent with the economic progress of collective bargaining, of occasional splits among union leaders on questions such as nuclear testing or other Cold liar issues. Second; and more important, are the social forces which prompt these feelings of unrest. Foremost is the permanence of unemployment, and the threat of automation, but important too is the growth of unorganized ranks in white collar fields with steady depletion in the already-organized fields. Third, there is the tremendous challenge of the Negro movement for support from organized labor: the alienation from and disgust with labor hypocrisy among Negroes ranging from the NAACP to the Black Muslims (crystallized in the formation of the Negro American Labor Council) indicates that labor must move more seriously in its attempts to organize on an interracial basis in the South and in large urban areas. When this task was broached several years ago, "jurisdictional" disputes prevented action. Today, many of those disputes have been settled – and the question of a massive organizing campaign is on the labor agenda again.

These threats and opportunities point to a profound crisis: either labor continues to decline as a social force, omit must constitute itself as a mass political force demanding not only that society recognize its rights to organize but also a program going beyond desired labor legislation and welfare improvements. Necessarily this latter role will require rank-and-file involvement. It might include greater autonomy and power for political coalitions of the various trade unions in local areas, rather than the more stultifying dominance of the international unions now. It might include reductions in leaders salaries, or to rotation from executive office to shop obligations, as a means of breaking down thee hierarchical tendencies which have detached elite from base and made the highest echelons b$ labor more like businessmen than workers. It would certainly mean an announced independence of the center and Dixiecrat wings of the Democratic Party, and a massive organizing drive, especially in the South to complement the growing Negro political drive there.

But such is not the case at present. Few anticipate it, and fewer still exhort labor to begin. Labor continues to be the most liberal – and most frustrated – mainstream institution in America.

4. Since the Democratic Party sweep in 1958, there have been exaggerated but real efforts to establish a liberal-left force in Congress, not to balance but to at least voice criticism of the conservatives. The most notable of these efforts was the Liberal Project begun early in 1959 by Representative Kastenmeier of Wisconsin. The Project was

neither disciplined, nor very influential, but it was concerned at least with confronting basic domestic and foreign problems, in concert with several liberal intellectuals.

The Project was never more than embryonic. If 1960 five of its members were defeated (for reasons other than their membership in the Project), Then followed a "post mortem" publication of a collection of *The Liberal Papers*, materials discussed by the Project when it was in existence. The Republicans called the book "further out than communism". The New Frontier Administration repudiated any connection with the *Papers*. Former members of the Project even disclaimed their roles, except two. A hopeful beginning came to a shameful end.

But during the demise of the Project, a new spirit of Democratic Party reform was occurring in several places: New York City, Ithaca, Massachusetts, Connecticut, Texas, California, and even in Mississippi and Alabama where Negro candidates for Congress challenged racist political power. Some were for peace, some for the liberal side of the New Frontier, some for realignment of the parties – and in most cases they were supported by students.

Americans for Democratic Action and *The New Republic*, pillars of the liberal community, took stands against the President on nuclear testing. A split, slight thus far, developed in organic labor on the same issue. The Rev, Martin Luther King Jr. preached against the Dixiecrat-Republican coalition across the nation. Here and there were stirrings of unprogrammatic discontent with the political stalemate.

5. From 1960 to 1962, the campuses experienced a revival of idealism among an active few. Triggered by the impact of the sit-ins, students began to struggle for integration, civil liberties, students' rights, peace and against the fast-rising right-wing "revolt" as well. The liberal students, too, have felt their urgency thwarted by conventional channels from student governments to congressional committees. Out of this sense of alienation from existing channels has come the creation of new ones; the most characteristic forms of liberal-radical student organizations

are the dozens of campus political parties, political journals, and peace demonstrations. In only a few cases have students built bridges to powers an occasional election campaign, or a show of action by campus ADA or the Young Democrats, or infrequently through the United States National Student Association whose notable work has not been focused on political change,

These contemporary social movements – for peace, civil rights, civil liberties, labor – have in common certain values and goals. The fight for civil rights is also one for social welfare for all Americans; for free speech and the right to protest; for the shield of economic independence and bargaining power; for reduction of the arms race which takes national attention and resources away from the settlement of domestic injustice. The fight of labor for jobs and wages is also one to end exploitation of the Negro as a source of cheap labor; for the right to petition and strike; for world industrialization; for the stability of peacetime economy instead of the insecurity of a war economy; for expansion of the Welfare State. The fight for a liberal congress is a fight for a platform from which these concerns can issue. And, the fight for student rights, for internal democracy in the university, is a fight too university a potential base and agency for a movement of social change.

1. Any new left in America must be, in large measure, a left with real intellectual skills, committed to deliberativeness, honesty, reflection as working tools. The university permits the political life to be an adjunct to the academic one, and action to be informed by reason.

2. A new left must be distributed in significant social roles throughout the country.

3. A new left must consist of younger people who matured in the postwar worlds and partially be directed to the recruitment of younger people. The university is the obvious beginning point.

4. A new left must include liberals and socialists, the farmer for their relevance, the latter for their sense of thoroughgoing reforms in the system. The university is a more sensible place than a political party for

these two traditions to discuss their differences and look for political synthesis.

5. A new left must start controversy across the land, if national policies and national apathy are to be reversed. The ideal university is a community of controversy, within itself in its effects on communities .beyond.

6. A new left must transform modern complexity into issues that can be understood and felt close-up by every human being. It must give form to the feelings of helplessness and indifference, so that people may see the political, social, and economic sources of their private troubles and organize to change society. In a time of supposed prosperity, moral complacency and political manipulation, a new left cannot rely on aching stomachs to be the engine force of social reform. The case for changes, for alternatives that will involve uncomfortable personal efforts, must be argued as never before. The university is a relevant place for all of these activities.

To turn these possibilities into realities will involve national efforts at university reform by an alliance of students and faculty. They must wrest control of the educational process from the administrative bureaucracy. They must legitimize the right to speak and act in public, partisan ways. They must make fraternal and functional contact with allies in labor, civil rights, and other liberal farces outside the campus,, They must import major public issues into the curriculum – research and teaching on problems of war and peace is an outstanding example. They must make debate and controversy, not dull pedantic cant, the common style of the educational life.

As students for a democratic society we are committed to stimulating this kind of social movement, this kind of vision and program in campus and community across the country.

If we appear to seek the unattainable, it has been said, then let it be known that we do so to avoid the unimaginable.

Transcribed by Jim Kalafus, May 2006

Questions for discussion:

How do the authors of this document perceive themselves?

What can we deduce about them, including their age, education, social background?

Why in their view has the old Left failed?

What is their idea of revolution? Note the use of the lower-case 'n' in 'new Left'.

Historiography of World History

Q: How many historians does it take to change a light bulb?

A (by Dr. L): There is a great deal of debate on this issue. Up until the mid-20th century, the accepted answer was 'one': and this Whiggish narrative underpinned a number of works that celebrated electrification and the march of progress in light-bulb changing. Beginning in the 1960s, however, social historians increasingly rejected the 'Great Man' school and produced revisionist narratives that stressed the contributions of research assistants and custodial staff. This new consensus was challenged, in turn, by women's historians, who criticized the social interpretation for marginalizing women, and who argued that light bulbs are actually changed by department secretaries. Since the 1980s, however, postmodernist scholars have deconstructed what they characterize as a repressive hegemonic discourse of light-bulb changing, with its implicit binary opposition between 'light' and 'darkness,' and its phallogocentric privileging of the bulb over the socket, which they see as colonialist, sexist, and racist. Finally, a new generation of neo-conservative historians have concluded that the light never needed changing in the first place, and have praised political leaders like Ronald Reagan and Margaret Thatcher for bringing back the old bulb. Clearly, much additional research remains to be done.

Source: http://fundermental.blogspot.co.uk/2011/05/peer-review-changing-lightbulb.html?m=1 [accessed 13 July 2013]

Going further:

James Baldwin, *The Fire Next Time*, Dial Press, New York, 1963

Felipe Fernández-Armesto , *The World: A History*, Prentice Hall, Upper Saddle River NJ, second edition, 2010

Betty Friedan, *The Feminine Mystique*, W.W. Norton, New York, 1963

Ian MacDonald, *Revolution in the Head: The Beatles' Records and the Sixties*, third edition, Vintage, London, 2005

Robert Pascoe, *The Manufacture of Australian History*, Oxford University Press, Melbourne, 1979

Robert Pascoe, *The Feasts & Seasons of John F. Kelly*, Allen & Unwin, Crows Nest NSW, 2006

Charles A. Reich, *The Greening of America*, Random House, New York, 1970

Peter Robb, *Midnight in Sicily*, Duffy & Snellgrove, Sydney, 1996

Unit 24

Neo-liberalism and the New World Order

'A working class hero is something to be', sang John Lennon:

> As soon as you're born they make you feel small
> By giving you no time instead of it all
> Till the pain is so big you feel nothing at all
> A working class hero is something to be
>
> They hurt you at home and they hit you at school
> They hate you if you're clever and they despise a fool
> Till you're so ****ing crazy you can't follow their rules
> A working class hero is something to be

The Lennon Wall in Prague [Rosemary Clerehan]

> When they've tortured and scared you for twenty-odd years
> Then they expect you to pick a career
> When you can't really function you're so full of fear
> A working class hero is something to be
>
> Keep you doped with religion and sex and TV
> And you think you're so clever and classless and free
> But you're still ****ing peasants as far as I can see
> A working class hero is something to be
>
> There's room at the top they're telling you still
> But first you must learn how to smile as you kill
> If you want to be like the folks on the hill
>
> A working class hero is something to be
> If you want to be a hero well just follow me

Lennon expresses the angst of many young people faced with a future that seems depressingly similar to what had gone before.

Contemporary history should be a guide to our immediate future in the twenty-first century, and even into the twenty-second century for some young people. The future is just the past before we experience it. The point of history is partly to show us what might happen if present trends continue. For example, with the accelerating effect of globalisation, one retired European banker says that a world government is inevitable.[92]

From its nadir in 1975 the US re-invented itself and defeated the Soviet Union in the Cold War. The secrets of its success were the adoption of a neo-liberal economic policy and its political commitment to the New World Order. Neo-liberalism produced a massive shift in resources to the American middle class, while the New World Order after 2001 gave America the right to the pre-emptive strike against its enemies.

---

92 Jacques Attali, *A Brief History of the Future*, Arcade, 2009.

At an economic level, the American State moved from the Keynesianism that had produced the Marshall Plan to neo-liberalism, as advocated by the economic rationalists. Foremost amongst these was Milton Friedman, who advocated lower taxes and the privatisation of government assets. In broad terms, the excesses of the Sixties produced a counter-reaction in the American heartland, with the emergence of the neo-conservatives, calling for Christian fundamentalism, anti-abortion legislation, and the teaching of Creationism in schools.

After Nixon was succeeded by Vice-President Gerald Ford, the Democrats returned to the White House with the election in 1976 of the progressive Jimmy Carter. Unfortunately for Carter's chances of re-election, in 1979 American diplomats were taken hostage in Teheran during the Iranian Revolution. The following year the Soviet Union invaded Afghanistan; the Afghani rebels were supported by the US. The same year the Iran-Iraq war started, proving to be the longest war of the twentieth century.

Meanwhile the Republican conservative Ronald Reagan was elected President and began a massive military build-up. In 1981 the USSR imposed martial law in Poland, and in 1983 Reagan deployed missiles in Western Europe, beginning his program of SDI (the Strategic Defense Initiative) and invaded Grenada as a show of US military strength. In 1984 Reagan was rewarded with a re-election. In 1985 Mikhail Gorbachev was appointed Premier of the USSR; within a year he had introduced both 'glasnost' and 'perestroika' to open up the Soviet economy and improve relations with the West.

This was the context in which George Bush Sr was elected President in 1988. In 1989 the Berlin Wall was opened and the Eastern European regimes were overthrown without interference from Gorbachev. In 1990 Iraq, still feeling the cost of its pointless war with Iran, invaded Kuwait. Germany was reunified in 1990, and Soviet troops began to withdraw from Eastern Europe.

In 1991 the US liberated Kuwait from the Iraqis in the First Gulf War and the USSR finally collapsed in the face of the astonishing growth in American wealth and power. The Cold War seemed to be over, and the US had won.

In 1992 the Balkans Wars erupted, following the break-up of the former Yugoslavia. A Democrat, Bill Clinton was elected President, and began to renegotiate America's role in the world throughout the 1990s. He decade proved to be relatively peaceful, with some notable exceptions and minor episodes that were a harbinger of what was to follow. In the 2000 elections George W. Bush was elected President. In 2001 the September 11 attacks gave his Administration the opportunity to return to the style of world leadership Reagan and his father had pursued. In 2003 US-led forces mounted an invasion of Iraq on the pretext of a connection with the September 11 bombings. Before the Iraqi occupation was complete, the US took NATO troops also into Afghanistan.

In 2008 a progressive Democrat and American's first Black President, Barack Obama was elected. The US survived the Global Financial Crisis (GFC) and Obama was re-elected in 2012.

The US and al-Qa'ida

With the end of the Cold War, Islamic and American interests were coming into conflict during the 1990s. Ironically, the US had helped train and support Islamic warriors in Afghanistan fighting the Soviets in the 1980s – their victory here and the Islamic Revolution in Iran in 1979 gave the Muslims renewed confidence. The militant al-Qa'ida launched a series of attacks on American interests in Africa during the 1990s and the *USS Cole* in the port of Aden on 12 October 2000. September 11 was the next step.

9/11 was as difficult an event for the Americans to fathom as the assassination of President Kennedy in November 1963, and also gave rise to various 'conspiracy theories'. One was the World Trade Center buildings were detonated by the US Government as a pretext for war.

Satirical cartoon featuring Julian Assange (WikiLeaks founder)
and Mark Zuckerberg (Person of the Year, Time, 2010)

Another was that US Air Force planes were ordered to Stand Down that day. A third was that no Jewish-Americans were in the building that day.[93] Just as with the Kennedy assassination, the US Government has responded with the digital publication of hundreds of key documents.[94] This evidence establishes conclusively enough that the so-called Holy Tuesday Operation was undeniably an al-Qa'ida plot. The US was alleged

---

93 Marc Levin, dir. *Protocols of Zion*, 93 mins, 2005.
94 US. National Commission on Terrorist Attacks Upon the United States [9-11Commission.gov, archived 2004]; US. 911 Investigations.net, a repository of documents relating to the 9/11 attacks and the War on Terrorism [911digitalarchive.org].

to have committed various crimes: the military occupation of the Arabian peninsula in the First Gulf War; aggression against the Iraqi people; and support of Israel against the Palestinians.

'The Power of Nightmares' (a BBC series from 2005) argues that both sides have exaggerated the threats to peace. It places al-Qa'ida in the tradition of the French Jacobins and the late nineteenth century anarchists: they are in that sense 'modern' - they anticipate a better tomorrow. It is their asymmetrical power vis-a-vis the USA that gives them strength. Even with the killing of Osama bin Laden, Obama continues with the use of drones and raids to conduct extra-judicial killing. Osama bin Laden was killed by US forces without a process, as the Pakistani report into the incident makes clear.

During the Cold War, both sides used assassination. Israel's Mossad became quite skilled at extra-judicial killing. Suspicion now surrounds every death, including that of Princess Di.[95]

History as a guide to the future

What will the twenty-first century look like? What is the future of History as a discipline? Globalisation, from A to Z (Assange to Zuckerberg) has helped accentuate world-wide values. The environmental crisis has created a stronger sense of concern for the planet. Moreover, the world has been 'flattened' by forces such as the Internet and suddenly there is a degree of competition never seen before. The development of new instant journalism, with its pitfalls and promises, has made every part of the globe open to all.

This globalisation does not mean a blurring of values, for there are still profound differences across the globe in how people see themselves in terms of religion and their values orientation. For example, the Inglehart Values Map attempts to chart where the deo-centric view is still strong, and where survival remains a daily concern, as we shall see. These values reflect the embedded history in these respective cultures.

---

95 Richard Belfield, *Terminate with Extreme Prejudice*, Pan Macmillan, Sydney, 2005.

Globalisation is also dependent on a post-industrial model of innovation. This post-industrial model of innovation works on a different paradigm to the industrial model. Now innovation is less about new inventions and their applications, more the improvement of processes. Along the way technological genius gives way to knowledge-laden industries. The 'practical man' is being replaced by the 'symbolic analyst' made famous by Clinton's Secretary of Labor, Robert Reich.[96] There is not one centre of innovation whose technicians populate the New World, but many, perhaps two dozen in all.

Some of these new centres of post-industrial innovation are in China and India. Neither China nor India allowed themselves to be westernised. The British rule of India did not fundamentally alter that society: the caste system continues, and there is a widening gap between rich and poor. The story of Rupert Murdoch in China is instructive.[97] Despite his investment, the Government rebuffed his inducements: China will continue to resist the West. China is now investing heavily across Asia and Africa. This so-called China Model proposes a different paradigm, just as post-war America said it was different from France and Britain during its imperial growth.

China now has global ambitions. Chinese is producing for a world market, as exemplified by the Guangdong Enterprises royal mug minted for the last British royal wedding. The future of China is one of continued economic growth. China is due to overtake the US economy in size by the year 2020. Questions abound: Will China be able to sustain its precocious economic growth? Will its citizens continue to accept the current political regime? Will its leadership adopt environmentally sound policies?

Will China adopt economic neo-liberalism and the New World Order? What will be the role of Chinese cyber warfare in future conflicts?

---

96 Robert Reich, *The Work of Nations: Preparing Ourselves for 21st Century Capitalism*, A.A. Knopf, New York, 1991.
97 Bruce Dover, *Rupert's Adventures in China: How Murdoch Lost a Fortune and Found a Wife*, Viking, London, 2008.

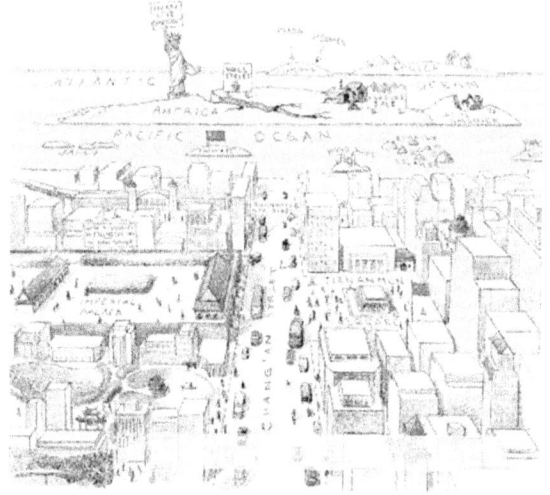

The spectre of a rising China in the twenty-first century [The Economist]

Economic Activity in a Spiky World

If we map the world with spikes to indicate places of economic significance, what results is a Spiky World. Beneath these spikes are particular histories of regions and societies across the globe that world historians have studied and written about. The values map of Ronald Inglehart suggests some of the cultural differences. There is still a division in Europe between Catholic and Protestant. There is the post-Communist legacy of the Russian Revolution. There are Spanish-speaking and English-speaking remnants of their respective empires. And there are Islamic, Buddhist, Confucian societies. Locating these on the Inglehart values map indicates how they cluster across the two axes.

The vertical axis measures societies in the deocentric/ anthrocentric spread, while the horizontal axis places them along the industrialising/ post-industrial spectrum. The cultural orientation of societies suggest they are at different points in the continuum from the deocentric to the anthro-centric. The deo-centric worldview is still strong in some Islamic and Spanish-speaking societies. Abraham Maslow contended that people's needs change as material survival ceases to be an issue. This is reflected in the survey data of people in societies that have become post-industrial. The Values Map is surprisingly consistent.

If we use categories such as the economic, the social, the cultural and the political, we can summarise the broad span of World History.

Economic theme in World History

Despite all the developments in what we call World History, there are still people who live as Primitive Communists. For instance, the Piraha

The commemorative mug prepared for the wedding of William and Kate in April 2011 by Guangdong Enterprises mixes up its royals

live in the Amazon valley with little contact with other languages, except some Portuguese. Their language appears to have very few numerals, or words for colour, or abstract nouns. The year 10,000 BCE marks the end of pre-patriarchal hunting and gathering societies. Patriarchy developed in urban centres, such as Sumer. From here it was a short step to the slave economies of Greece and Rome. The Spartacus revolt (73 BCE) demonstrated that there were always unresolved tensions between slaveholder and slave.

Feudalism emerged as a synthesis of the primitive communism of the nomadic Germans and the slave economy of the Roman Empire. Feudalism centred on France, but failed to develop outside Europe.

The Islamic and East Asian economies were less feudal and more proto-capitalist. Some have argued that the American South, with its slave economy, was closer to feudalism as a lived reality.

The Industrial Revolution in Britain (1780–1820) fundamentally changed the economic history of the world – especially when coupled with capitalism. Industrial capitalism developed on the Continent, and then in Japan and the USA – it broke clear from Europe in a way that feudalism could not. An industrial model of innovation explains the precocious economic success of the USA in the nineteenth century – immigration was also part of that formula. In the late twentieth century innovation began to occur according to a post-industrial model.

Social theme in World History

Human societies take on a surprising variety of forms. India's caste system is very old and well-established, while other social structures have been more changeable. For example, Classical Athens had an idealised view of men, while women's lives improved under the Romans. Roman social order was reflected in the town planning of cities like Lutetia (Paris). In the medieval period towns grew back following the end of the Roman Empire. Towns represented a separate culture from the world of the feudal countryside. The two dominant classes of this period (the peasantry, the gentry) were superseded in size and importance by the two dominant classes of industrial capitalism (the proletariat, the bourgeoisie). Western and non-Western cities seemed to take on different patterns throughout this medieval and early-modern period. Haussmann's refashioning of Paris in the mid-nineteenth century was very important, both for Paris and the cities worldwide that modelled themselves on it. In 2006 the majority of people were urbanites for the first time in world history. The 'demographic transition' should mean that the total population levels off in mid-twenty-first century and then steadily declines to around 6 billion.

Political theme in World History

Political systems have similarly varied widely throughout history. Direct democracy was a feature of Classical Athens, while Chinese bureaucratic rule is very old and efficient – based on meritocracy and Confucian learning. Medieval monarchs began to depend on parliaments to raise taxes; the English Civil War (1640s-1650s) reflected the failure of the monarch to understand how this could work in practice. The American Revolution (1776) and the French Revolution (1789) were crucial moments in this assertion of popular sovereignty, while the socialist Russian Revolution (1917) put power in the hands of the new proletariat. However, socialism failed elsewhere in Europe – especially in Germany, Italy, Spain – and in the USA. Decolonisation followed the break-up of European hegemony after the World Wars of the twentieth century, creating new centres of political power elsewhere. Future political power will not be confined to national boundaries, as al-Qa'ida has shown.

With changes in politics have come changes in the face of war. The twentieth century saw war changing from fixed armies ranged across wide battlefields to surgical strikes and guerrilla campaigns.[98] Despite the military might of America, it has failed in Vietnam, Iraq, and Afghanistan.

---

98 Martin Van Creveld, *The Changing Face of War: Lessons of Combat, from the Marne to Iraq*, Ballantine Books, New York, 2006.

Cultural theme in World History

More attention should be given to the history of languages in world history – how different people view the world differently through the prism of Arabic, Latin, English or another major language – as language certainly frames cultural understandings.[99] Religion is interwoven with language. For instance, India is the home of both Hinduism and Buddhism. In early times, monotheistic religions gradually replaced the polytheism of early paganism. The medieval Christian Church embarked on major imperial projects, such as the Crusades, but underneath the cover of Christendom European peasants continued to live 'la cultura contadina' into modern times.

In the aftermath of the industrial revolution, the nineteenth century saw the development of urban culture, such as the novel, to explain the profound changes taking place. Around 1910 avant-garde writers adopted Modernism, notably William Carlos Williams, James Joyce, Virginia Woolf. After the Second World War new writers emerged, such as the existentialists in Paris and the Beat generation in San Francisco, who fundamentally challenged the optimism of the Modernists. The new movements of twenty-first century were as likely to be separatist groups, such as the feminists and the environmentalists.

History's twin questions appeared in the film *Rear Window* (Alfred Hitchcock, dir. 1954) in the words of Lisa to her wheelchair-bound boyfriend Jeff who thought he saw a murder being committed: 'Tell me exactly what you saw -- and what you think it means.'

---

99 Nicholas Ostler, *Empires of the Word: A Language History of the World*, Harper Perennial, London, 2006 [2005].

Primary source:

Barack Obama, *A New Beginning*, 4 June 2009

Barack Obama's speech in Cairo, Egypt in front of the Muslim World is about building new relationships with and among Middle East countries to pursue peace not as single nations but as a unified people in pursuit of world peace and acceptance.

Thank you very much. Good afternoon. I am honored to be in the timeless city of Cairo, and to be hosted by two remarkable institutions. For over a thousand years, Al-Azhar has stood as a beacon of Islamic learning; and for over a century, Cairo University has been a source of Egypt's advancement. And together, you represent the harmony between tradition and progress. I'm grateful for your hospitality, and the hospitality of the people of Egypt. And I'm also proud to carry with me the goodwill of the American people, and a greeting of peace from Muslim communities in my country: Assalaamualaykum. (Applause.)

We meet at a time of great tension between the United States and Muslims around the world – tension rooted in historical forces that go beyond any current policy debate. The relationship between Islam and the West includes centuries of coexistence and cooperation, but also conflict and religious wars. More recently, tension has been fed by colonialism that denied rights and opportunities to many Muslims, and a Cold War in which Muslim-majority countries were too often treated as proxies without regard to their own aspirations. Moreover, the sweeping change brought by modernity and globalization led many Muslims to view the West as hostile to the traditions of Islam.

Violent extremists have exploited these tensions in a small but potent minority of Muslims. The attacks of September 11, 2001 and the continued efforts of these extremists to engage in violence against civilians has led some in my country to view Islam as inevitably hostile not only to America and Western countries, but also to human rights. All this has bred more fear and more mistrust.

So long as our relationship is defined by our differences, we will empower those who sow hatred rather than peace, those who promote conflict rather than the cooperation that can help all of our people achieve justice and prosperity. And this cycle of suspicion and discord must end.

I've come here to Cairo to seek a new beginning between the United States and Muslims around the world, one based on mutual interest and mutual respect, and one based upon the truth that America and Islam are not exclusive and need not be in competition. Instead, they overlap, and share common principles – principles of justice and progress; tolerance and the dignity of all human beings.

I do so recognizing that change cannot happen overnight. I know there's been a lot of publicity about this speech, but no single speech can eradicate years of mistrust, nor can I answer in the time that I have this afternoon all the complex questions that brought us to this point. But I am convinced that in order to move forward, we must say openly to each other the things we hold in our hearts and that too often are said only behind closed doors. There must be a sustained effort to listen to each other; to learn from each other; to respect one another; and to seek common ground. As the Holy Koran tells us, "Be conscious of God and speak always the truth." (Applause.) That is what I will try to do today – to speak the truth as best I can, humbled by the task before us, and firm in my belief that the interests we share as human beings are far more powerful than the forces that drive us apart.

Now part of this conviction is rooted in my own experience. I'm a Christian, but my father came from a Kenyan family that includes generations of Muslims. As a boy, I spent several years in Indonesia and heard the call of the azaan at the break of dawn and at the fall of dusk. As a young man, I worked in Chicago communities where many found dignity and peace in their Muslim faith.

Barack Obama speaking in Cairo, 4 June 2009 [Foreign Policy Association]

As a student of history, I also know civilization's debt to Islam. It was Islam – at places like Al-Azhar – that carried the light of learning through so many centuries, paving the way for Europe's Renaissance and Enlightenment. It was innovation in Muslim communities – (applause) – it was innovation in Muslim communities that developed the order of algebra; our magnetic compass and tools of navigation; our mastery of pens and printing; our understanding of how disease spreads and how it can be healed. Islamic culture has given us majestic arches and soaring spires; timeless poetry and cherished music; elegant calligraphy and places of peaceful contemplation. And throughout history, Islam has demonstrated through words and deeds the possibilities of religious tolerance and racial equality. (Applause.)

I also know that Islam has always been a part of America's story. The first nation to recognize my country was Morocco. In signing the

Treaty of Tripoli in 1796, our second President, John Adams, wrote, "The United States has in itself no character of enmity against the laws, religion or tranquility of Muslims." And since our founding, American Muslims have enriched the United States. They have fought in our wars, they have served in our government, they have stood for civil rights, they have started businesses, they have taught at our universities, they've excelled in our sports arenas, they've won Nobel Prizes, built our tallest building, and lit the Olympic Torch. And when the first Muslim American was recently elected to Congress, he took the oath to defend our Constitution using the same Holy Koran that one of our Founding Fathers – Thomas Jefferson – kept in his personal library. (Applause.)

So I have known Islam on three continents before coming to the region where it was first revealed. That experience guides my conviction that partnership between America and Islam must be based on what Islam is, not what it isn't. And I consider it part of my responsibility as President of the United States to fight against negative stereotypes of Islam wherever they appear. (Applause.)

But that same principle must apply to Muslim perceptions of America. (Applause.) Just as Muslims do not fit a crude stereotype, America is not the crude stereotype of a self-interested empire. The United States has been one of the greatest sources of progress that the world has ever known. We were born out of revolution against an empire. We were founded upon the ideal that all are created equal, and we have shed blood and struggled for centuries to give meaning to those words – within our borders, and around the world. We are shaped by every culture, drawn from every end of the Earth, and dedicated to a simple concept: E pluribus unum – "Out of many, one".

Now, much has been made of the fact that an African American with the name Barack Hussein Obama could be elected President. (Applause.) But my personal story is not so unique. The dream of opportunity for all people has not come true for everyone in America, but its promise exists for all who come to our shores – and that includes nearly 7 million

American Muslims in our country today who, by the way, enjoy incomes and educational levels that are higher than the American average. (Applause.)

Moreover, freedom in America is indivisible from the freedom to practice one's religion. That is why there is a mosque in every state in our union, and over 1,200 mosques within our borders. That's why the United States government has gone to court to protect the right of women and girls to wear the hijab and to punish those who would deny it. So let there be no doubt. (Applause.)

Let there be no doubt: Islam is a part of America. And I believe that America holds within her the truth that regardless of race, religion, or station in life, all of us share common aspirations – to live in peace and security; to get an education and to work with dignity; to love our families, our communities, and our God. These things we share. This is the hope of all humanity.

Of course, recognizing our common humanity is only the beginning of our task. Words alone cannot meet the needs of our people. These needs will be met only if we act boldly in the years ahead; and if we understand that the challenges we face are shared, and our failure to meet them will hurt us all.

For we have learned from recent experience that when a financial system weakens in one country, prosperity is hurt everywhere. When a new flu infects one human being, all are at risk. When one nation pursues a nuclear weapon, the risk of nuclear attack rises for all nations. When violent extremists operate in one stretch of mountains, people are endangered across an ocean. When innocents in Bosnia and Darfur are slaughtered, that is a stain on our collective conscience. (Applause.) That is what it means to share this world in the 21st century. That is the responsibility we have to one another as human beings.

And this is a difficult responsibility to embrace. For human history has often been a record of nations and tribes – and, yes, religions – subjugating one another in pursuit of their own interests. Yet in this new age, such attitudes are self-defeating. Given our interdependence, any world order that elevates one nation or group of people over another will inevitably fail. So whatever we think of the past, we must not be prisoners to it. Our problems must be dealt with through partnership; our progress must be shared. (Applause.)

Now, that does not mean we should ignore sources of tension. Indeed, it suggests the opposite: We must face these tensions squarely. And so in that spirit, let me speak as clearly and as plainly as I can about some specific issues that I believe we must finally confront together.

The first issue that we have to confront is violent extremism in all of its forms.

In Ankara, I made clear that America is not – and never will be – at war with Islam. (Applause.) We will, however, relentlessly confront violent extremists who pose a grave threat to our security – because we reject the same thing that people of all faiths reject: the killing of innocent men, women, and children. And it is my first duty as President to protect the American people.

The situation in Afghanistan demonstrates America's goals, and our need to work together. Over seven years ago, the United States pursued al Qaeda and the Taliban with broad international support. We did not go by choice; we went because of necessity. I'm aware that there's still some who would question or even justify the events of 9/11. But let us be clear: Al Qaeda killed nearly 3,000 people on that day. The victims were innocent men, women and children from America and many other nations who had done nothing to harm anybody. And yet al Qaeda chose to ruthlessly murder these people, claimed credit for the attack, and even now states their determination to kill on a massive scale. They have affiliates in many countries and are trying to expand their reach. These are not opinions to be debated; these are facts to be dealt with.

Now, make no mistake: We do not want to keep our troops in Afghanistan. We see no military – we seek no military bases there. It is agonizing for America to lose our young men and women. It is costly and politically difficult to continue this conflict. We would gladly bring every single one of our troops home if we could be confident that there were not violent extremists in Afghanistan and now Pakistan determined to kill as many Americans as they possibly can. But that is not yet the case.

And that's why we're partnering with a coalition of 46 countries. And despite the costs involved, America's commitment will not weaken. Indeed, none of us should tolerate these extremists. They have killed in many countries. They have killed people of different faiths – but more than any other, they have killed Muslims. Their actions are irreconcilable with the rights of human beings, the progress of nations, and with Islam. The Holy Koran teaches that whoever kills an innocent is as – it is as if he has killed all mankind. (Applause.) And the Holy Koran also says whoever saves a person, it is as if he has saved all mankind. (Applause.) The enduring faith of over a billion people is so much bigger than the narrow hatred of a few. Islam is not part of the problem in combating violent extremism – it is an important part of promoting peace.

Now, we also know that military power alone is not going to solve the problems in Afghanistan and Pakistan. That's why we plan to invest $1.5 billion each year over the next five years to partner with Pakistanis to build schools and hospitals, roads and businesses, and hundreds of millions to help those who've been displaced. That's why we are providing more than $2.8 billion to help Afghans develop their economy and deliver services that people depend on.

Let me also address the issue of Iraq. Unlike Afghanistan, Iraq was a war of choice that provoked strong differences in my country and around the world. Although I believe that the Iraqi people are ultimately better off without the tyranny of Saddam Hussein, I also believe that events in Iraq have reminded America of the need to use diplomacy and build international consensus to resolve our problems whenever possible. (Applause.) Indeed, we can recall the words of Thomas Jefferson, who said: "I hope that our wisdom will grow with our power, and teach us that the less we use our power the greater it will be."

Today, America has a dual responsibility: to help Iraq forge a better future – and to leave Iraq to Iraqis. And I have made it clear to the Iraqi people – (applause) – I have made it clear to the Iraqi people that we pursue no bases, and no claim on their territory or resources. Iraq's sovereignty is its own. And that's why I ordered the removal of our combat brigades by next August. That is why we will honor our agreement with Iraq's democratically elected government to remove combat troops from Iraqi cities by July, and to remove all of our troops from Iraq by 2012. (Applause.) We will help Iraq train its security forces and develop its economy. But we will support a secure and united Iraq as a partner, and never as a patron.

And finally, just as America can never tolerate violence by extremists, we must never alter or forget our principles. Nine-eleven was an enormous trauma to our country. The fear and anger that it provoked was understandable, but in some cases, it led us to act contrary to our traditions and our ideals. We are taking concrete actions to change course. I have unequivocally prohibited the use of torture by the United States, and I have ordered the prison at Guantanamo Bay closed by early next year. (Applause.)

So America will defend itself, respectful of the sovereignty of nations and the rule of law. And we will do so in partnership with Muslim communities which are also threatened. The sooner the extremists are isolated and unwelcome in Muslim communities, the sooner we will all be safer.

The second major source of tension that we need to discuss is the situation between Israelis, Palestinians and the Arab world.

America's strong bonds with Israel are well known. This bond is unbreakable. It is based upon cultural and historical ties, and the recognition that the aspiration for a Jewish homeland is rooted in a tragic history that cannot be denied.

Around the world, the Jewish people were persecuted for centuries, and anti-Semitism in Europe culminated in an unprecedented Holocaust.

Tomorrow, I will visit Buchenwald, which was part of a network of camps where Jews were enslaved, tortured, shot and gassed to death by the Third Reich. Six million Jews were killed – more than the entire Jewish population of Israel today. Denying that fact is baseless, it is ignorant, and it is hateful. Threatening Israel with destruction – or repeating vile stereotypes about Jews – is deeply wrong, and only serves to evoke in the minds of Israelis this most painful of memories while preventing the peace that the people of this region deserve.

On the other hand, it is also undeniable that the Palestinian people – Muslims and Christians – have suffered in pursuit of a homeland. For more than 60 years they've endured the pain of dislocation. Many wait in refugee camps in the West Bank, Gaza, and neighboring lands for a life of peace and security that they have never been able to lead. They endure the daily humiliations – large and small – that come with occupation. So let there be no doubt: The situation for the Palestinian people is intolerable. And America will not turn our backs on the legitimate Palestinian aspiration for dignity, opportunity, and a state of their own. (Applause.)

For decades then, there has been a stalemate: two peoples with legitimate aspirations, each with a painful history that makes compromise elusive. It's easy to point fingers – for Palestinians to point to the displacement brought about by Israel's founding, and for Israelis to point to the constant hostility and attacks throughout its history from within its borders as well as beyond. But if we see this conflict only from one side or the other, then we will be blind to the truth: The only resolution is for the aspirations of both sides to be met through two states, where Israelis and Palestinians each live in peace and security. (Applause.)

That is in Israel's interest, Palestine's interest, America's interest, and the world's interest. And that is why I intend to personally pursue this outcome with all the patience and dedication that the task requires. (Applause.) The obligations – the obligations that the parties have agreed to under the road map are clear. For peace to come, it is time for them – and all of us – to live up to our responsibilities.

Palestinians must abandon violence. Resistance through violence and killing is wrong and it does not succeed. For centuries, black people in America suffered the lash of the whip as slaves and the humiliation of segregation. But it was not violence that won full and equal rights. It was a peaceful and determined insistence upon the ideals at the center of America's founding. This same story can be told by people from South Africa to South Asia; from Eastern Europe to Indonesia. It's a story with a simple truth: that violence is a dead end. It is a sign neither of courage nor power to shoot rockets at sleeping children, or to blow up old women on a bus. That's not how moral authority is claimed; that's how it is surrendered.

Now is the time for Palestinians to focus on what they can build. The Palestinian Authority must develop its capacity to govern, with institutions that serve the needs of its people. Hamas does have support among some Palestinians, but they also have to recognize they have responsibilities. To play a role in fulfilling Palestinian aspirations, to unify the Palestinian people, Hamas must put an end to violence, recognize past agreements, recognize Israel's right to exist.

At the same time, Israelis must acknowledge that just as Israel's right to exist cannot be denied, neither can Palestine's. The United States does not accept the legitimacy of continued Israeli settlements. (Applause.) This construction violates previous agreements and undermines efforts to achieve peace. It is time for these settlements to stop. (Applause.)

And Israel must also live up to its obligation to ensure that Palestinians can live and work and develop their society. Just as it devastates Palestinian families, the continuing humanitarian crisis in Gaza does not serve Israel's security; neither does the continuing lack of opportunity in the West Bank. Progress in the daily lives of the Palestinian people must be a critical part of a road to peace, and Israel must take concrete steps to enable such progress.

And finally, the Arab states must recognize that the Arab Peace Initiative was an important beginning, but not the end of their responsibilities. The Arab-Israeli conflict should no longer be used to distract the people of Arab nations from other problems. Instead, it must be a cause for action to help the Palestinian people develop the institutions that will sustain their state, to recognize Israel's legitimacy, and to choose progress over a self-defeating focus on the past.

America will align our policies with those who pursue peace, and we will say in public what we say in private to Israelis and Palestinians and Arabs. (Applause.) We cannot impose peace. But privately, many Muslims recognize that Israel will not go away. Likewise, many Israelis recognize the need for a Palestinian state. It is time for us to act on what everyone knows to be true.

Too many tears have been shed. Too much blood has been shed. All of us have a responsibility to work for the day when the mothers of Israelis and Palestinians can see their children grow up without fear; when the Holy Land of the three great faiths is the place of peace that God intended it to be; when Jerusalem is a secure and lasting home for Jews and Christians and Muslims, and a place for all of the children of Abraham to mingle peacefully together as in the story of Isra – (applause) – as in the story of Isra, when Moses, Jesus, and Mohammed, peace be upon them, joined in prayer. (Applause.)

The third source of tension is our shared interest in the rights and responsibilities of nations on nuclear weapons.

This issue has been a source of tension between the United States and the Islamic Republic of Iran. For many years, Iran has defined itself in part by its opposition to my country, and there is in fact a tumultuous history between us. In the middle of the Cold War, the United States played a role in the overthrow of a democratically elected Iranian government. Since the Islamic Revolution, Iran has played a role in acts of hostage-taking and violence against U.S. troops and civilians. This history is well known. Rather than remain trapped in the past, I've made it clear to Iran's leaders and people that my country is prepared to move forward. The question now is not what Iran is against, but rather what future it wants to build.

I recognize it will be hard to overcome decades of mistrust, but we will proceed with courage, rectitude, and resolve. There will be many issues to discuss between our two countries, and we are willing to move forward without preconditions on the basis of mutual respect. But it is clear to all concerned that when it comes to nuclear weapons, we have reached a decisive point. This is not simply about America's interests. It's about preventing a nuclear arms race in the Middle East that could lead this region and the world down a hugely dangerous path.

I understand those who protest that some countries have weapons that others do not. No single nation should pick and choose which nation holds nuclear weapons. And that's why I strongly reaffirmed America's commitment to seek a world in which no nations hold nuclear weapons. (Applause.) And any nation – including Iran – should have the right to access peaceful nuclear power if it complies with its responsibilities under the nuclear Non-Proliferation Treaty. That commitment is at the core of the treaty, and it must be kept for all who fully abide by it. And I'm hopeful that all countries in the region can share in this goal.

The fourth issue that I will address is democracy. (Applause.)

I know – I know there has been controversy about the promotion of democracy in recent years, and much of this controversy is connected to the war in Iraq. So let me be clear: No system of government can or should be imposed by one nation by any other.

That does not lessen my commitment, however, to governments that reflect the will of the people. Each nation gives life to this principle in its own way, grounded in the traditions of its own people. America does not presume to know what is best for everyone, just as we would not presume to pick the outcome of a peaceful election. But I do have an unyielding belief that all people yearn for certain things: the ability to speak your mind and have a say in how you are governed; confidence in the rule of law and the equal administration of justice; government that is transparent and doesn't steal from the people; the freedom to live as you choose. These are not just American ideas; they are human rights. And that is why we will support them everywhere. (Applause.)

Now, there is no straight line to realize this promise. But this much is clear: Governments that protect these rights are ultimately more stable, successful and secure. Suppressing ideas never succeeds in making them go away. America respects the right of all peaceful and law-abiding voices to be heard around the world, even if we disagree with them. And we will welcome all elected, peaceful governments – provided they govern with respect for all their people.

This last point is important because there are some who advocate for democracy only when they're out of power; once in power, they are ruthless in suppressing the rights of others. (Applause.) So no matter where it takes hold, government of the people and by the people sets a single standard for all who would hold power: You must maintain your power through consent, not coercion; you must respect the rights of minorities, and participate with a spirit of tolerance and compromise; you must place the interests of your people and the legitimate workings of the political process above your party. Without these ingredients, elections alone do not make true democracy.

AUDIENCE MEMBER: Barack Obama, we love you!

PRESIDENT OBAMA: Thank you. (Applause.) The fifth issue that we must address together is religious freedom.

Islam has a proud tradition of tolerance. We see it in the history of Andalusia and Cordoba during the Inquisition. I saw it firsthand as a child in Indonesia, where devout Christians worshiped freely in an overwhelmingly Muslim country. That is the spirit we need today. People in every country should be free to choose and live their faith based upon the persuasion of the mind and the heart and the soul. This tolerance is essential for religion to thrive, but it's being challenged in many different ways.

Among some Muslims, there's a disturbing tendency to measure one's own faith by the rejection of somebody else's faith. The richness of religious diversity must be upheld – whether it is for Maronites in Lebanon or the Copts in Egypt. (Applause.) And if we are being honest, fault lines must be closed among Muslims, as well, as the divisions between Sunni and Shia have led to tragic violence, particularly in Iraq.

Freedom of religion is central to the ability of peoples to live together. We must always examine the ways in which we protect it. For instance, in the United States, rules on charitable giving have made it harder for Muslims to fulfill their religious obligation. That's why I'm committed to working with American Muslims to ensure that they can fulfill zakat.

Likewise, it is important for Western countries to avoid impeding Muslim citizens from practicing religion as they see fit – for instance, by dictating what clothes a Muslim woman should wear. We can't disguise hostility towards any religion behind the pretence of liberalism.

In fact, faith should bring us together. And that's why we're forging service projects in America to bring together Christians, Muslims, and Jews. That's why we welcome efforts like Saudi Arabian King Abdullah's interfaith dialogue and Turkey's leadership in the Alliance of Civilizations. Around the world, we can turn dialogue into interfaith service, so bridges between peoples lead to action – whether it is combating malaria in Africa, or providing relief after a natural disaster.

The sixth issue – the sixth issue that I want to address is women's rights. (Applause.) I know – I know – and you can tell from this audience, that there is a healthy debate about this issue. I reject the view of some in the West that a woman who chooses to cover her hair is somehow less equal, but I do believe that a woman who is denied an education is denied equality. (Applause.) And it is no coincidence that countries where women are well educated are far more likely to be prosperous.

Now, let me be clear: Issues of women's equality are by no means simply an issue for Islam. In Turkey, Pakistan, Bangladesh, Indonesia, we've seen Muslim-majority countries elect a woman to lead. Meanwhile, the struggle for women's equality continues in many aspects of American life, and in countries around the world.

I am convinced that our daughters can contribute just as much to society as our sons. (Applause.) Our common prosperity will be advanced by allowing all humanity – men and women – to reach their full potential. I do not believe that women must make the same choices as men in order to be equal, and I respect those women who choose to live their lives in traditional roles. But it should be their choice. And that is why the United States will partner with any Muslim-majority country to support expanded literacy for girls, and to help young women pursue employment through micro-financing that helps people live their dreams. (Applause.)

Finally, I want to discuss economic development and opportunity.

I know that for many, the face of globalization is contradictory. The Internet and television can bring knowledge and information, but also offensive sexuality and mindless violence into the home. Trade can bring new wealth and opportunities, but also huge disruptions and change in communities. In all nations – including America – this change can bring fear. Fear that because of modernity we lose control over our economic choices, our politics, and most importantly our identities – those things we most cherish about our communities, our families, our traditions, and our faith.

But I also know that human progress cannot be denied. There need not be contradictions between development and tradition. Countries like Japan and South Korea grew their economies enormously while maintaining distinct cultures. The same is true for the astonishing progress within Muslim-majority countries from Kuala Lumpur to Dubai. In ancient times and in our times, Muslim communities have been at the forefront of innovation and education.

And this is important because no development strategy can be based only upon what comes out of the ground, nor can it be sustained while young people are out of work. Many Gulf states have enjoyed great wealth as a consequence of oil, and some are beginning to focus it on broader development. But all of us must recognize that education and innovation will be the currency of the 21st century – (applause) – and in too many Muslim communities, there remains underinvestment in these areas. I'm emphasizing such investment within my own country. And while America in the past has focused on oil and gas when it comes to this part of the world, we now seek a broader engagement.

On education, we will expand exchange programs, and increase scholarships, like the one that brought my father to America. (Applause.) At the same time, we will encourage more Americans to study in Muslim communities. And we will match promising Muslim students with internships in America; invest in online learning for teachers and children around the world; and create a new online network, so a young person in Kansas can communicate instantly with a young person in Cairo.

On economic development, we will create a new corps of business volunteers to partner with counterparts in Muslim-majority countries. And I will host a Summit on Entrepreneurship this year to identify how we can deepen ties between business leaders, foundations and social entrepreneurs in the United States and Muslim communities around the world.

On science and technology, we will launch a new fund to support technological development in Muslim-majority countries, and to help transfer ideas to the marketplace so they can create more jobs. We'll open centers of scientific excellence in Africa, the Middle East and Southeast Asia, and appoint new science envoys to collaborate on programs that develop new sources of energy, create green jobs, digitize records, clean water, grow new crops. Today I'm announcing a new global effort with the Organization of the Islamic Conference to eradicate polio. And we will also expand partnerships with Muslim communities to promote child and maternal health.

All these things must be done in partnership. Americans are ready to join with citizens and governments; community organizations, religious leaders, and businesses in Muslim communities around the world to help our people pursue a better life.

The issues that I have described will not be easy to address. But we have a responsibility to join together on behalf of the world that we seek – a world where extremists no longer threaten our people, and American troops have come home; a world where Israelis and Palestinians are each secure in a state of their own, and nuclear energy is used for peaceful purposes; a world where governments serve their citizens, and the rights of all God's children are respected. Those are mutual interests. That is the world we seek. But we can only achieve it together.

I know there are many – Muslim and non-Muslim – who question whether we can forge this new beginning. Some are eager to stoke the flames of division, and to stand in the way of progress. Some suggest that it isn't worth the effort – that we are fated to disagree, and civilizations are doomed to clash. Many more are simply skeptical that real change can occur. There's so much fear, so much mistrust that has built up over the years. But if we choose to be bound by the past, we will never move forward. And I want to particularly say this to young people of every faith, in every country – you, more than anyone, have the ability to reimagine the world, to remake this world.

All of us share this world for but a brief moment in time. The question is whether we spend that time focused on what pushes us apart, or whether we commit ourselves to an effort – a sustained effort – to find common ground, to focus on the future we seek for our children, and to respect the dignity of all human beings.

It's easier to start wars than to end them. It's easier to blame others than to look inward. It's easier to see what is different about someone than to find the things we share. But we should choose the right path, not just the easy path. There's one rule that lies at the heart of every religion – that we do unto others as we would have them do unto us. (Applause.) This truth transcends nations and peoples – a belief that isn't new; that isn't black or white or brown; that isn't Christian or Muslim or Jew. It's a belief that pulsed in the cradle of civilization, and that still beats in the hearts of billions around the world. It's a faith in other people, and it's what brought me here today.

We have the power to make the world we seek, but only if we have the courage to make a new beginning, keeping in mind what has been written.

The Holy Koran tells us: "O mankind! We have created you male and a female; and we have made you into nations and tribes so that you may know one another."

The Talmud tells us: "The whole of the Torah is for the purpose of promoting peace."

The Holy Bible tells us: "Blessed are the peacemakers, for they shall be called sons of God." (Applause.)

The people of the world can live together in peace. We know that is God's vision. Now that must be our work here on Earth.

Thank you. And may God's peace be upon you. Thank you very much. Thank you. (Applause.)

[Courtesy of The White House]

Questions for discussion:

Why is the US distrusted in the Middle East?

How does Obama deal with this distrust in this speech?

How well-known was his admission of US involvement in Iran in the early 1950s?

What are some of the rhetorical strategies he uses to persuade his audience he is sympathetic to them and their culture?

How well does he use classical rhetorical devices?

How does an Ongian analysis of his speech help us understand these rhetorical strategies and devices?

Going further:

Jacques Attali, *A Brief History of the Future*, Arcade, 2009

Richard Belfield, *Terminate with Extreme Prejudice*, Pan Macmillan, Sydney, 2005

Geoffrey Blainey, *A Short History of the World*, Viking, Camberwell, Vic., 2000

Bruce Dover, *Rupert's Adventures in China: How Murdoch Lost a Fortune and Found a Wife*, Viking, London, 2008

Felipe Fernández-Arnesto, *Civilizations: Culture, Ambition, and the Transformation of Nature*, The Free Press, New York, 2001

John Gray, *Al-Qaeda and What It Means to be Modern*, Faber and Faber, London, 2003

Paul Greengrass, dir. *United 93*, 2006

Marc Levin, dir. *Protocols of Zion*, 93 mins, 2005

Abraham Maslow, Abraham, 'A theory of human motivation', *Psychological Review*, 50 (1943) pp. 370-396

[online at http://psychclassics.yorku.ca/Maslow/motivation.htm]

Barack Obama, *Dreams From My Father: A Story of Race and Inheritance*, Crown, New York, 2004 [1995]

Nicholas Ostler, *Empires of the Word: A Language History of the World*, Harper Perennial, London, 2006 [2005]

Robert Reich, *The Work of Nations: Preparing Ourselves for 21st Century Capitalism*, A.A. Knopf, New York, 1991

US. National Commission on Terrorist Attacks Upon the United States [9-11Commission.gov, archived 2004]

US. 911 Investigations.net, a repository of documents relating to the 9/11 attacks and the War on Terrorism [911digitalarchive.org]

Martin Van Creveld, *The Changing Face of War: Lessons of Combat, from the Marne to Iraq*, Ballantine Books, New York, 2006

Peter Watson, *Ideas: A History from Fire to Freud*, Weidenfeld & Nicolson, 2005

Acknowledgements

The author wishes to thank many colleagues in this project: Chris Absell, Mark Armstrong-Roper, Peter Betros, Geoffrey Bolton, Thor Haakon Baake, Rob Bollard, Caterina Cafarella, Conall Cash, Bruno Cataldo, Richard Chauvel, Rosemary Clerehan, Sean Clerehan, Lachlan Clohesy, Bryon Cunningham, Jim Davidson (who introduced World History to Victoria University a decade ago), Michael Deery, Phillip Deery, Geoff Gallop, Marita Grafe-tshur, Michele Grossman, Dianne Hall, the late Irwin Herrman, Giuliano Iacuzzi, Bill Logan, Chris McConville, Brendan McGloin, John McLaren, Firas Massouh, Yoni Molad, Aurélien Mondon, Carla Pascoe, Stephen Pascoe, Susan Pascoe, Howard Prosser, Virginie Rey, Ron Ridley, Jenny Sharples, Deborah Staines, Mark Stevenson, Adrian Threlfall, John Tully, Christopher Wood.

Permissions

The author and publisher acknowledge ownership of the illustrations and extracts in this book as indicated within square brackets.

Index

A Tree Grows in Brooklyn (1945) 313-4
Abdullah, King of Saudi Arabia 388
'Abdu-r-Razzāq Ma'mūrī 111-3
Abdu-s-Samad 112
Aborigines, Australian 198
Absolutism 3-38
Abu-Lughod, Janet L. 337
Academy Awards 312
Acre 56
Aden 366
Afghanistan 96, 365-6, 373, 380-1
Agincourt 17
Agra 99, 105
Akbar the Great 96
Alabama 356
Al-Azhar University 375, 377
Albania 265
Albany, NY 43
Alexander (Aleksandr) I, Russia 78
Alexander (Aleksandr) II, Russia 78
Alexander (Aleksandr) III, Russia 240
Alexandra, Tsarina 240
al-Qa'ida (Al Qaeda) 380
Alsace-Lorraine 225, 236
American Civil War 227ff
American Declaration of Independence 45, 50, 58ff, 200, 226

American War of Independence 15, 53
Aminu-d-daula 111
Amiru-I-umara 111, 115
Amsterdam 289
Anatolia 80
ancien regime 40, 46, 55
Andalusia 387
Anderson, Benedict 337
Anderson, Perry 337
Ankara 380
Anschluss 268
Antilles 4
ANZACs 238
ANZUS 302
Arabic 374
Ardennes 274
Argentina 192, 195
Armenians 263
Arms Control and Disarmament Agency 303
Arnold, Matthew 132, 134
Arthur, Jean 315
Āṣaf Khān 109, 113
Assange, Julian 368
Atlantic Crossing 192, 226, 233
Augustine of Hippo 333, 335
Aurangzeb 97, 100

Auschwitz 279, 289ff
Australia 12, 45, 132, 135-6, 161, 189ff, 226. 238, 245, 262, 273-5, 304, 311, 31, 319, 335
Austria-Hungary 237
Aztecs 303

Babur 95-6
Bach, Johann Sebastian 46
Baden-Baden 327
Baez, Joan 307, 327
Baghdad Pact 302-3
Baldwin, James 329-30
Balkan Wars, 1990s 366
Balkans War of 1912 237
Banfield, Edward 303
Bangladesh 388
Barbarossa, Operation 270-1
Bardot, Brigitte 297
Baseball 233
Basques 263
Bastille 54, 57
Battle of Britain 270
Bauhaus 263
Beat Generation 307
Beatles, The 310, 327
Bedouin 333
Beirut 159, 197
Belgium 317
Bengal 112
Benjamin, Walter 227

Bentham, Jeremy 131
Berkeley Student Revolt 325
Berlin Wall 299-301
Bernstein, Eduard 236
Béthune, France 242
Bhabha, Homi K. 278
Bihar 111, 115
Bill of Rights, English 41
Birmingham 125
Black Power 329-30
Blake, William 123, 132
Bland, Bill 241, 254
Boer War 197, 237
Bogota, Colombia 13
Bohemia, see Austria 74
Bohr, Niels 236
Bolivia 51
Bolkestein, Gerrit 288
Bologna 5, 264
Bolshevism 104, 225, 259, 263
Bonapartism 194
Bonn 160
Booth, Paul 324
Bosnia 293, 379
Boston 43, 305
Boulton, Matthew 125, 154
bourgeoisie 4-4, 10, 20, 52, 103, 130-31, 134, 198, 202ff, 234, 264, 373
Boxer Rebellion 102

Brando, Marlon 297, 315
Braudel, Fernand 335, 338
Braveheart (1995) 46
Brazil 91, 192, 195
Brecht, Bertolt 235
Britain (or England) 56-9, 63, 103-4, 123ff, 153, 156, 186, 191, 197-201, 226, 233, 237, 263-4, 268-70, 275, 310-11, 327, 335, 369, 372
British East Africa 195
Brittany 53
Buchenwald 383
Budapest 297
Buenos Aires 159, 197
Bulgaria 263
Bush Sr, George 365
Bush, George W. 226, 366
Byzantine Empire 10, 130, 235
Byzantium, see also Constantinople 130

Cairo 197, 375-6, 390
Calas, Jean 42
Calatafimi, Italy 157
California 191, 229, 314, 326, 356
Cambodia 329
Campanella, Roy 297
Canada 50-1, 192, 195, 304
Capet, Hugh 14
capitalism 74, 129ff, 157, 162-5, 186, 190, 223, 233ff, 276, 298, 372-3
Capra, Frank 314

Caribbean 51, 230, 278
Carmichael, Stokely 330
Carter, Jimmy 365
Castile, Spain 11-12, 17
Catalans 263
Catherine (Yekaterina) I, Russia 78
Catherine (Yekaterina) II (the Great), Russia 42, 71-5, 79-81
Chaplin, Charlie 132
Charles (Carlos) III, Spain 11
Charles I and V, Spain 11, 12, 81
Charles I, England 15
Charles II, England 15, 40-1
Charles II, Spain 11
Charles IX, Sweden 19
Charles XI, Sweden 20
Chartists 155-6
Chechik, Jeremiah S. 315
Chicago 234, 330, 336, 376
Childe, Vere Gordon 335
China 41, 51, 82, 95, 101-4, 115, 130, 195, 298, 303, 311, 324, 328-9, 369
Chodelros de Laclos, Pierre 45
Christina, Sweden 19
Christmas, 25 December 48, 314-5
Churchill, Winston 271, 275, 299
CIA (Central Intelligence Agency) 299
Clapton, Eric 305
Clinton, Bill 331, 366, 369
Clive, Robert 100

Code Napoleon 56
Cohen, Joseph 280
Cohn, Roy 297
Cold War 299-302, 325, 332, 342, 364, 366, 368, 375, 385
Collingwood, Victoria 197
Cologne 160
colonialism 104, 135, 189ff, 199-201, 335, 375
Colorado 233, 348
Columbian Exchange 131, 337
Columbus, Christopher 337
command or coercion (*dominio*) 31, 71, 113, 170, 176, 210, 239, 265-6, 269-70, 302, 387
Communism 129, 162, 202, 264, 270, 274, 299, 306, 325, 334, 351, 356, 372
Confucianism 101
Congo 317
Connecticut 62, 233, 356
Conrad, Joseph 235
conservatism 264, 307, 311
Constantinople 40, 80
Cook, Captain James 47-8
Copernicus, Nicolaus 41
Cordoba, Spain 387
Corleone family 192
Cornwall, the Cornish 125-8, 191, 233
Corsica 55
Corso, Gregory 306-7
Cortés, Hernán 12

Cossacks 78-9
Crawshay, Francis 127
Crécy 17
Crimea 75
Cromer, Lord 197
Cromwell, Oliver (Old Ironsides) 15, 40
Cromwell, Richard 15
Crusades, the 206, 337, 374
Cultural Revolution, China 328-9
Curtin, John 274-5
Curtis, Tony 317
Czechoslovakia 263, 268

Dallas 312
Darfur 379
Darwin, Charles 135, 195, 234
Dawson, Christopher 334
Day, Doris 297-8
de Carvalho e Melo, Sebastião José 73
De Gasperi, Alcide 327
de Gaulle, Charles 327
de Staël, Anne Louise Germaine 45
de Winter, Rosa 289-90
Dean, James 297
Declaration of the Rights of Man and Citizen 58ff
Delbo, Charlotte 279, 290ff
DeLillo, Don 306
Denmark 73, 270
deWilde, Brandon 315

Diana of Wales, Princess
Dickens, Charles 134, 190
Diderot, Denis 44
Dien Bien Phu 297
DiMaggio, Joe 207-8
Disraeli, Benjamin 134
Dresden 275
Dubai 389
Dublin 83ff, 134
Duchamp, Henri 235-6
Dunn, James 313
Dylan, Bob 327

East Germany 74
East India Company 100, 102
Edinburgh 335
Edward I, England 18
Edward III, England 18
Egypt 55, 103, 129, 190, 195, 197, 206, 237, 251, 332-5, 375ff
1848 Revolution 104, 135, 153ff
Einstein, Albert 236, 297
Eisenhower, Dwight D. 300, 354
El Alamein 273
Eliot, George 190
Eliot, T.S. 235
Elizabeth (Yelisaveta) Petrovna, Russia 78
Elizabeth I (The Virgin Queen) 15
Ellis Island 304, 323
Ellis, Havelock 218

Emilia-Romagna 265
Engels, Friedrich (Frederick) 135, 160-2
English 5-7, 13-18, 36, 39ff, 55-6, 61, 93, 128, 132-5, 151, 153, 163, 172-3, 189ff, 225, 233, 241ff, 265, 286, 370, 373-4
English Radicals, the 45, 151, 153, 157, 223
English Revolution or Civil War 6-7, 16-18, 40, 373
Enlai, Zhou 51
Enlightenment, the 68, 72-3, 103, 124, 129, 160, 195, 213, 276, 329, 333-4, 377
Entente Cordiale 237
Eric XI, Sweden 19
Ethiopia 197, 265
Eyes Wide Shut (1999) 235

Fanon, Frantz 278
Farīd Bukhārī 110
Fascism 251, 264ff, 325
Fatehpur Sikri 99
Faulkner, William 235
FBI 332
Ferdinand I of Aragon 11
Ferdinand, Archduke Franz 237
Fergana 95
Ferlinghetti, Lawrence 306-7
Fernández-Armesto, Felipe 337
feudalism 4, 8-9, 20, 37, 40, 52, 74-5,

104, 129, 190, 210, 337, 372
Final Solution, the 268
Finch, Peter 317
Finland 263
First Gulf War 365, 368
First World War, see Great War 237ff, 243ff, 254, 259ff, 271, 293, 334
Fitzgerald, F. Scott 261
Five Eyes 304
Flanders 53
Florence 19, 306
Ford, Gerald 332, 365
Ford, John, film director 315, 321
Ford, John, playwright 39
Foucault, Michel 337
Fragment Thesis 198ff
France 8, 14ff, 40, 42, 46, 50ff, 64ff, 74, 76, 104, 132, 163-4, 197, 201, 205, 214, 223, 226, 237, 241, 243ff, 263, 268, 270, 275-6, 311, 335, 369, 372
Franco, Francisco 69
Franco-Prussian War 159
Frank, Anne 279ff
Frank, Edith 289-90
Frank, Margot 281ff
Frank, Otto 289-90
Frankfurt School 263, 276ff, 307
Frankfurt-on-Main 281
Franklin, Benjamin 43, 62
Franklin, William 43
Frederick I, Prussia 72, 75-6

Frederick II (the Great), Prussia 72-3, 75-6
Frederick VI, Denmark 73
Frederick William I, Prussia 76
Frederick William II, Prussia 76
French Revolution 51ff, 71, 73, 123, 125, 130, 135, 151, 158, 194, 373
Freud, Sigmund 234-5, 276
Friedan, Betty 329
Friedman, Milton 365
Fukuyama, Francis 337

Galileo Galilei 41
Gallipoli 238
Gandhi, Mahatma 200
Garbo, Greta 19
Garden City 263
Gardner, Ava 317-8
Garfield, James 312
Garibaldi, Giuseppe 157
Gaskell, Elizabeth 134
Gaza 383-4
Gela, Sicily 274
General Agreement on Tariffs and Trade (GATT) 302
Genoa 19, 130
Germany 46, 56, 72ff, 132, 159-60, 164, 205, 214, 225-6, 236ff, 263ff, 278, 299, 327, 334, 365, 373
Gettysburg Address 230-1
Ginsberg, Allen 307
Gitlin, Todd 34

Glorious Revolution, the 40, 42, 123, 125, 194
Godfather II, 1974 192, 306
Gorbachev, Mikhail 365
Grace, Princess of Monaco 297
Gramsci, Antonio 265-6
Granada, Spain 12, 269
Graves, Robert 241ff, 254
Great Chain of Being 11
Great Depression 263, 266, 299
Great Game, the 100
Great War (see First World War)
Greece 280, 300, 372
Greek 130, 200, 231, 321, 333-4
Greenwich 199
Greer, Germaine 329
Grenada 365
Gropius, Walter 235
Guizot, François 202
Gustav I, Sweden 19
Gustavus Adolphus 7, 19-20
Guthrie, Woody 307

Haber, Alan 324, 339
Habsburg dynasty (also spelt Hapsburg) 74, 77
Hamburg 275
Handlin, Oscar 331
Hansen, Marcus Lee 330
Harlem 304-6
Harvard 228, 278, 304-7, 331, 334-5

Haussmann, Georges-Eugène 159, 197, 373
Hawaii 47
Hayden, Tom 324
Hegel, G.W.F. 162, 333-4
Hegemony (*egemonia*) 265, 306, 311, 323ff, 373
Hemingway, Ernest 259
Henry IV, England 3, 15
Henry IV, France 14
Henry V, England 3, 15
Henry VII, England 15
Henry VIII, England 15, 17
Hepburn, Audrey 317
Herodotus 333, 338
Hersh, Seymour 324
Hindustan 112
Hiroshima 275, 302
Hitchcock, Alfred 319, 374
Hitler, Adolf 266-72, 281, 286
Ho Chi Minh 200
Hobbes, Thomas 7, 21ff, 36-7
Hodgson, Marshall G.S. 336
Hogarth, William 128
Hohenzollern dynasty 74, 76, 236
Hollywood 233, 293, 304-7, 313ff, 329
Holocaust, the 268, 293, 382
Holy Roman Empire 56, 236
Homer, Winslow 232
Hong Kong 103
Hongwu 101

Horkheimer, Max 276
House Un-American Activities Committee (HUAC) 344
Hudson Bay 4
Hudson Valley 48
Huguenots 76
Humayun 97
Hundred Years' War 14, 17
Hungary 263
Hussein, King 332

Ibn Khaldun 333
India 95ff, 129, 165, 190, 192, 195, 200, 204, 311, 368, 372, 374
Indians, American 48-9, 146-7, 233
Indonesia 329, 376, 384, 387-8
Industrial Revolution 41, 103-4, 123ff, 153ff, 186, 190-2, 198-9, 226, 372, 374
Inglehart Values Map 368, 370
International Atomic Energy Treaty 303
Internet, the 334, 368-9
Iowa 229
Iran 366, 385-6
Iranian Revolution 364
Iran-Iraq War 365
Iraq invasion 366, 381-2
Ireland 17, 83ff, 331
Irish Famine 135
Iron Curtain speech 299
Isabella I of Castile 11-12

Israel 68, 324, 331-2, 368, 382-5, 391
It's a Wonderful Life, 1946 315
Italy 19, 55-6, 130, 157, 192, 205, 237, 263ff, 273, 327, 373
Ithaca, NY 356
Ivan III (the Great), Russia 77
Ivan IV (the Terrible), Russia 77

Jahāngīr 97ff, 104ff
James I, England 15, 40
Japan 41, 102, 132, 239-40, 263, 274-5, 327, 372, 389
Jefferson, Thomas 45, 62, 226, 378, 381
Jena 75
Jews 91, 130, 233, 267-8, 281ff, 307, 325, 330, 383ff
Joanna the Mad, Spain 11
Joel, Billy 298
John III, Sweden 19
John of Gaunt 3
John XXIII 324-5
Johnson, Lyndon Baines 324
Johnson, Robert 305
Joseph II, Austria 73, 75
Joyce, James 235, 374
Joyeux Noël, 2005 226
Justinian, Emperor 6
Juvenal 93

Kamara, Kande 242, 254
Kandinsky, Wassily 235

Kangxi 102, 105, 115ff
Kant, Immanuel 44
Kashmir 99
Kastenmeier, Robert 355
Kazan, Elias 313
Kennedy, John F. 300-1, 312
Kent State killings 324
Kerouac, Jack 307
Keynesianism 342, 365
Khusrau 110ff
Khwājagī Fathu-llah 111
King, Martin Luther 330, 356
Kingdom of Serbs, Croats and Slovenes (see also Yugoslavia) 263
Klimt, Gustav 235
Korea (North and South) 274, 297, 389
Korean War 300
Kosovo 293
Kramer, Stanley 317
kristallnacht 268
Krushchev, Nikita 297
Kuala Lumpur 389
Kuwait 365

Ladd, Alan 315
Lady's Day, 25 March 48
Latin 74, 81
Lawrence, D.H. 235
Le Corbusier (Charles-Édouard Jeanneret-Gris) 235

League of Nations 240, 263
Lebanon 388
Led Zeppelin 305
Leigh, Janet 320-1
Lemmon, Jack 319
Lenin, V.I. 165, 239-40
Lennon, John 363-4
Lepanto 13
Liberace (Władziu Valentino Liberace) 297
liberalism (see also neoliberalism) 123, 135, 363ff, 369, 388
Lichenstein, Roy 310
Lin Zexu 102
Lincoln, Abraham 230
Locke, John 42, 50
London 86ff, 101, 123. 125, 134, 154, 160, 199, 202, 235, 288
Long Boom 297ff, 306ff, 323
Lorenzini, Carlo (Collodi) 158
Lost generation, the 259ff
Louis XIV (the Sun King) 14, 73
Louis XV, France 14
Louis XVI, France 14, 51ff, 73
Louisiana 4, 309
Luddites 154
Lutetia (Paris) 372
Lynch, E.P.F. 245ff, 250, 254
Lyon 278
Lyotard, Jean-François 336

Macedonians 263

Machiavelli, Niccolò 3, 6, 19
MacLaine, Shirley 319
Madhi, the 242
Madho Singh 113
Madrid 11, 268
Mai '68 327
Maktūb Khān 110
Malenkov, Georgy 297
Malthus, Thomas 131, 180, 186
Manchester 125, 241
Manchuria 102
Manet, Édouard 159
Manohar 114
Mao 328
Maori Wars 201, 245
March on Rome 265
Marciano, Rocky 297
Marcuse, Herbert 307
Margaret, Sweden 19
Maria Carolina, Austria 73
Maria Theresa, Austria 73
Marie Louise, Austria 55
Marshall Plan 300, 303, 365
Marvin, Lee 321
Marx, Karl 334ff
Maslow, Abraham 371
Massachusetts 37, 51, 62, 356
Matisse, Henri 235
Maurice of Orange 7
McCarthy, Senator Joseph 297, 300
McCarthyism 306, 325, 348

McGuire, Dorothy 313
McKinley, William 312
McNeill, William H. 336
Medici 19
Melbourne 133, 197, 199, 268, 317-9, 324
Mengele, Josef 290
Mexico 12
Michael (Mikhail) Romanoff, Russia 78
Michaelmas, 29 September 48
Michigan 191
Middle Colonies 47
Midsummer, 24 June 48
Milan 264
Miles, Vera 321
Mill, John Stuart 186
Ming dynasty 101
Mīrān Ṣadr Jahān 108
Missouri 299
Modern Times, 1936 132
modernism 235-6, 259, 374
Mongols 95
Monroe Doctrine 227, 298
Monroe, Marilyn 297
Monsonis, Jim 324
Moro, Aldo 328
Morocco 237, 269, 377
Moscow 71, 274
Mughals 82, 95ff
Muhammad, Elijah 330

Mukhtar Beg 113
Mumtaz Mahal 100
Munich 268
Muqīm 111
Murdoch, Rupert 369
Mussolini, Benito 264ff
Mutual Assured Destruction (MAD) 302
My Lai massacre 324

Nagasaki 275, 302
Nanking 274
Nanterre 327
Naples 56, 73
Napoleon Bonaparte 14, 17, 40, 54ff, 73, 75, 163
Napoleon III, France 158
Napoleonic Wars 124, 199
Nasser, Gamal Abdel 297
Nation of Islam 330
National Italian American Foundation (NIAF) 331
National Lampoon's Christmas Vacation, 1989 315
National Socialism (Nazism) 264-6
neo-liberalism (see liberalism)
neo-Marxism 265-6, 276-8, 307
Netherlands or Holland 42, 280-1, 286
New England 47ff
New Guinea 274-5
New Jersey 62, 306, 323
New Left 325ff, 332, 357ff

New World Order 363-4, 369
New York 51, 62, 191, 233, 235, 304, 314, 325, 356
New Zealand 201, 245, 304
Newcastle, England 137
Newcomen, Thomas 125
Newton, Isaac 41
Nicholas (Nikolai) I, Russia 78
Nicholas (Nikolai) II, Russia 78
Nixon, Richard 297, 300, 323-4, 332, 365
Noah 42
North Atlantic Treaty Organisation (NATO) 300
Norway 270
Nuremberg trials 303

Obama, Barack 231, 366, 368, 375ff
On The Beach (1959) 317-8
OPEC oil crisis 323-4, 332
Opium Wars 102
Orwell, George 269
Osama bin Laden 368
Osborn, Emily Mary 127
Ottoman Empire 129, 226, 237, 262-3
Owen, Robert 157
Owen, Wilfred 243ff, 254

Pacific War 274ff
Padua, Italy 41
Page, John 226

Paglia, Camille 306
Paine, Thomas 45, 137, 145ff, 151, 153
Pakistan 368, 381, 388
Palance, Jack 315
Palestine 383-4
Palmer, Attorney-General A. Mitchell 240
Panmunjom, Korea 297
Paris Commune 104, 135, 159, 163, 236
Parma, Italy 39
Parry, J.H. 335
Parsons, Talcott 303
Pascoe surname 191
Paterson, NJ 305
Paul (Pavel), Russia 78
Pearl Harbor 240, 312
peasantry 4, 20, 41, 74, 78, 126-7, 198, 239, 333, 373
Peck, Gregory 317
Peel, Robert 189-90
Peel, Thomas 189, 198
Pennsylvania 43, 48, 62, 191
Pentagon Papers 324
Pepys, Samuel 9
Perkins, Anthony 321
Peron, Juan 297
Persia 97ff, 110, 114, 333
Peru 12, 51
Peter (Pyotr) I (the Great), Russia 73, 78

Philadelphia 43, 51
Philip VI, France 14
Philippines 13, 200
Phillip I, Spain 11
Phillip II, Spain 11
Phillip III, Spain 11
Phillip IV, Spain 11
Picasso, Pablo 235-6
Piraha people 371
Pirandello, Luigi 235
Pizarro, Francesco 12
Plassey 100
Poitier, Sidney 317
Pol Pot 293, 329
Poland 74ff, 263, 268ff, 365
pop art 307, 310
Pope, Alexander 131
Port Huron Statement 323, 329, 339ff
Portugal 13, 17, 73
Portuguese 13, 125, 165, 192-3, 372
postcolonialism 190, 259, 278
Pound, Ezra 235
Presley, Elvis 297
Primitive Communism 334, 372
Prima de Rivera, Miguel 269
Pripet Marshes 271
Prokofiev, Sergei 297
proletariat or working class 128, 134, 153, 162
Protectorate, the 40, 193, 195

Proudhon, Pierre-Joseph 163
Proust, Marcel 235
Provence 53
Prussia (East Germany) 64, 67, 72-5, 159, 276
Psycho, 1960 317
Ptolemy 41
PTSD 238
Puzo, Mario 306

Qara Khan Turkman 113
Qing dynasty 101-4

Radishchev, Alexsander 71-2
Raja Bhagwān Dās 112-3
Raja Bihari Mal 112-3
Raja Jagannath 113
Raja Man Singh 112
Rakewell, Tom 128
Rānā Shankar 113
Rasputin, Grigori 240
Ray, Johnnie 297
Read, Deborah 42
Reagan, Ronald 326, 360, 365-6
Rear Window (1954) 374
Reconquista 12
Red Brigades 327
Reformation 17, 20, 334
Reich, Charles A. 331
Reich, Robert 369
Remarque, Erich Maria 244, 254
Renaissance 19, 306, 337, 377

Rennie, John 154
Rhineland 268
Ricardo, David 131, 163, 166-7, 186, 223
Richard I (The Lionheart) 15
Richard II, England 15
Riis, Jacob 234
Rilke, Rainer Maria 235
Risorgimento 157
Rizal, José 200
Robespierre, Maximilien de 54
Robinson, Sugar Ray 297
Rockefeller, John D. Jr 297
Rodham, Hilary (Clinton) 331
Rolling Stones 306, 327
Roman Law 5-6, 20, 195
Romania 263
Romanov dynasty (also spelt Romanoff) 74, 77, 78
Romans, Rome 28, 30, 37, 74, 129, 203, 265, 280, 303, 311, 324-5, 372
Roosevelt, F.D. 274, 304
Rosenberg, Julius and Ethel 297
Rostow, W.W. 303
Rousseau, Jean-Jacques 43ff, 51, 276
Ruknu-d-dīn 113
Russia 57, 71-80, 100, 104, 132, 184, 193, 195, 201, 226, 237, 263-4, 268-71, 273-4, 300
Russian Revolution 135, 238ff, 370, 373
Rwanda 293

Sa'īd Khān 110
Sacco, Nicola 240
Saddam Hussein 381
Sadiq Khān 113
Said, Edward 278
Saigon 324, 332
Salem, Massachusetts 49
Salmanaazor (George Psalmanazar) 88
San Francisco 307, 374
Sanskrit 100, 200
Sarajevo 238
Sartre, Jean-Paul 276
Sassoon, Siegfreid 243, 250, 254
Saudi Arabia 332, 388
Schiller, Friedrich 46
Scientific Revolution 41ff, 129
Scotland 17
Scottish Enlightenment 46, 124
Scramble for Africa, the 189ff, 237
SDI (the Strategic Defense Initiative) 365
SDS (Students for a Democratic Society) 324, 327, 339ff
SEATO 302
Second Vatican Council 324-5
Second World War 200, 237, 266ff, 279ff, 293, 299, 302, 374
Seljuk Turks 80
Senate Internal Security Committee 344
September 11 366, 375

Serbia 238
serfs, serfdom 74ff, 204, 238
Seven Years' War 8
Seville 269
Shah Jahan 97-100
Shakespeare, William 3
Shane, 1953 313-7
Sharīf Khān 111
Shelley, Mary Wollstonecraft 49
Siberia 71
Sicily 157, 274
Sigmund, Sweden 19
Silesia 76
Sinclair, Upton 234
Six-Day War 332
slaves, slavery 36, 49-51, 74, 78, 99, 14, 129, 141, 165, 192, 202-3, 210, 216, 227ff, 305, 334, 372, 384
Smith, Adam 10, 124, 129, 131, 166ff, 186, 223
SNCC (Student Non-Violent Coordinating Committee) 330
social darwinism 135, 195-6
social democracy 264
socialism 124, 157, 164, 237, 373
Sorbonne 327
South Africa 195, 197, 226, 384
South Melbourne, Victoria 199
Soviet Union (see also Russia) 270-6, 299-300, 311, 338, 364-5
Spain 7, 11-14, 17, 40, 56, 73, 269, 373

Spanish Civil War 269
Spanish Inquisition 12, 41
Spence, Thomas 137ff, 151, 153
Spengler, Oswald 334-8
Spivak, Gayatri Chakravorty 278
Springsteen, Bruce 306, 323
Sputnik 300
St Helena 57
St Kilda, Victoria 199
St Petersburg 71, 239
Stalin, Joseph 264, 270-6, 293, 311
Stalingrad 274
Stavrianos, L.S. 336
Steffens, Lincoln 234
Stein, Gertrude 235
Stephen, James 193
Stevens, George 315
Stewart, James 314, 321
Stravinsky, Igor 235-6
Sudan 197, 242
Sudetenland 268
Suez Crisis 297, 311
Suharto, General 329
Sulanu-n-nisa Begam 112
Suleiman I, Ottoman Empire 81
Sultan Parwiz 112
Sumer 335, 372
Swan River (Perth, WA) 189
Sweden 19-20, 73
Swift, Jonathan 83ff, 93-4, 186
Taiping Rebellion 102

Taj Mahal 100
Taliban, the 380
Tawhiao, King 201
Tawney, R.H. 131
Teheran 365
Tennessee Valley Authority 348
Tertullian 93
Texas 312, 356
Thanksgiving 49
The Apartment (1960) 319
The Cabinet of Dr Caligari (1920) 293
The Defiant Ones (1958) 317
The King and I (1956) 297
The Man Who Shot Liberty Valance (1962) 321
The New Republic 356
The Nun's Story (1959) 317
The Searchers (1956) 315
The Sixth Sense (1999) 293
Third Reich 267-8, 383
Third World War 311
Thirty Years' War 6-7, 14, 20
Thompson, E.P. 128
3M 233
Thucydides 333
Timur 96
Tokyo 275
Toscanini, Arturo 297
Toulouse 42
Tower of London 17-18
Toynbee, Arnold J. 335-6

Travers, Henry 314
Treaty of Tripoli 378
Triple Alliance 237
Trotsky, Leon 239
Truman Doctrine 300
Truman, Harry S. 297-300
Turan 110
Turkey 81, 300, 388
Turner, Frederick Jackson 232-3
Tuscany 265
Twain, Mark 233

Ungaretti, Giuseppe 235, 251ff, 254-5
United Kingdom (see also England and Britain) 191
Urabi, Ahmad 103, 197
Urdu 100
Uzbekistan 99

van Daan, Mrs (Auguste van Pels) 285, 289
van der Rohe, Mies 235
Vanzetti, Bartolomeo 240
Vatican 275
Vendée 54
Venice 19, 130
Versailles, Treaty of 240, 263, 266-7, 269, 298, 303
Vienna 234-5, 268
Vietnam 57, 102
Vietnam War 303, 323-4, 327, 332, 373

Voltaire (François-Marie Arouet) 42, 72
von Bismarck, Otto 159, 236
von Hindenburg, Paul 267
von Metternich, Klemens 56, 202
von Stauffenberg, Claus 274
von Wallenstein, Albrecht 7

Wales, the Welsh 127, 233, 242
War of 1812 298
Warhol, Andy 310
Washington DC 227
Washington, George 230
Watergate scandal 324, 332
Waterloo, Battle of 7, 57
Watt, James 125
Wayne, John 321
Wazir Jamil 113
Weathermen, the 327
Weimar Republic 267, 293
Wells, H.G. 334
West Bank 383-4
Westerbork 285, 289
Western Australia 189-90, 198
Western Front 228, 238, 244, 268
Wheen, Francis 162-3
Whigs 123, 156
White, Thomas 262
William and Mary, England 40
William I (The Conqueror) 15
Williams, Cara 317

Williams, William Appleman 237
Williams, William Carlos 235-6, 374
Wilson, Woodrow 240
Winchell, Walter 297-8
Winfrey, Oprah 44
Wisconsin 355
Wollstonecraft, Edward 45
Wollstonecraft, Mary 45, 329
Wood, Grant DeVolson 261
Woolf, Virginia 235, 374
Wyatt, Samuel 154

Yankees 47

Years of the Bullet, the 327
Yeats, William Butler 235
Yom Kippur War 332
Yongle 101

Zāhid Khān 113
Zenelli family 323
Zheng He 101
Zhu Yuanzhang 101
Zinnemann, Fred 317
Zionism 56
Zola, Émile 202, 218ff
Zuckerberg, Mark 368

www.ingramcontent.com/pod-product-compliance
Lightning Source LLC
Chambersburg PA
CBHW052054300426
44117CB00013B/2120